TEACHER EVALUATION IN MUSIC

Teacher Evaluation in Music

A GUIDE FOR MUSIC TEACHERS IN THE U.S.

Cara Faith Bernard

and

Joseph Michael Abramo

OXFORD
UNIVERSITY PRESS

Oxford University Press is a department of the University of Oxford. It furthers
the University's objective of excellence in research, scholarship, and education
by publishing worldwide. Oxford is a registered trade mark of Oxford University
Press in the UK and certain other countries.

Published in the United States of America by Oxford University Press
198 Madison Avenue, New York, NY 10016, United States of America.

Library of Congress Cataloging-in-Publication Data
Names: Bernard, Cara Faith, author. | Abramo, Joseph (Joseph M.) author.
Title: Teacher evaluation in music : a guide for music teachers in the U.S. /
Cara Faith Bernard, Joseph Michael Abramo.
Description: New York : Oxford University Press, [2019] |
Includes bibliographical references and index.
Identifiers: LCCN 2018023208 (print) | LCCN 2018025329 (ebook) | ISBN 9780190867119 (updf) |
ISBN 9780190867126 (epub) | ISBN 9780190867102 (pbk. : alk. paper) |
ISBN 9780190867096 (cloth : alk. paper)
Subjects: LCSH: Music teachers—Rating of—United States. |
Music—Instruction and study—Evaluation—United States.
Classification: LCC MT3.U5 (ebook) | LCC MT3.U5 B416 2019 (print) | DDC 780.71—dc23
LC record available at https://lccn.loc.gov/2018023208

9 8 7 6 5 4 3 2 1

Paperback printed by Sheridan Books, Inc., United States of America
Hardback printed by Bridgeport National Bindery, Inc., United States of America

Contents

Foreword

FOR MORE THAN a century it has been the responsibility of school administrators to evaluate teachers (Cubberley, 1915), but in the early 2000s, as US states were in the midst of sorting out the No Child Left Behind Act (2001)—what would constitute adequate yearly progress and who could be counted as a highly qualified teacher—came reports on the nightly news that most teachers' performance in the classroom was considered "satisfactory." This finding raised seemingly contradictory questions for educators, administrators, politicians, and the general public: Was this a concerted attempt to blame the problems of schools on teachers and further deprofessionalize them? Yet how could high school graduation rates and standardized test scores be so low if teaching was truly satisfactory?

Some answers came with a deeper investigation of teacher evaluation policies. For example, Brant and colleagues (2007) found that school district policies addressed who was empowered to conduct evaluations and how often evaluations should be conducted, but not how results would be used. Furthermore, they found that most school administrators were not required to obtain specific training in how to evaluate teaching. As Donaldson (2009) commented, this finding was especially troublesome given the complexities of teaching and how school administrators were frequently called upon to evaluate teachers in academic subject areas with which they were not familiar.

Perhaps the thorniest issue of teacher evaluation has been connecting teacher effectiveness to student learning. At least some of the problem arises from the way that *effective teaching* has been defined since the 1960s. A model of direct instruction originated with Engelmann and colleagues at the University of Illinois, perhaps most famously implemented in a model called Direct Instruction System for Teaching and Remediation (DISTAR; Engelmann & Bruner, 1969; Engelmann & Carnine, 1969; Engelmann & Osborn, 1977). Brophy (1979) related the findings of a host of studies surrounding direct instruction: "Those who receive most of their instruction directly from the teacher do better than those expected to learn on their own or from one another" (p. 735). But eventually the emphasis on direct instruction focused exclusively on teacher behaviors: their brisk pacing from step to step in instruction, keeping instructional steps within reach of a majority of students, displaying enthusiasm or high intensity, and providing immediate feedback to students. These teaching behaviors were sequenced as follows:

1. A review of prerequisite knowledge and skills
2. Introduction of the main concept, reinforced with several examples
3. Opportunity for students to respond, or guided practice
4. Teacher feedback and correction
5. Opportunity for students' independent practice

This basic sequence appeared not only as Englemann's direct instruction model, but also in Rosenshine's explicit teaching (1987), Good and Grouws' (1979) strategies for effective teaching, and Hunter's (1982) design of effective teaching. In all cases, lessons were intended to be highly scripted.

Yarbrough and Price (1989), borrowing direct instruction principles, modeled their sequential patterns of instruction in music similarly and noted: "Given the amount of research data supporting use of complete and correct teaching cycles, the authors believe it is of paramount importance to develop techniques for teaching prospective teachers to present musical information, allow student response time, and appropriately reinforce acquisition of that information" (p. 185). In all cases, direct instruction rests on behaviorist principles; that is, if teaching is conducted in this sequence, teacher behaviors should promote on-task student learning. The model, therefore, is based on the idea that student learning is invariant across academic subject areas and learner characteristics. The emphasis on teacher behaviors has been so strong, in fact, that the qualities of student learning have all but disappeared from consideration. It comes as no surprise that MacLeod and Nápoles (2015), relying on a model of direct instruction in music education, find that "experienced teachers rated excerpts with high teacher delivery and less student progress higher in effectiveness than excerpts with low teacher delivery and more student progress" (p. 32). Our ideas of what constitutes effective teaching have become skewed.

A new focus on teacher accountability for students' learning, then, may be interpreted as a hopeful sign for education. Yet as Cara Bernard and Joseph Abramo suggest in this volume, how teacher evaluation policies are implemented makes a difference. Do teachers view implementation only as a set of tools for personnel decisions—for "measuring and sorting"—or do they see principals and other administrators who are committed to supporting their teaching and professional development? As Reinhorn, Johnson, and Simon (2017) indicate, "a principal who knows instruction well can engage the teachers in a process of inquiry, self-reflection, and improvement, which ultimately benefits the entire school. However, principals must help teachers see opportunity in a comprehensive evaluation system and feel confident about seeking help, taking risks, and acting on good advice. How principals frame the purpose and character of evaluation for their teachers will influence teachers' readiness to benefit from it" (p. 403). And yet Bernard and Abramo offer their wise advice that music teachers also have a role to play in making evaluation beneficial. They can familiarize themselves with state policies surrounding teacher evaluation as well as components of the model in use in their school districts. Moreover, teachers have ample opportunity to become acquainted with a primary evaluator, whether that is a principal or a performing arts supervisor: What is the evaluator's primary academic area? What is his or her understanding of music education? How does the school culture influence the evaluator's interpretation of teacher evaluation guidelines? Music teachers have opportunities to be advocates, not only for themselves but also for their performing arts colleagues.

Bernard and Abramo do not write from a detached, academic perspective, but from the perspective of music educators who are concerned that evaluation criteria do not apply to music teaching, and that evaluators have little experience in music classrooms. They honor music teachers' pedagogical content knowledge while at the same time challenging them to invest in a broader school culture and remain open to feedback so they can grow professionally. The authors offer abundant recommendations for navigating areas of evaluation that can be tricky for music teachers: questioning, differentiated instruction, literacy, and assessment. Their advice and examples are relentlessly positive and pragmatic—just what music educators need to thrive in their chosen profession.

Susan Wharton Conkling
Boston, Massachusetts

Acknowledgments

THIS BOOK WOULD not be possible without the guidance and inspiration of others. We would like to thank those who read early drafts of the book and provided valuable guidance on the content, structure, and tone. Thank you to Joe's wife, Melissa Natale Abramo, for her reminders of what music teachers truly need in a book on teacher evaluation and for her emotional support throughout the writing process, and to Travis Sherwood, who read every word of this book multiple times, listened to and challenged our thinking, and added continuous support, always with a touch of levity.

Special thanks to Matt Rotjan for his review of and input on the examples and lesson plans included in this book; to Mark Robin Campbell for his conceptual advice; and to the reviewers of this book, for their careful attention to detail and feedback on our manuscripts. Without each of these persons' expertise, the book would not have been possible.

We thank the University of Connecticut's Neag School of Education for continued support. Thank you to current department head of curriculum and instruction, Suzanne Wilson, and former head Mary Anne Doyle, who encouraged us to take this idea and run with it. Thank you to our colleagues, David Moss and Rachael Gabriel, who as book authors themselves provided advice on all steps of the writing and publishing process.

Thank you to Susan Wharton Conkling for writing the foreword to our book. She has been a constant source of encouragement throughout this project as well as other aspects of our careers and is the ultimate model of a teacher educator. Thank you to Norm Hirschy, our editor at Oxford University Press, who approached us with the idea for this book. His vision, along with his patience, enthusiasm, and sense of humor helped guide this book from inception to production.

Finally, thank you to the teachers and students we work with. Thank you to the music teachers whose narratives and experiences with teacher evaluation shaped this research and writing. Their difficulties and successes helped us create the vignettes and stories throughout this book and helped to make the book more illustrative and embedded in the "real world." We thank our students, whose enthusiasm and hard work as they strive to become better music teachers inspire us to better ourselves as researchers and practitioners. Some of our students read portions of early drafts of this book and provided valuable feedback, helping us focus our content and tone on what readers need from this book. Their dedication and insights remind us that the ultimate goal of teacher evaluation and all educational scholarship is to better serve students.

INTRODUCTION

Teacher Evaluation and Music Teachers

On a warm September morning, music teachers from across the region gather for a professional development session. Before the meeting, four colleagues discuss their excitement about the coming academic year. Their conversation quickly turns to their teacher evaluation requirements. Maria, a general music teacher, takes a deep breath and sighs, then says, "I'm dreading it; my principal always tells me to change my teaching. She wants me to ask more high-level questions, differentiate more, let the students have more say in the class, blah, blah, blah. Those things don't work in music classes. But how would she know? She was a math teacher. How is she supposed to evaluate my teaching if she doesn't know anything about the content?" Jacob, an orchestra teacher, agrees, saying, "I'm not looking forward to it either. My principal does what all the teachers call a 'doorknob' observation. He only comes for a few minutes and stands by the door, with his hand never leaving the doorknob, and then returns to his office. He never sees the larger picture of what I'm trying to accomplish that day or in general. On top of that he's always asking me to incorporate some idea—his 'flavor of the month' as we like to call it—but he quickly loses interest and moves on to pushing another strategy." Band director Terrence gets a little red in the face and adds, "Right, they don't get it! I'm tired of being asked to incorporate literacy and other school-wide initiatives into my class- room. I don't have time for that; I've got a concert in December, and I can't waste rehearsal time with those kinds of things! And then the most frustrating part is that my principal doesn't listen to me when I advocate for myself and my program in the post-observation. I mean, I've been doing this a long time and I know what I'm doing. We've gotten into arguments over this." In a calmer voice, chorus teacher Sarah says, "I hear all of you; I've had these problems, too. But you know, I've come to realize through talking with my principal that he has some good things to say about teaching that I can apply, even though there are times when I have to explain to him how teaching music is different than teaching other subjects. You know, I once invited him to sit in with the altos, and he's been able to observe in a different way by surrounding himself with the students. He's pointed to how students can navigate and decode a score and adapt their sound by listening to others around them, something he took for granted when observing from the back of the room. The students got a kick out of him singing with them, and we had some really great conversations about how some of these teaching ideas look in music."

THIS VIGNETTE CAPTURES music teachers' varying experiences of teacher evaluation. Like Maria, Jacob, and Terrence, many music teachers are frustrated with teacher evaluation. They feel that the evaluation system is not well-suited for the subject of music and does not acknowledge the unique challenges of music teaching. Some music teachers also feel that their evaluators do not know enough about music to make informed judgments about their teaching and to provide advice to help them improve. They feel that the evaluators do not devote enough observation time to music teachers' work to understand fully the challenges they face and the reasons for their pedagogical decisions. Music teachers are also often bombarded with the mixed messages of different initiatives and different conceptions of good teaching. They become even more frustrated because these initiatives often are not sustained. As a result, teachers often see these initiatives as "flavors of the month" that will eventually disappear.

Music teachers' frustrations with teacher evaluation can lead to stress and to strained professional relationships (Shaw, 2016). They may feel considerable pressure because their employment, salary, and professional reputation are contingent on arbitrary rules and standards beyond their control (Robinson, 2015). In addition to lesson planning, dealing with classroom management, preparing for concerts, calling parents, and balancing budgets, music teachers are now required to prove their effectiveness. This can lead to resentment toward evaluators and administrators, the people who have immediate control over a teacher's evaluation. In some cases it can even lead to yelling, as in the case of the band director, Terrence, described in the vignette.

While music teachers are often frustrated with their administrators and evaluators, the evaluators also face pressures that make their work in teacher evaluation difficult. Like music teachers, administrators and evaluators are often constrained by rules and standards beyond their control (Ravitch, 2013). They, too, might feel the criteria and procedures are unfair to them and the teachers that they evaluate. Because of these pressures on music teachers and evaluators alike, teacher evaluation can be a stressful experience for all.

However, as Sarah demonstrates, when handled with care, the evaluative process can be constructive. As a survey conducted by the RAND Corporation suggests, a majority of teachers find feedback through evaluation systems helpful for improving their instructional practice (Tuma, Hamilton, & Tsai, 2018). The process can be beneficial for all when music teachers take the time to communicate with evaluators. This will help evaluators understand music teachers' thinking and their challenges. Open communication also helps music teachers keep open minds so they can take advice and improve their teaching. Teacher evaluation processes and open communication can help music teachers grow professionally, resulting not in frustration, as experienced by Maria, Jacob, and Terrence, but in positive professional development, as in Sarah's case. With the correct care, teacher evaluation can serve as an opportunity for music teachers to reflect on practice and to improve their teaching.

APPLYING TO PRACTICE I.1

- Do you identify with Maria, Jacob, Terrence, or Sarah in the vignette? Do you feel that some of the experiences they described are similar to your experiences?
- Take stock of your initial opinions about teacher evaluation:
  - What is your general attitude about feedback from evaluators, teachers, and administrators who are not music teachers? Do you think an evaluator must have a music background to provide valuable feedback?
  - How effective do you think evaluators with and without music backgrounds can be in providing feedback on your teaching?
  - What are the areas in which you believe evaluators with and without music backgrounds may help?
  - Do you believe teacher evaluation is harmful, can be used for professional development, a combination of these, or something else?

WHY A BOOK ON TEACHER EVALUATION AND MUSIC TEACHERS?

We wrote this book because we know from firsthand experience how difficult and frustrating teacher evaluation can be for music teachers. We approach teacher evaluation from our experience as former public school teachers and current teacher educators and researchers. As music teachers who have been evaluated under the new generation teacher evaluation systems, we found it daunting to demonstrate knowledge, measure students' growth, create yearly goals, and talk to evaluators, all while engaging with the difficult work to be done in classrooms, preparing for performances, and completing all other duties. As teacher educators, we have thought much about the skills, knowledge, and dispositions future teachers need to succeed within teacher evaluation systems.

As researchers, we have studied teacher evaluation. One of the authors, Cara, has conducted research in which she talked with music teachers and evaluators about their experiences with teacher evaluation (Bernard, 2015). She found that unfortunately, music teachers perform lower than their colleagues in certain areas in evaluations. As she talked to administrators, she found they did not always know how to communicate about teacher evaluation and music. Music teachers explained to her that they, too, had a hard time rationalizing to their evaluators their pedagogical choices in the music classroom. As we have read other research (Cote & Bernard, 2017; NAfME, 2016a, 2016b; Shuler, 2012; Shaw, 2016) and traveled the country to talk with other music educators and administrators and observe classrooms, we have found that these themes return again and again. These experiences suggest that blending teacher evaluation and music teaching is particularly difficult.

The difficulties of blending music teaching and teacher evaluation arise for several reasons. First, teacher evaluation is politically contentious. The general public argues about teacher evaluation from a policy perspective, sometimes vitriolically. People debate the political agendas of teacher evaluation, the role of corporations in the process, and the validity of the measurements of student growth and teacher effectiveness. Regardless of these issues, music teachers are mandated by laws and policies to participate in these systems. They are required, perhaps unfairly, to find individual solutions within what some people see as a flawed system that can only be fixed through legal and political reform. This book is intended to

---

Teacher evaluation is difficult because . . .

1. Although it is politically contentious, teachers are still required to fulfill its mandates.
2. The policies, rules, and interpretations are continually changing.
3. It is often created to evaluate not specifically music teaching, but rather teaching in general.
4. It potentially creates an adversarial relationship between teachers and evaluators, or evaluators are not effective communicators.
5. Evaluators often do not have a background teaching music.

help music teachers with this difficult task. While we touch upon larger political issues, our intention is to cut through the political noise and focus primarily on helping music teachers with the everyday task of successfully completing teacher evaluation.

Second, there is much uncertainty within teacher evaluation because of changing requirements, conceptions, uses, and interpretations. All teachers, whether they are in the early years of teaching or seasoned veterans, are required to participate in teacher evaluation. However, completing teacher evaluation is not something learned in the first year of teaching and then repeated each year until retirement. With changing evaluators and policies, each completed year is different. Because of that, this book is intended for all music teachers. It is difficult for early career teachers to learn all the nuances of teacher evaluations. Figuring out all the requirements and unwritten rules, then determining how evaluators and administrators understand those rules and requirements, can be stressful. Veteran teachers might want to raise their scores or use teacher evaluation to improve their teaching. They might feel comfortable with their current systems but might become uncertain because of changes in procedures, criteria, administration, or evaluators. Veteran teachers might want to find ways to effectively communicate with new administrators and evaluators or decipher new requirements. This book is intended to help music teachers, novice or veteran, understand these systems and communicate effectively.

Third, as we noted about Cara's research, music teachers struggle to apply the requirements of teacher evaluation. Though these are designed to be applicable to all teaching regardless of the academic subject, music teachers often have a difficult time adapting these requirements to the uniqueness of music teaching. The language of teacher evaluation is often difficult to decipher and apply to music teaching. In particular, Cara has found that music teachers have issues in four key areas: questioning strategies, differentiated instruction, literacy, and assessment (Bernard, 2015). These four pedagogical tools are prevalent across varying teacher evaluation systems. This book aims to help teachers understand the language and practice of these four key areas to improve practice.

Fourth, all these difficulties complicate the daunting task of communicating with evaluators and administrators. Anger toward the political environment of teacher evaluation and evaluators' and administrators' differing interpretations of what counts as good teaching are some of the difficulties music teachers face in pre- and post-observation meetings. The ambiguity of teacher evaluation requirements and "systems of accountability" can strain relationships between teachers and administrators, leading to breakdowns in communication, unpleasant experiences, and sometimes catastrophic results, including poor reviews and even termination.

Fifth, this difficulty in communicating is frequently exacerbated by the fact that music teachers are often evaluated by educators who do not have experience teaching music. Often they are assessed by administrators who have backgrounds in math, science, physical education, English, or other subject areas. Communicating with and receiving feedback from those who have experience as educators but lack knowledge of teaching music is a difficult and sometimes frustrating experience for music teachers. Effectively communicating and receiving feedback requires a delicate balance of advocating for what is done in music education while also remaining open to sound pedagogical advice and an outsider's perspective that might improve practice. While this book addresses different types of evaluators, we especially focus on working with evaluators without music backgrounds.

In sum, this book intends to help music teachers understand and address these difficulties in order to proactively minimize negative experiences. However, it also aims to help teachers move beyond mere completion and compliance. This book can help music teachers use these systems to grow as educators and become better teachers. While teacher evaluation is sometimes used to punish, it ultimately can be—and should be—used to help teachers to dialogue with other educators and improve their teaching. When educators dialogue, teacher evaluation becomes less about fulfilling requirements and checking boxes and more a tool for improvement. We want to provide music teachers with the ability to look past the fads and use teacher evaluation policies to improve their own practice. Overall, we want music teachers to be responsive—not reactive—to these evaluation systems. We aim to help them rely on their expertise as music teachers to improve their teaching and advocate for their teaching choices in productive conversations with their evaluators and, most important, to grow as professional educators. In this way, this book is intended to help people not just to *survive*, but also to *thrive*.

> Music teachers need to be responsive—not reactive—to teacher evaluation, to better advocate and communicate with evaluators, and to allow themselves potential to grow as educators.

HOW TO USE THIS BOOK

How, then, do music teachers thrive in teacher evaluation? In this book we provide advice that teachers can apply to understanding these systems, working on areas where music teachers tend to struggle, learning how to productively converse with evaluators and administrators. Throughout this book we explore ways music teachers can successfully engage in teacher evaluation. In the first two chapters we provide background on teacher evaluation that will help teachers begin to understand the varying uses of teacher evaluation and an overall strategy for responding to these uses. In chapter 1 we explore teacher evaluation in the United States, including a brief history and criteria common to policies and teacher evaluation systems. In chapter 2 we suggest a mindset or approach that will help music teachers make teacher evaluation work for them to spark professional growth and ultimately be successful.

In chapters 3 through 6 we delve into details of the four key areas that music teachers often struggle with in order to prepare them for observations and discussions with evaluators. Chapter 3 explores how teachers can ask quality, varied questions. Chapter 4 discusses how music educators might apply a variety of methods to implement robust differentiation in their lessons. Chapter 5 discusses the sometimes thorny area of literacy in the music classroom. We examine how music teachers can implement reading and writing in the music curriculum in authentic and useful ways that advance students' *musical* education, and how they can properly incorporate and advocate for broader definitions of literacy. Chapter 6 addresses the controversial topic of assessment in teacher evaluation. This includes ways music teachers might fulfill the requirements of evaluators who observe the teacher's assessment practices in the classroom, as well as how to address the components of teacher evaluation that assess student growth through standardized tests or other means.

In the final chapter we discuss how to talk to evaluators. We explore in depth how to balance this tension of educating evaluators about the unique pedagogical content knowledge of music while remaining open to their insights in pedagogical knowledge and other areas. We discuss how to approach this with both arts and non-music evaluators, helping to put music teachers' knowledge into context for the evaluator. These productive dialogues might create opportunities for mutual understanding, leading to growth and advocacy. We address how teachers might create such opportunities with ideal evaluators who are master teachers, are open to dialogue, and provide good feedback. We also discuss how music teachers might accomplish this with evaluators who lack pedagogical knowledge, are poor communicators, or may even be hostile. This final chapter also synthesizes information in the previous chapters to help music teachers communicate effectively in the four key areas.

As noted, chapters 3–6 focus on areas that research suggests music teachers typically struggle with in teacher evaluation (Bernard, 2015; Katz-Cote, 2016; Martin, 2014; Shaw, 2016). In this book we do not focus on places in the evaluation systems where music teachers tend to do well or received a lot of in teacher education preparation, including score study, history, conducting, and other musical content knowledge. Music teachers traditionally do well in the professional responsibilities sections, such as communicating with parents and involving the community. As such, these are not aspects music teachers need great support with in relation to evaluation systems. Instead, we focus on targeted areas that music teachers often need extra support to flourish within teacher evaluation systems.

Throughout the chapters we present vignettes like the one at the beginning of this introduction. These vignettes feature the following fictitious characters: general music teacher Maria, orchestra director Jacob, band director Terrence, chorus director Sarah, and their evaluators. The vignettes are intended to demonstrate the issues surrounding talking to evaluators and implementing the four key areas of teaching. These vignettes are based on the combined experiences of teachers and administrators derived from Cara's research (Bernard, 2015) and our own experiences of speaking and working with in-service music teachers. We have combined these stories into characters to highlight themes and common occurrences in these processes. This strategy of combining the stories of real people into fictional characters is often employed by researchers to distill and demonstrate ideas captured in qualitative research (Finley, 2011; for an excellent example in education, see Sizer's [1997] character Horace). Toward the end of each chapter, we rewrite these narratives using the information in the chapter so that they express a more positive outcome.

Within the chapters, we provide guidance on how teachers can synthesize the ideas in this book and apply them to their teaching. Throughout each chapter we include "Applying to Practice" exercises. These are designed to help readers apply concepts described in the book to a music teacher's practice in and out of the classroom and to help them create, modify, and reflect on lesson plans and prepare for their pre- and post- observation meetings with evaluators. At the ends of chapters 3, 4, 5, and 6 we provide lesson plans that serve as examples for implementing these strategies in various music classrooms. These include lesson plans using well-known, standard repertoire for elementary and secondary grade levels in general music, chorus, and instrumental ensembles. These lessons are adaptable to the varying ways that music teachers might be required or prefer to craft their lesson plans. The lessons incorporate components music teachers commonly use in lesson plans. We have included both behavioral and conceptual objectives; crafted essential questions and enduring understandings, as outlined in *Understanding by Design* (Wiggins & McTighe, 2005); and identified the US *National Core Arts Standards* (National Coalition for Core Arts Standards, 2014) that each lesson fulfills.

Finally, we aim to provide information that teachers can apply regardless of their required teacher evaluation systems. There are many different systems, including Danielson, Marzano, Stronge, and McREL; some school districts and states modify these common systems to their unique work environments, while others create their own. Because of this variety, although we reference specific teacher evaluation systems throughout the text, we do not emphasize one specific evaluation system or tool. Rather, we focus on the salient themes embedded within the most prominent and widely used systems and the ways in which teachers may improve upon them in their teaching, regardless of the system they are required to complete.

APPLYING TO PRACTICE I.2

- Why have you decided to read this book?
  - Are you finding difficulty in certain aspects of teacher evaluation?
  - Are you having difficulty with a particular administrator or evaluator?
  - Are you looking to improve your scores?
  - Do you want to understand how to improve your teaching using teacher evaluation?
  - Do you have some other motivation?

Pinpointing the specific reasons you have decided to read this book will help you address your concerns and goals while also remaining open to differing points of view and areas you had not considered.

1

TEACHER EVALUATION

History, Policy, and Practice

Terrence the band director meets with his instructional coach for his post-observation. After some pleasant discussion, the instructional coach asks, "How have you fulfilled Domain 1 in our evaluation framework?" Not knowing the specifics of Domain 1, Terrence shares how he and his ensemble are active within the community: "Let me think. We play at all the pep rallies and football games. This year we were invited to march in the town parade. They've been ambassadors for our school by playing in the community. On top of that, I conduct the pit for the school musical, staying after school until 7:00 p.m. almost every night for rehearsals." "This is all a wonderful testament to your dedication," the instructional coach responds, "but I'm interested in the ways you've thought through your planning and preparation, which is a requirement of Domain 1 in our evaluation framework." Terrence responds, "Hmm. Well, I have to plan for the concerts by picking different styles and levels of music. Once I pick my repertoire I have to make sure the students are well rehearsed and know their parts. I can't plan for the next rehearsal until I hear how they sound in the current rehearsal." The instructional coach explains that "thinking through the specific goals for the semester and year will help you with the day to day teaching, and will improve your professional practice." Terrence responds that he practices his professionalism daily, and that "concerts sell out every season with standing room only. And, the band has gotten gold with distinction for the last three years we have gone to the state festival. We are on the

top of our game." Terrence's instructional coach again praises his profession-
alism and commitment to building a musical community, but reminds him that
he was being evaluated on his planning and preparation: "It seems to me you
haven't thought much about planning. I'm giving you a developing rating for
planning and preparation," she adds. "To improve on that, I want you to submit
to me a planning map that shows your learning goals for the year and describes
how the students will reach them through the music you choose throughout the
year." Feeling defeated, Terrence sighs. As he leaves, he thinks to himself, "She
doesn't understand how hard I work. Why does she keep harping on planning?"

FOR TERRENCE—AND many music teachers—the pressure of concerts, music
festivals, and other performances often drives planning, preparation, and
lesson and rehearsal plans. Despite these difficulties, for many years Terrence
was positively evaluated by how well his concerts sounded and his high level of
involvement in the community. As a result, he identified himself as a successful
teacher. However, with the new generation evaluation systems, a rating is no
longer based solely on the professional responsibilities of a music teacher, such
as putting in long hours, conducting concerts, or performing at community
events. Instead, current evaluation systems focus on the quality of teaching,
including planning and instruction, in order to improve practice. Terrence has
been reluctant to acknowledge these changes in how teachers are evaluated.
He never learned the requirements of the evaluation system and was unable
to answer his instructional coach when she asked him how he fulfilled the
planning and preparation requirements in Domain 1. He could not easily digest
his instructional coach's feedback or advocate for his teaching accordingly, and
he left the meeting frustrated that she did not rate him as successful.

How might Terrence learn about teacher evaluation and its uses to better respond to his instructional coach's comments and improve his professional practice? In this chapter we provide background on teacher evaluation in the US. This
background may help music teachers navigate teacher evaluation systems and
avoid the types of situations in which Terrence found himself. First, we provide
a brief history of federal and state education law and education policy. Second,
we look at how history and policy have led to tensions, disagreements, and
contradictions within teacher evaluation processes and policies. Finally, we describe how these tensions have resulted in the common characteristics of teacher
evaluation systems found throughout the country. By understanding this background and history, music teachers may begin to actively participate in teacher
evaluation.

A BRIEF HISTORY OF TEACHER EVALUATION POLICY
IN THE UNITED STATES

The evaluation of teachers is not a new concept. For almost as long as there has been teaching, there has been both formal and informal teacher evaluation. In the US, for much of the twentieth century there was a patchwork of evaluation systems. Teachers in Alabama, for example, were evaluated based on different criteria than were used for teachers in California (Taebel, 1990a, 1990b). Even within states there were different criteria. Teachers in New York City schools that lacked resources were held to different standards and criteria than teachers in the affluent suburbs less than thirty miles away (Otterman, 2011; Polikoff & Porter, 2014). Eventually people became critical of this patchwork of evaluation systems. Critics argued that teachers were not evaluated in the same way as other professionals. As the argument goes, the systems were not rigorous and did not accurately and adequately evaluate teachers; the result was uneven education for students based on where they lived (Darling-Hammond, 2013; Kohn, 2011; Prince et al., 2009).

Because of these concerns, for better or worse lawmakers began to look for ways to improve education by more systematically evaluating teachers. The result of these efforts was a series of federal policies and laws that can be divided into four stages. The first phase aimed to standardize public education. The second phase then aimed to evaluate the standards through students' performance on standardized tests and other measures. In the third phase, students' outcomes were then further tied to teachers' effectiveness through teacher evaluation systems. Finally, in the last phase many of these efforts were rolled back, and lawmakers gave powers back to the individual states to make decisions about how to approach and structure student growth and teacher evaluation. Table 1.1 summarizes these phases.

In the first phase, the focus was on making the standards of education throughout the country more uniform. In 1983 the Reagan administration produced a document called *A Nation at Risk: The Imperative for Educational Reform* (US National Commission on Excellence in Education, 1983). This publication focused on improving student performance outcomes through "better curriculum standards, higher graduation requirements, better teacher training, higher teacher pay, and other customary improvements" (Ravitch, 2013, p. 10). As a result, schools increased testing and created standards and benchmarks for learning (Gabriel & Woulfin, 2017). Twelve years later, during the Clinton administration, Congress followed *A Nation at Risk* with *Goals 2000: Educate America Act* (USDOE, 1995). *Goals 2000* aimed to create "clear and rigorous standards for what every child should know and be able to do" (USDOE, 1995, sec. 2) in core subjects. In music education, this move toward standardization resulted in the publication of

TABLE 1.1.

Four phases of contemporary teacher evaluation in the United States

	Phase 1: Standardizing Public Education	Phase 2: Standardized Tests	Phase 3: Teacher Evaluation	Phase 4: Rollback
Description	An aim to standardize the curricula throughout the nation.	An aim to make these standards "accountable" through standardized tests.	An aim to tie the results of these standardized tests to the evaluation of teachers.	A rollback of teacher evaluation, in which the states, rather than the federal government, make the criteria for how they fulfill teacher evaluation requirements.
Key Documents, Policies, and Legislation	• *A Nation at Risk: The Imperative for Educational Reform* (1983) • Goals 2000: Educate America Act (1995) • Music National Standards (1994)	No Child Left Behind Act (NCLB) (2001)	Race to the Top (R2T) (2012)	Every Student Succeeds Act (ESSA) (2016)

the 1994 National Standards in Music by the Music Educators National Conference (MENC), now named NAfME (National Association for Music Education). The creation of these music standards was an attempt to respond to the political climate of the time and create more uniform standards in music throughout the country.

The second phase was an attempt to tie the standards outlined in *A Nation at Risk* and *Goals 2000* to student performance. In 2001, during the George W. Bush administration, Congress passed the *No Child Left Behind* (NCLB) Act (USDOE, 2001), which aimed to make schools "accountable" to these "high standards." NCLB required that students complete standardized tests to determine if a school provided them an adequate education. It also aimed to ensure that students from all backgrounds received an equal education. Schools had to demonstrate that students from different subpopulations—such as students of different races, genders, and socioeconomic backgrounds, as well as special education students— could perform sufficiently on these tests. Lawmakers thought that schools, by having to demonstrate that all subgroups could pass standardized tests in sufficient numbers, could not hide that they were educating students of certain populations better than others. This way, "no child was left behind" because of his or her race, disabilities, or other characteristic of circumstance. If students continually did not perform successfully on tests, schools could lose federal funding or be taken over by the government, and teachers could be terminated.

While NCLB's purported aim was to improve education for all students, it failed to produce large improvements in student achievement as outlined by the National Assessment of Education Progress (U.S. DOE, 2015), was publically unpopular, and became a politically contentious law. Because of its unpopularity, the Obama administration instituted Race to the Top (R2T) in 2011 (Civic Impulse, 2017). An education document called *The Widget Effect* (Weisberg et al., 2009) exposed that few teachers were actually evaluated in schools. In fact, there was no basis or data to show how teachers received tenure or were promoted or retained. In response to *The Widget Effect*, R2T shifted the focus from student testing to teacher ability and its effects on student achievement. Simply stated, the teacher's impact influenced and affected student growth, progress, and product.

Similar to NCLB, R2T became politically contentious. In 2016 Congress passed the Every Student Succeeds Act (ESSA; US Congress, 2016), which aimed to provide more flexibility to the states. Many political conservatives believed that R2T and NCLB had created too much regulation at the federal level. The ESSA granted states more flexibility in how they demonstrate that their schools meet standards and evaluate teachers. It laid out four ways to measure teacher quality and student progress: (1) formal and informal observations; (2) rubrics to measure instruction; (3) feedback given to teachers by evaluators; and (4) teacher goal setting for student achievement. Policymakers believed that these four factors would lead to capturing and measuring student learning and document teachers' work to create more effective teachers. The evaluation systems currently employed in school districts embody these factors, focusing more on teacher growth and reflection and student engagement rather than on achievement. These evaluation systems make direct connections between the policy and pedagogy, providing a basis for observing student engagement, giving teachers feedback on their instruction, and allowing space for teacher improvement.

> Current teacher evaluation policies allow states more flexibility in how they implement policies, focusing more on teacher growth and student achievement and less on test scores.

CONTEMPORARY TEACHER EVALUATION: "MEASURE AND SORT" VERSUS "SUPPORT AND DEVELOP"

We have painted a tidy history of the development of teacher evaluation over the last several decades. As we explained this history, it might look like a series of policies and laws were passed rather routinely and logically. The truth, however, is messier. As these laws were proposed, debated, and then passed, people and organizations approached them with different interests and motivations. On one side, some lawmakers wanted to enact more "accountability" for teachers through laws like NCLB and R2T. These laws aimed to objectively measure student learning and teacher effectiveness. However, these notions of accountability often did not take into account the complexity of teaching and learning, including how students' socioeconomic background, funding, and other factors outside of teachers' control affect learning. Meanwhile, professional educators, concerned with the lack of nuance in these systems, pushed to make teacher evaluation a professional development tool. This approach, backed by research (Hall, Dirksen, & George, 2008), aimed to use teacher evaluation to create dialogue between educators to improve their practice.

The systems that teachers currently work within are the results of these political battles; they are uneven and contradictory in aims and purposes. On the one hand, teacher evaluation is more closely directed toward collegiality and teacher professional development than during the NCLB and R2T years. There are more flexible ways of demonstrating competency and progress that relate more to school and classroom situation and context. On the other hand, the many assumptions and language of NCLB and R2T still remain in teacher evaluation. Teacher evaluation is more uniform than it was prior to ESSA. Yet for better or worse, educators are left to work within a system that is influenced by this history.

As a result, today teacher evaluation is used in two contradictory ways: as a checkpoint or standard to measure teachers or as a tool for the professional development and improvement of teachers. Gabriel and Woulfin (2017) describe these two contradictory approaches to evaluation as "measure and sort" and "support and develop" (p. xvi). A *measure and sort* approach uses observations as a means to assess the quality of teaching and to assign a rating to the teacher's quality of instruction. The evaluation rubrics become a sort of checklist to collect data about a teacher. A measure and sort approach allows evaluators to make personnel decisions about the teacher, including hiring, firing, and promotion and tenure. On the other hand, a *support and develop* approach, as Gabriel and Woulfin describe it, uses "observations to gain data on what to support teachers on" (2017, p. xvi) and includes giving feedback and having conversations with teachers. Support and develop allows the teacher to be a professional learner and to use the evaluation process as a means for growth and reflection. A survey by the RAND Corporation (Tuma et al., 2018) suggests that teachers prefer a "support and develop" approach that provides them feedback to help them improve their practice.

> A *measure and sort* approach uses observations as a means to assess the quality of teaching and to assign a rating to the teacher's quality of instruction.
>
> A *support and develop* approach uses "observations to help teachers improve and professional develop" (Gabriel & Woulfin, 2017, p. xvi)

These contradictions often cause confusion and competing uses of teacher evaluation both district-wide and at the school-wide levels. Everyone from teachers to the superintendent has different pressures, goals, and responsibilities in schools. Teachers are charged with the immediate care and instruction of children; evaluators and instructional coaches must help teachers professionally develop and create consistency within curricula; and administrators are tasked with supervision of teachers and must verify that laws and policies are enacted and followed by all members of the school community. Because of these different goals, these participants in teacher evaluation may use it differently. Teachers might see it as a procedure to follow, instructional coaches as a professional development tool, and administrators as a procedure that can create uniformity among curriculum and instruction. These uses of teacher evaluation sometimes conflict with one another, creating tensions. Each of these three groups might expect different outcomes from teacher evaluation.

While these different groups may have differing conceptions of teacher evaluation, they do not always effectively articulate these varying perspectives. Sometimes because of lack of time, administrators do not clearly communicate what they hope teacher evaluation will accomplish. At other times educators have not communicated to themselves what they hope it might accomplish. They may see it as another law or mandate to comply with and have not taken the time to think about their assumptions regarding teacher evaluation.

Goldstein (2008) calls this lack of communication the "telephone game" of teacher evaluation. As teacher evaluation policies are passed from administrators to instructional coaches to teachers, each group attaches its own interpretation and goals to them. Much like the children's game of telephone, this sometimes distorts the process, and by the time these laws and policies reach teachers, the message is quite different than how it was originally conceived, leading to miscommunication and sometimes resentment, because each group is looking for different outcomes from the teacher evaluation procedure.

The "telephone game" of teacher evaluation requires teachers to be aware of additional influence on teacher evaluation. Evaluators and administrators have differing goals for and interpretations of teacher evaluation, and they may or may not be clear in communicating their expectations. They may see it as a tool to measure and sort or to support and develop. Because of this, music teachers should be extra aware of the pressures, expectations, and assumptions evaluators may have. For example, if an evaluator is required to raise test scores, he or she may use teacher evaluation as a way to motivate or force teachers to improve their students' scores. However, evaluators may not be explicit in communicating that they are using teacher evaluation in this way. We return to this crucial point in chapter 7, where we discuss how music teachers might communicate with evaluators to determine what their goals and expectations are, even if they are not particularly effective communicators.

The tension between the measure and sort and support and develop approaches to teacher evaluation—both on a policy level and in how individual people use and interpret the system—leaves music educators in a difficult position. In chapter 2 we discuss in more detail the right mindset to deal with this tension. For now it is important to note that music teachers should aim to use the system as a way to support and develop their own growth as teachers. By understanding that a key contradiction between the measure and sort and support and develop approaches exists, music teachers can begin to see patterns and begin to push teacher evaluation toward being a tool for professional development rather than for punishment. This is not an easy task. But by understanding these systems, understanding evaluators' different motivations and pressures, learning how to communicate, and having an open mind toward growth, teachers can exploit the support and develop aspects and minimize the measure and sort uses of teacher evaluation.

APPLYING TO PRACTICE 1.1

Conduct an initial review of your evaluation experience thus far. Has your experience been more a process to "measure and sort" or to "support and develop"? What about your experience makes you categorize it this way?

COMPONENTS OF TEACHER EVALUATION SYSTEMS

The history and contradictions we just reviewed have direct impacts on the components commonly found in current teacher evaluation systems. In this section we look at some of the common attributes and requirements of teacher evaluation. While we do enumerate common components, there is great variety in the types of teacher evaluation systems currently employed throughout the US. As we noted, ESSA has given states flexibility in how to implement teacher evaluation and policies; as such, implementation may vary depending on school district and even within individual schools. Within these differing systems, teachers are given a wide variety of degree of freedom and input into how they are assessed. Sometimes teachers can select or create their own assessments, form the criteria for how they will be assessed, and set their own yearly goals for teacher evaluation. At other times more is predetermined; the criteria of assessment are set by district policies or state laws with little or no input from teachers.

While there is variety among the systems, some characteristics are commonly found throughout the US. This is because NCLB and R2T policies created some uniformity that remains to this day. In addition, states and districts often adopt commercially available teacher evaluation systems to serve as the basis for evaluation of criteria. The most commonly used systems are by Danielson (2007, 2013) and Marzano (2013). In addition, systems like 5D+ (University of Washington Center for Educational Leadership, 2017), Stronge (Stronge & Associates, 2016), and McREL (McREL International, 2017) are also widely used. These common components of many of the teacher evaluation systems include *inputs* (or observations), *outcomes* (or

> A teacher's overall evaluation score may be comprised of *inputs* (observation and meetings with evaluators), *outcomes* (student test scores), or how he or she fulfills his or her *yearly goals*.

TABLE 1.2.

Common components of teacher evaluation

	Description	How It Is Evaluated
Input	Evaluates whether the teacher uses effective teaching strategies, planning, and interactions with others.	Classroom observations by an evaluator.
Outcomes	Evaluates whether students can demonstrate growth and that they have learned materials.	• Standardized tests. • Student learning outcomes (SLOs).
Yearly Goals	Involves formation of a yearly plan to improve practice.	Formation of yearly goals to improve teaching practice, followed by meetings to decide if these goals were met.

assessment of student growth), and the requirement for teachers to create and/or achieve *yearly goals*. Table 1.2 summarizes these common components.

INPUTS: OBSERVATION AND MEETINGS WITH EVALUATORS

First, teacher evaluation aims to assess teacher *inputs* into the learning environment. These might include the teaching strategies teachers use, their classroom management, how they contribute to the atmosphere of the school, and other factors that the system believes are under their control. Each system emphasizes different aspects of these inputs and construes them in different ways. The two most common systems, Danielson and Marzano, for example, both consist of four domains on which that evaluators must evaluate the teachers on. Each domain has subgroups that more specifically enumerate the components of each of these requirements. These domains and brief descriptions of them are shown in table 1.3.

These two systems, and many others, have the following attributes in common as part of the inputs:

- They require strong planning for lessons based on educational theory.
- Instruction is flexible, driven by assessment, and based on knowledge of students.

TABLE 1.3.

Marzano and Danielson evaluation domains

Marzano (2013)	Danielson (2007, 2013)
Domain 1: Classroom Strategies and Behaviors The teacher demonstrates strong classroom management and effective communication with students, creating positive relationships with students, engaging students in meaningful learning, and tracking student progress.	**Domain 1: Planning and Preparation** The teacher creates strong lesson plans based on knowledge of education theory and students' backgrounds, and designs strong assessment.
Domain 2: Planning and Preparing The teacher demonstrates that he or she plans lessons by using educational theory to create strong lessons; uses a variety of resources; and puts into place strategies that support English Language Learners, special education students, and students who lack supports for schooling.	**Domain 2: The Classroom Environment** The teacher demonstrates that the classroom is well managed, and there is respect between teacher and students.
Domain 3: Reflecting on Teaching The teacher demonstrates that he or she evaluates his or her own teaching and implements better strategies to improve his or her teaching.	**Domain 3: Instruction** The teacher communicates with students, asks good questions and facilitates dialogue, uses assessment to determine the trajectory of instruction, and demonstrates flexibility in teaching.
Domain 4: Collegiality and Professionalism The teacher demonstrates that he or she positively contributes to the school community and parents and promotes the sharing of ideas.	**Domain 4: Professional Responsibilities** The teacher demonstrates that he or she positively contributes to the school community and parents, shows the ability to grow professionally, keeps accurate records, and reflects on his or her teaching to implement better strategies to improve teaching.

- Instruction supports learners who need extra attention.
- Teachers have strong classroom management.
- Teachers are able to reflect on and improve their teaching and grow professionally.
- Teachers positively contribute to the community by communicating with parents and other professionals.

Teachers' abilities in these areas are primarily assessed through observation by an evaluator (Coggshall, Ott, & Lasagna, 2010; Prince et al., 2009; Steinberg & Donaldson, 2016). The evaluator is most commonly a school administrator, but it might also be another teacher, a department supervisor, or a third party hired by the district. These evaluators may or may not have a background in teaching music. These observations usually consist of an evaluator coming to the teacher's classroom to watch him or her teach a full lesson or part of a lesson. Sometimes these observations are announced; the teacher and evaluator agree that a specific lesson will be observed. Sometimes they are unannounced, and the teacher does not know when he or she will be observed. Most evaluation systems include a combination of both announced and unannounced observations.

These observations are usually coupled with meetings outside of the classroom between the teacher and the evaluator. Typically, there is a pre-observation meeting ("pre-ob") at which the teacher discusses his or her plans for the lesson to be observed and any information about that class or the students that will help the evaluator in his or her comments and evaluation. There is commonly a post-observation meeting ("post-ob") as well, at which the evaluator provides evidence of his or her observation, feedback, and strategies for future improvement.

APPLYING TO PRACTICE 1.2

- What evaluation system is used in your school or district? Is it one of the common frameworks, like Marzano or Danielson; an adapted version of these frameworks; or something specifically designed for your district?
- Look through the evaluation tool. What are the overarching parts of the tool? Does it evaluate teachers based on planning, instruction, creating a learning environment, and displaying professionalism? Are there other large evaluative components?

OUTCOMES: EVALUATING STUDENT GROWTH THROUGH TESTING

In addition to the inputs of observation, a second common component aims to assess *outcomes*. In other words, teacher evaluation systems often also seek to assess whether the teacher's inputs affect students' learning and growth. This component often aims to measure the teacher's instruction in a more numerical way, because it is more difficult to measure the ways in which inputs yield student learning.

The practices for assessing student learning and growth vary widely based on location and academic subject. In certain disciplines, such as math or English, standardized tests are used to measure student growth; however, these tests are uncommon in music. Instead, in subjects where there are no standardized tests, including music, individual teachers, schools, and districts create their own assessments of student growth. This may include pre- and post-tests intended to measure student growth. These assessments are commonly known as "student learning outcomes" or "student learning objectives" (SLOs). The SLOs are often based on a learning objective (such as reading rhythms or improvising on three notes), and students are tested at the beginning of the unit or year to determine what they know. Known as a baseline assessment, a test that evaluates the same content is given again at the end of the unit or year to assess students' growth. We discuss SLOs more in chapter 6, on assessment.

Sometimes the evaluations of student growth are based on factors outside the teacher's direct control. For example, even though a teacher might teach music, students' performance on a math or English Language Arts (ELA) state test may determine the student growth component of the teacher's evaluation. At other times the assessment is based on parameters not directly related to the teaching process, including attendance or other school-wide factors like school climate. Regardless of how it is assessed, a teacher's evaluation—including inputs and outcomes—makes up a percentage of a teacher's overall effectiveness.

YEARLY GOALS

In addition to the inputs and outcomes components, another common aspect of evaluation is the teacher's creation of yearly goals. For example, the Marzano model requires teachers to create a "growth and development plan," which requires teachers to target areas they want to improve in their teaching or set goals for student growth and create a strategy to achieve that goal. Sometimes yearly goals are district or school based, in which the superintendent or principal wants teachers to work toward a common goal, such as incorporating ten minutes of writing per class period or using unit questions to drive lesson planning and instruction. On an individual basis, a teacher's yearly goal, for example, might be to improve her communication with parents. To accomplish this goal, she might create a plan in which she implements a classroom newsletter, social media account, or other way of easily disseminating communication with parents. A teacher might also look to create more equitable and fair classroom management strategies. He might seek out professional development that will help him become sensitive to issues and devise strategies that make all students feel connected to the classroom and ready to learn. These yearly goals sometimes are created by the teacher with input and guidance from an evaluator. At other times schools or districts dictate what these goals will be.

APPLYING TO PRACTICE 1.3

- What percentage of your overall evaluation rating is based on outcomes, or student test scores? How is this score calculated?
- Does your school or district require its teachers to create a list of yearly goals, including an action plan for reaching these goals? If so, what are your own current yearly goals?

PUTTING IT TOGETHER: BECOMING AN ACTIVE PARTICIPANT IN TEACHER EVALUATION

We have described a brief history of teacher evaluation and policy in the US and the competing uses of teacher evaluation and have identified some common components. By knowing these influences, music teachers might begin to actively participate in teacher evaluation. Rather than it seeming like a random, punitive system, by knowing these different contexts, music teachers might see patterns and begin to shift the evaluation process from a tool used to measure and sort to a procedure used to support and develop their teaching. Table 1.4 lists some questions music teachers might answer as they prepare for teacher evaluation. These guidelines apply to teacher evaluation in general. In the following chapter we turn to some specific challenges and issues that arise when music teachers are evaluated in these systems. We return to these questions in the final chapter to discuss in greater detail the strategies music teachers can use to engage in discussions and seek out this information.

SUMMARY

Music teachers have different experiences and feelings about teacher evaluation. Teacher evaluation policies can be enacted, implemented, and interpreted

TABLE 1.4.

Overarching principles for music teachers to keep in mind when participating in teacher evaluation

Questions for Actively Participating in Teacher Evaluation	Resources to Find the Answers
Requirements	
• What are the requirements of the teacher evaluation?	• Read the agreed-upon teacher evaluation system in the district or school.
• What are its components?	
• How are these components evaluated?	• Consult resources if it is a commercially available system (like Marzano, Danielson, etc.).
	• Consult representatives of your union if you have one.
Regional or State Context	
• What are the state laws and requirements of teacher evaluation?	• Read state policies and laws by consulting the state education department website.
• What is the general view of the public about teacher evaluation?	
• Do teachers' unions or other teacher advocacy groups in the area have official positions?	
School-wide Context	
• How have administrators, evaluators, and teachers used teacher evaluation in the past?	• Discuss with other teachers.
	• Consult representatives of your union if you have one.
• Has it been used to measure and sort, support or develop, or both?	
Evaluators' Perspective	
• What pressures, goals, and expectations of teacher evaluation do evaluators and administrators have, but have not clearly articulated?	• Consult administrators or evaluators.
	• Read school reports.
	• Discuss with other teachers what they believe are the pressing issues in the district.

differently from federal to state to district to school levels. Having a working knowledge and understanding of the background and history of the policies and their purposes can help music teachers to better live within and navigate current evaluation processes. The current teacher evaluation systems can be used as a checkpoint (measure and sort) or as a means for teacher reflection and growth (support and develop). Individual evaluators may use them in different ways, depending on their pressures and expectations. In the "telephone game" of teacher evaluation, evaluators might not have taken the time to examine their own assumptions about teacher evaluation or have clearly communicated their expectations. Finally, teachers might not know that the actual requirements of teacher evaluation. Teacher evaluation systems typically consist of three components: the teacher's observation, measurement of student growth, and the creation of yearly goals. Knowing the makeup of these evaluation systems and how different people use them helps teachers and evaluators understand the process in their schools and classrooms. With this knowledge, music teachers might be better prepared to "rewrite" situations like the one Terrence encountered in the vignette at the beginning of this chapter.

Terrence the band director meets with his instructional coach for his post-observation. After some pleasant discussion, the instructional coach asks, "How have you fulfilled Domain 1 in our evaluation framework?" Terrence remembers that as a yearly goal his school has been preoccupied with teachers sequencing lessons, so he responds, "Okay, Domain 1 is planning, right? I have the framework right here. Domain 1c in the Danielson specifically calls for setting instructional outcomes, including 'value, sequence, and alignment.' As a teacher with such a busy performance schedule, I have to think about sequence a lot. I need to plan the repertoire ahead of time for these events and lay out how we will learn the pieces in an effective way, creating goals for each piece." His instructional coach asks, "How do you organize this for your planning?" Terrence responds, "I put an agenda on the board every day with the goals for the day to help the students know what they're working toward daily. I put an overall goal that we're working toward over an extended period of time, such as creating a balanced sound, and then smaller goals to accomplish during the actual class period. So, today, the students applied their work on musical balance to a new section of 'Amazing Grace' while also focusing on sight reading and playing legato musical lines." He continues, "Also, since we play so often in the community, I plan my goals to be not only musical, but also community based." He takes out a chart: "Here's a calendar chart of when the performances are. I work backward from there, making sure to target my goals while also working toward performance. Right now the overall goal is musical balance, so I will make sure the students feel comfortable with this concept by the time they perform next." The instructional coach thanks Terrence for the explanation and says he looks forward to seeing how Domain 1 is realized in Terrence's teaching next week in the observation.

2

DEVELOPING A MINDSET TO SUCCEED IN TEACHER

EVALUATION SYSTEMS

As part of chorus director Sarah's evaluation system, the principal is required to conduct one unannounced observation. One afternoon the principal comes to observe Sarah's beginner level chorus. He stays for fifteen minutes and then leaves without making a comment. A week later, the principal calls Sarah down to his office for the post-observation meeting. "I only have a minute to talk, but I wanted to tell you 'Great job'," he says. "But I wonder about one thing: How do you know the students were engaged?" Sarah sighs. "Of course they're engaged; they're singing. They're automatically engaged." "But how do you really know that they're engaged?" the principal responds. "They could be lip-syncing and you might not know. I think you need to take steps to show they're engaged more. I need you to incorporate more dialogue by having them fill out a sheet that reviews all the notes you want to teach them and then have a discussion about them. Then you'll know that they're engaged more." Sarah begins to get a little angry and raises her voice. "What you're saying won't work in a music class because it's an unproductive use of rehearsal time. There's no need for a sheet; I know they're engaged. You're welcome to stay the entire period—then you can see more of what I'm doing with the students." "OK," says her principal, "I do think the sheet will provide another way to get students engaged. You should try it." Sarah leaves the meeting feeling like she received unsound advice on teaching music.

LIKE SARAH, MANY music teachers are evaluated by their principals or other administrators who have no background in music. For Sarah this is a frustrating experience because the evaluator is giving advice that is not informed by a deep knowledge of music and is contrary to effective and often-used teaching strategies in music education. Sarah feels that fifteen minutes is not enough time for her principal to understand these nuances of music education and to accurately evaluate her. However, with the right mindset, there are valuable things to draw from an evaluator even if he or she does not know much about teaching music or has not spent much time observing. In this chapter we first discuss some of the common problems music teachers have with teacher evaluation and then provide an overall framework or approach that can help music teachers develop the best mindset and strategies to overcome these problems. In doing this, music teachers can use teacher evaluation to not just survive but thrive, to successfully use teacher evaluation to advocate for their teaching, and to grow professionally.

MUSIC TEACHERS' CONCERNS WITH TEACHER EVALUATION

As we noted in chapter 1, there is a contradiction between the measure and sort and support and develop approaches to evaluating teachers (Gabriel & Woulfin, 2017). On one side, evaluators and administrators might use teacher evaluation as an accountability tool to measure teacher effectiveness and remove ineffective teachers. On the other side, evaluators and administrators might use teacher evaluation to spark dialogue between professionals in order to improve practice. This contradiction is a result of the history of federal policies and has resulted in the input/output format of observation and measurement of student growth commonly found in contemporary teacher evaluation systems. Problems arise because various actors—policymakers, administrators, team leaders, and teachers— interpret this contradiction in differing ways and emphasize different aspects in the teacher evaluation process (Spillane, 2006).

These contradictions in the aims and interpretations of teacher evaluation often lead to concerns that music teachers have with these systems. In her research, Cara (Bernard, 2015) interviewed music educators and administrators about their experiences with teacher evaluation. She found that music educators felt evaluation tools and ratings did not provide specific enough guidelines and evaluators lacked enough knowledge related to specific subjects to sufficiently implement teacher evaluation in effective ways. By acknowledging and naming these frustrations, teachers can pinpoint difficulties and begin to craft strategies to deal with them.

CRITERIA ARE NOT APPLICABLE TO MUSIC

Teacher evaluation systems are often not specifically designed for music. Instead, they are framed so that evaluators and administrators may apply the criteria to all teachers in a school, regardless of the subject they teach. For example, as Charlotte Danielson (The Danielson Group, n.d.) notes, her framework for teaching "is grounded in the simple fact that teaching, in whatever context, requires the same basic tasks, namely, knowing one's subject, knowing one's students, having clear outcomes, establishing a culture for learning, engaging students in learning, etc. . . . [W]hile teaching is highly contextualized, the basic work of teaching is universal" (n.p.). For many music teachers, this "simple fact" of evaluating music teaching through a "universal" approach is insufficient. Music has unique teaching strategies and content. As a result, music teachers often feel that teacher evaluation does not apply to them or that music teaching does not "fit" into teacher evaluation. For example, when Cara discussed evaluation with an orchestra director, he noted that he disagreed with Danielson's assessment of the "same basic tasks" of teaching: "designing coherent instructions, creating an environment of respect and rapport, managing student behavior, using questioning and discussion techniques. . . . I don't think really fits into what we do. . . . [I] think that we need performing arts-specific components" (Bernard, 2015, p. 121). For this teacher and many music teachers, music requires specific pedagogies and therefore needs music-specific ways of assessing a music educator's quality.

NON-MUSIC EVALUATORS

Similar to the problem of lack of specific applicability to music, music teachers sometimes feel that evaluators without a background in music cannot effectively evaluate music teaching. Without sufficient knowledge of music and of the teaching strategies unique to it, evaluators might not understand and accurately evaluate good music teaching. An evaluator, for example, might have spent her career teaching English and might bring or even impose her own experience when observing a music classroom. The evaluator's own knowledge of English and teaching English may drive the way she reads, understands, and interacts with the evaluative tool, without her considering the uniqueness of the subject, classroom, or group of students at hand. As a result, she may feel that her knowledge and teaching may fit and work in any classroom, regardless of area or location. An evaluator's background may eliminate the musical aspects of music teaching completely, making it difficult to present a whole picture of what happens in the music classroom. As one band director shared about his evaluator: "I'm a little nervous about having to defend my actions to someone who doesn't understand them. My current supervisor is not necessarily looking for anything negative, she's a very intelligent person and I think she's just using a critical eye when she's observing, as she should . . . and that's what I'm afraid of . . . there's pedagogy going on that she's not aware of because she's not a musician" (Bernard, 2015, p. 171). Just as many music teachers believe music teaching needs music-specific standards to evaluate teacher effectiveness, they feel they should be evaluated by someone who understands the musical subject matter, as Terrence described. In other words, music teachers want to receive feedback from an evaluator who can appreciate and pick up on the nuances that occur in a music classroom.

APPLYING TO PRACTICE 2.1

- Do you have other concerns or frustrations about teacher evaluation not mentioned here? What might be some of the reasons for those frustrations?
- Based on your answers, make a list of your concerns in one column and in another list some possible solutions to these concerns. It is likely that you will not have solutions to all or even many of these concerns. That is to be expected, and this book is intended to help you to generate those solutions. However, identifying concerns and discovering the lack of a solution may help you focus as you read the other chapters of this book.

DEVELOPING A PRODUCTIVE ATTITUDE TOWARD TEACHER EVALUATION

How might music teachers react in light of these frustrations and contradictions? These limitations are, of course, annoying. However, despite these limitations, as Cara found, teachers who tried to use teacher evaluation in positive ways in their everyday teaching despite its negative aspects had the right attitude to succeed (Bernard, 2015). Conversely, those who struggled did not believe teacher evaluation was valuable. As a result, they barely complied and communicated poorly with administrators and evaluators. Essentially, successful teachers—as the saying goes—"made lemonade out of lemons." Similar results were recently found among teacher in general in a survey conducted

> Teachers who try to use and incorporate elements of teacher evaluation in positive ways in their everyday teaching to improve practice take on the right attitude to succeed.

by the RAND Corporation (Tuma et al., 2018). This attitude of directly and proactively engaging with teacher evaluation is a crucial—maybe even the *most* crucial—component of succeeding in teacher evaluation systems.

One teacher Cara interviewed, named Linda, is an example of a teacher who struggled because she was unwilling to participate fully in teacher evaluation efforts (Bernard, 2015). Linda was a high school choral director in an affluent town, where she spent her entire career building a program that was well respected by the community, her colleagues, and other music teachers throughout the region. Because Linda's program was strong and many of her singers went on to earn music scholarships, she felt she did not need to take the new evaluation processes seriously. One year Linda's evaluator provided her with feedback on ways to make sure all students beyond just the strong ones participated equally in class. Linda was annoyed by this feedback. She thought, "I've been teaching for twenty years. My programs are successful and challenging. This evaluator knows nothing about teaching music, and these rubrics don't have anything to do with music." So she ignored this feedback. The evaluator noticed that Linda's teaching did not change after this process and called her into his office numerous times to discuss the importance of making these small changes. Both Linda and her evaluator became frustrated by the tone and repetition of these discussions. They stopped listening to and respecting each other and failed to find common ground. As a result, despite her thriving choral program and years as a successful teacher, Linda received low ratings in her year-end evaluation.

Contrary to Linda's story, elementary general music and band teacher Miguel found success. Although he had reservations about teacher evaluation, he knew he had to comply with the new policies. Miguel decided to engage in many conversations with his evaluator and principal about curriculum and teaching and what the evaluation components could—and do—look like in a music class. As Miguel took the time to speak with his evaluators, they began to show openness to learning and to treating him as an expert in music teaching. When the new teacher evaluation system rolled out in Miguel's district, he joined the faculty team as the music and art representative to determine how the evaluation components and student learning objectives fit into music. Miguel found being a member of this team important because he did not want general ideas of teaching imposed on the music department. He and his department tried to visualize what they already did through the requirements of the system, building a vocabulary to use in discussions with non-music colleagues and evaluators. When it came time for his observation, Miguel was able to objectively listen to feedback, and his evaluator was able to listen to how some ideas needed to be modified for music. As a result,

Miguel happily incorporated the evaluator's comments, grew as a teacher, and received superior ratings in his evaluations.

Despite any reservations music teachers might have, those who are successful with teacher evaluation, like Miguel, approach it pragmatically. Conversely, music teachers like Linda, who are unwilling to engage in teacher evaluation because of its negative aspects, struggle and miss an opportunity to use a potentially flawed system for positive aims. Some readers might see this willingness to engage in teacher evaluation as capitulating to negative forces. However, music educators might simultaneously work within the system and change it from the outside. For example, they may choose to advocate politically for major structural reforms while leveraging the current system in ways that are helpful rather than harmful to their teaching and their program.

APPLYING TO PRACTICE 2.2

Assess your initial attitude toward teacher evaluation and form some preliminary strategies to increase the likelihood of success in the evaluation process:
- Do you identify with Linda's or Miguel's story? Has your experience been similar to Linda's or Miguel's, or is it something else entirely?
- Rate your current willingness to participate in teacher evaluation on a scale of 1 to 10. What are some positive steps you can take to be more open to the teacher evaluation process to increase your likelihood of success?

A FRAMEWORK FOR PROACTIVELY ENGAGING IN TEACHER EVALUATION

In the previous section we suggested that teachers who are successful in teacher evaluation move past their difficulties and reservations and actively participate in the process. Music teachers who proactively address teacher evaluation rather than thinking it does not apply to them or have anything positive to offer can succeed and use teacher evaluation for positive ends. However, this is more easily said than done. Many obstacles hinder teachers from achieving this success. How do music teachers develop the right mindset to address the limitations of teacher evaluation so that they may grow as professionals and ultimately thrive? How do music teachers apply and adapt the guidelines of teacher evaluation to music teaching? How do they convey the unique aspects of teaching music to evaluators not experienced in music? How do they juggle the demands of teaching music—like concerts and skills—with the more general aims of pedagogy outlined in teacher evaluation systems? To answer these questions, we propose a heuristic—a tool or way of framing—that will help music teachers name and understand these difficulties in teacher evaluation and begin to address them. By proposing this way of looking at teacher evaluation, we provide an avenue for music teachers to balance openness to feedback and change with advocacy for what they believe is effective teaching.

TYPES OF TEACHER KNOWLEDGE

Key to understanding how to balance these different aspects of teacher evaluation is categorizing the various types of knowledge teachers and evaluators possess. Teachers' knowledge is inexhaustible. They need to know what motivates students and how to effectively manage a classroom. They must possess a deep understanding of the material they teach and know how to clearly explain difficult concepts so that the students "get it," among many other types of knowledge.

Educational researcher Shulman (1986, 1987) suggested that teacher knowledge can be divided into broad three categories: content knowledge, general pedagogical knowledge, and pedagogical content knowledge. Table 2.1 provides an overview of these knowledges.

Content knowledge is a teacher's knowledge of the material being taught to students, such as the intervals in a major triad, the correct hand position on the violin, the sections of sonata form, or the stylistic characteristics of the Baroque era. Content knowledge is knowledge of *what* to teach. The importance of content knowledge is why music education preparation usually consists of theory and history classes, private tutelage on a major instrument, and ensemble experiences. Importantly, content knowledge is not a memorization of facts, but rather a deeply competent understanding of content, in this case music. It allows music teachers to model singing and demonstrate on instruments, detect errors, and find solutions. Content knowledge is the ability to weigh different perspectives, make connections, and form valuable judgments based on information and facts. In terms of Bloom's Taxonomy, music teachers have command of the higher part of the taxonomy; they have deep knowledge of the information so that they can synthesize, create, and evaluate (Wendell, 2007).

According to Shulman (1987), in addition to content knowledge, teachers also possess *general pedagogical knowledge*, including "broad principles and strategies of classroom management and organization that appear to transcend subject matter" (p. 8). Pedagogical knowledge is a deep understanding of *how* to teach. Understanding child development and learning theories, knowing how to structure a lesson plan, conducting class discussions, and implementing differentiation

TABLE 2.1.

Shulman's (1987) content knowledge, general pedagogical knowledge, and pedagogical content knowledge

	Definition	Examples
Content Knowledge	Knowledge of the material being taught.	• How to form a major triad. • The correct hand position on the violin. • The sections of sonata form. • Stylistic characteristics of the baroque era.
General Pedagogical Knowledge	General knowledge of teaching and educational theory, regardless of subject.	• Classroom management strategies. • Knowing how people best learn and remember material. • Strong assessment strategies. • Knowledge of best pedagogies based on students' developmental stages.
Pedagogical Content Knowledge	The unique pedagogical knowledge required for teaching a specific subject area.	• Effective strategies to teach brass players to play in the upper range. • Leading kindergartners to feel the beat and sing in tune. • Helping students learn to write a beautiful melody.

are examples of general pedagogical knowledge. General pedagogical knowledge is a general sense of good teaching, regardless of the content taught; it is good teaching that "transcends subject matter." Teachers are often prepared to gain general content knowledge by taking courses in educational psychology, learning theories, classroom management, assessment, and other general courses in education.

Content knowledge and general pedagogical knowledge probably seem commonsensical; they are knowledge of *what* to teach and *how* to teach. In a less obvious way, Shulman (1987) says teachers also possess *pedagogical content knowledge,* which he describes as "that special amalgam of content and pedagogy that is uniquely the province of teachers, their own special form of professional understanding" (p. 8). Pedagogical content knowledge links both content and general pedagogy together; it is the unique pedagogical knowledge required for teaching a specific subject area. For example, in music, teachers gain and execute effective strategies to teach brass players to play in the upper range, to lead kindergartners to feel the beat and to sing in tune, and to help students learn to write a beautiful melody. Choosing repertoire, teaching a folk song, and running a rehearsal are other examples of pedagogical content knowledge. Music teachers rely on their musical and pedagogical knowledge, skills, and resources to deliver effective instruction and to communicate with students through musical material. This knowledge informs the ways music educators, for example, may decide to ask students questions or when it is better to simply model or use language to explain how a student might play a musical passage.

Having pedagogical content knowledge in music is necessary to function as an effective music teacher. This is why music education preparation programs usually include methods and techniques courses specific to music, even narrowed down within musical subdisciplines such as choral, instrumental, or elementary methods. Music teachers need a high-level working knowledge, understanding, and application of music, coupled with tools, strategies, and best practices to enact pedagogical content knowledge. There is a specific organization and sequence to these activities, but they are musically rooted. Pedagogical content knowledge, then, bridges and balances skill-based techniques with a multitude of approaches to allow students to actively experience, learn, and name musical content and concepts.

> Teachers may apply three types of knowledge when teaching (Shulman, 1986, 1987): *Content knowledge*, knowledge of the subject material being taught; *pedagogical knowledge*, general knowledge of teaching; and *pedagogical content knowledge*, subject-specific pedagogical knowledge.

The process of teacher evaluation—the rubrics and instruments used by evaluators—when viewed through Shulman's (1986, 1987) three areas of teacher knowledge begins to show why and where music teachers may find the process frustrating, unhelpful, and sometimes unfair. Teacher evaluation rubrics and guidelines are aimed primarily or exclusively at assessing general pedagogical knowledge. Because they are often designed for all teachers regardless of subject, the evaluation tools address how teachers execute broader fundamentals of pedagogy, such as asking good questions or including student input into the direction of the lesson. They are often not tailored to the pedagogical content knowledge needed in teaching music. In addition, evaluators with no background in music are often charged with evaluating music teachers. While these evaluators often have great general pedagogical knowledge, they might lack content knowledge and pedagogical content knowledge in music. Music teachers, then, are often left to bridge the gap between the general pedagogical knowledge outlined in the rubrics and guidelines and the pedagogical content knowledge in their teaching.

Musical pedagogical content knowledge might not be easily acknowledged and valued in rubrics and guidelines by evaluators without music backgrounds. An example of this is the use of gesture and performance versus talk in ensembles. Some research in music education has shown that ensembles perform at a higher level when teachers minimize the time they talk and maximize the time students play (Duke, Prickett, & Jellison, 1998; Goolsby, 1996, 1997). Teachers achieve this by providing concise feedback and by using gestures during conducting that convey meaning to the students without uttering a word. A music teacher's ability to do this might be understood as a form of pedagogical content knowledge. Converse to this uniquely musical way of teaching, the current evaluation systems construe communication differently. These systems encourage dialogue among teachers and students, often looking for *more* talking rather than less, and do not consider how teachers might communicate through nonverbal means, such as conducting. In addition, as we mentioned previously, evaluators without music backgrounds may bring their own content biases and may not understand the meanings and knowledge executed in music teachers' conducting gestures. They may see less dialogue as lacking, while the music teacher thinks it marks sound pedagogy. In this sense, the rubrics and evaluator may simply miss music teachers' execution of pedagogical content knowledge and their effectiveness as educators.

Though evaluation systems might not best capture a music teachers' execution of pedagogical content knowledge, opportunities to grow as a music teacher still exist. Music educators must not use the uniqueness of content knowledge as an excuse to retreat from thinking about pedagogy or pedagogical content knowledge, as in Linda's experience, described earlier. While music teachers conduct, make music, and communicate nonverbally, they also talk and give directions. They have much to learn from other educators about "teacher talk moves" or the way teachers use questions and prompts to engage student growth. General pedagogical knowledge and dialogue with non-music teachers are valuable because they point music teachers in the direction of how students learn best, regardless of the content or the context.

APPLYING TO PRACTICE 2.3

- While this book examines how you execute types of knowledge in more detail in the following chapters, as an initial exercise, videotape your teaching. While reviewing the tape, find places where you think you effectively execute content knowledge. For example, if you are helping students play in tune, you are demonstrating knowledge of intonation.
  - Make a list of content knowledge you have demonstrated.
  - Repeat this process, this time looking for pedagogical knowledge. Find places where you are demonstrating general ideas about teaching that would be understandable by educators in subjects other than music. For example, are you using the zone of proximal development, using effective questioning, accessing students' schemas to introduce a concept, and so forth?
  - Finally, repeat the process with pedagogical content knowledge. Where are there places you are applying pedagogical knowledge to teach unique content knowledge? For example, to combine the previous two examples, how are you using students' schemas to teach students about intonation?
- Look at the teacher evaluation system used in your school that you are required to complete. Note where pedagogical knowledge is specified. While referencing a lesson you often teach, write down next to the requirement the pedagogical content knowledge you employ to fulfill that requirement.
- Note some places where you think your teacher evaluation system does not capture your teaching and pedagogical content knowledge. What are some ways you can begin to explain to educators not in music how those parts are missing in the evaluation system?

USING TEACHER KNOWLEDGE TO BE SUCCESSFUL IN TEACHER EVALUATION

Using these different areas of teacher knowledge—content knowledge, general pedagogical knowledge, and pedagogical content knowledge—might be a way to help teachers begin to understand how to maneuver teacher evaluation systems. As we have noted, these systems focus on general pedagogical knowledge because they need to apply broadly to the teaching of various subjects. However, this can leave the guidelines and rubrics open and vague when applied to specific academic subjects. In other words, teacher evaluation systems often do not directly address specific content knowledge or pedagogical content knowledge. In music, this means the evaluation systems do not address standards or the unique strategies and theories music teachers employ every day.

In the face of this general approach to teaching, some music teachers simply think that these evaluation systems do not apply to them and provide no information to improve their teaching. An example of this attitude is demonstrated by a middle school band teacher named Enrique. During a recent conversation, Enrique complained that the evaluation system's general pedagogical knowledge requirements and the non-music-specific advice he receives from evaluators do not capture how music is taught. After observing a middle school band rehearsal, Enrique's evaluator suggested that he think about adjusting his questioning techniques. She wanted him to ask questions that could have multiple correct answers. Enrique thought this was impossible and argued, "How can I ask higher-level, nuanced questions when my beginning band students don't possess the basic musical skills to read or play?" Enrique ultimately felt that his evaluator's advice was ill-suited for teaching music and that he could ignore her feedback on his teaching because she had no background in music. Like Linda, throughout the year he continually argued with his evaluator, and it became a frustrating experience for both of them.

Contrast Enrique's concerns about not receiving valuable feedback from evaluators without music backgrounds to Anna's. For Anna, the opposite is true; she prefers feedback from evaluators without backgrounds in music:

> I think music teachers too often think that nobody understands them, they're their own thing and they disconnect themselves from the larger school culture. And that's a problem. And we as a field, we keep saying, "nobody understands me." And you want your music administrator to observe you because they understand you, but that's insular. I think as music educators, we need to be aware of not only the culture of our school, but what's going on in education. We need to open our eyes a little bit more and be ready and willing to see what's happening around us and situate ourselves in that. So, I think in some ways, only having music people observe music people perpetuates this isolation. (Bernard, 2015, p. 119)

When Anna mentions school culture, she does not mean being a part of school functions and other essential aspects of school life. In fact, music teachers are often quite involved in this way. Their ensembles play at pep rallies, assemblies, and other school functions. Instead, Anna is describing an attitude she has observed from some music teachers who think non-music educators have little to offer them in professional development. For Anna, observations from non-music evaluators are useful. They help her to keep connected to the larger school culture and to ideas outside music education, to not be "insular," as she described it. While knowledge of music is valuable for an evaluator to have, being closed off from non-music evaluators can negatively affect the teacher evaluation process and harm music teachers. Because of Anna's attitude of being open to different perspectives, she felt she had an open dialogue with her evaluator, and she found it to be a valuable part of her professional development.

There is probably some truth in the perspectives of both Enrique and Anna. Enrique is right that there are specific ways to teach and learn music that are different than those in other disciplines. There are times that an evaluator might not fully understand those specific ways to teach music—in other words, the pedagogical content knowledge of music. For example, an evaluator may have excelled in classroom management when he or she taught math but might not know about the idiosyncrasies of classroom management in music. He or she does not know how to manage a classroom of sixty students with instruments in their hands or how to pace a rehearsal so students are engaged the entire time. An evaluator might have been a master at how to sequence a series of subject-specific instructional activities to help students complete complex skills and thinking. However, he or she might not know what order to sequence a lesson plan so that an ensemble can play in a concert or a student can compose a chord progression. An evaluator might know what successful differentiation looks like in a science class that meets requirements for teacher evaluation but might miss entirely the ways music teachers differentiate for their students. In other words, an evaluator might have great pedagogical knowledge but need help understanding what that looks like through content knowledge and pedagogical content knowledge in music. There are times, unfortunately, when administrators and evaluators lack even general pedagogical knowledge, so that music teachers must deal with the difficult task of educating their evaluators in constructive ways and advocating for themselves and their interpretation of teacher evaluation rubrics and guidelines.

However, as Anna suggests, there are valuable strategies and theories to learn from experienced educators, regardless of which academic subjects they have taught. Their general content knowledge and experience can provide fresh insight into music teaching. Because evaluators without music backgrounds are not habituated into the standard procedures, strategies, and pedagogies of music education, they might be able to provide inventive, insightful, and exciting new ways to teach music, improve music teachers' practice, and connect those teaching practices to the larger educational community in their schools.

Anna's and Enrique's perspectives highlight a tension that we suggest music teachers must balance if they are to be successful in teacher evaluation and grow from the experience. Music teachers need to negotiate the gap between the general pedagogical knowledge of the rubrics and evaluators with their own pedagogical content knowledge. In bridging this gap, music teachers need to balance the seemingly opposite goals of advocating for their teaching while remaining open to feedback and growing professionally through the process. In other words, they need to know when they need to stand up for the uniqueness of music education and the ways teacher evaluation systems may not capture sound musical pedagogy, *and* they need to balance this with a growth mindset and openness to using positive aspects of teacher evaluation to improve their practice. They need to balance both advocacy and openness even when the evaluator has no experience as a music teacher.

> Music teachers need to balance advocating for their teaching with remaining open to receiving feedback from evaluators in order to grow professionally through the evaluation process.

This balance is not always easy. When facing the evaluation system, a music teacher's first reaction might be only to advocate, much like Enrique. He or she might say as a reflex, "This isn't about general music, so it doesn't apply to me" or "I already do what the evaluation system requires, there's no need for me to change anything," or might hold onto practices simply because "that's what music teachers do." However, as Anna's perspective suggests, while advocacy is necessary at appropriate times, an unwillingness to grow from teacher evaluation can ossify a teacher's development and hinder his or her ability to be successful. Thinking about general pedagogical knowledge and taking advice from other educators, whether or not they are music teachers, can be valuable. The process can allow music teachers to wonder, for example, "perhaps there are other strategies besides conducting that will allow me to achieve my objectives," and to ask: "How can I improve my teaching strategies by learning about and implementing what we know about how children learn best regardless of the content?" Discussions, even with a teacher who has general pedagogical knowledge but may lack pedagogical content knowledge in music, provide opportunities for music teachers with the right mindset to improve their practice.

APPLYING TO PRACTICE 2.4

What do you think of Anna's view that music teachers too often disconnect themselves from the larger school culture? Do you think, as Anna puts it, "nobody understands me"? If so, how can you begin to engage with non-music colleagues so that they do understand you and you may learn from them to grow professionally?

BALANCING ADVOCACY AND GROWTH TO IMPROVE PRACTICE

We have suggested that active participation in teacher evaluation requires music teachers to address concerns by balancing advocacy and openness to growth. In music education there are patterns in which music educators might balance advocacy and openness in different degrees. In her discussions with teachers, Cara found there are particular places that music teachers struggle and others where they excel with common requirements of teacher evaluation (Bernard, 2015). For example, they tend to do well in communication with parents and community, as we mentioned in the introduction. They also tend to fare well with classroom procedures. Music teachers, and in particular ensemble directors, manage a variety of equipment and have developed many strategies to deal with complicated classroom configurations.

While music teachers excel in some areas, there are others in which both evaluators and music teachers have reported that they struggle. In the next four chapters we address these key areas. They include questioning strategies, differentiation, implementation of literacy, and effective assessment. Each of these areas has specific requirements or parameters that are commonly used in teacher evaluation and have broad application to many aspects of teacher evaluation.

SUMMARY

Because rubrics and criteria often do not specifically address music, many music educators think evaluation systems do not accurately evaluate music teaching or provide useful feedback to improve their teaching. Similarly, music teachers might argue that evaluators without backgrounds in teaching music cannot effectively evaluate music educators or help them improve their practice. Despite these concerns, teachers who try to use teacher evaluation in positive ways in their everyday teaching take on the right attitude to succeed. They do this through balancing advocacy with an openness to feedback. They accomplish this balance by possessing robust content knowledge, general pedagogical knowledge, and pedagogical content knowledge. Importantly, this knowledge includes understanding how to bridge general pedagogical knowledge specified in teacher evaluation systems with how it is enacted in musical content knowledge and pedagogical content knowledge. This requires music teachers to be open to general pedagogical knowledge from evaluators and to have the imagination to translate it into musical pedagogical content knowledge. It also requires music teachers to advocate for themselves and to educate their evaluators so they understand how music teachers enact that pedagogical knowledge in ways evaluators might miss. The areas of questioning, literacy, differentiated instruction, and assessment are particularly difficult for teachers and require focused attention. Through careful attention, music teachers like Sarah can begin to reshape their negative experiences and find success in teacher evaluation systems.

As part of Sarah the chorus director's evaluation system, the principal is required to conduct one unannounced observation. One afternoon the principal comes to observe Sarah's beginner level chorus. She stays for fifteen minutes and then leaves without making a comment. A week later, the principal calls Sarah down to her office for the post-observation meeting. "I only have a minute to talk, but I wanted to tell you 'Great job'," she says. "But I wonder about one thing: How do you know the students were engaged?" Sarah responds, "I was changing my conducting, showing different dynamics—changes in the levels of sound—that I want them to sing. Their sound was changing in response to my conducting, which showed me that they were paying attention by watching me, listening to one another, and making changes to their singing in the moment without my having to tell them what to do. So that showed me that they were engaged." Sarah's principal responds, "Ah, ok, very good. But couldn't some students be lip-syncing and zoning out?" Sarah agrees, "Sure. But I moved around the room while conducting so I could hear each individual voice part more clearly. And since I know the singers' voices, I could hear and assess who was singing, who was shaky on this part and needs to review the notes, and so on. We actually focused on another section of the piece after you left where we had to address some incorrect pitches from the alto section, and they made real improvements." Sarah's principal thanks her for giving some evidence and says she looks forward to "visiting longer next time and seeing how the students responded to your nonverbal cues."

3

QUESTIONING STRATEGIES

High school orchestra teacher Jacob is observed by his evaluator, an assistant principal who taught social studies. In the observation, Jacob keeps a brisk rehearsal pace, addresses musical ideas and issues as he hears them, and polishes a section of Alshin's arrangement of "Danny Boy," focusing on the movement of the melodic lines. In Jacob's post-observation discussion, his evaluator addresses the questions asked in his beginning orchestra class: "I notice that you started and stopped a lot to fix spots, often singing parts to show what you want. It would be helpful to incorporate more questions. Instead of singing their parts to them, could you ask something about how the music is written to help them see how it should be played? You can layer your questioning by moving from simple questions to more discussion-based ones, applying it to students' playing. Because of this, the questioning component is the only area where I'm going to mark you with a developing rating." Jacob answers, "Open-ended questions don't always work in an ensemble because of issues like technique—holding a bow or creating an embouchure—that takes precedence. Asking questions with no distinct answer or with multiple entry points doesn't work. If I ask a student, 'What did you think of that F sharp? Was it in tune?,' the answer is either yes or no." Jacob continues, arguing that asking questions is "difficult with challenging music, or even beginning level music for that matter. The students aren't ready to make connections on their own. I need to tell them." He further explains that "we are more product-driven. We evaluate student progress through sound and performance. There isn't much time for discussion-type questions, but I know the evaluation tool doesn't reflect that." Jacob's principal ends the conversation, saying, "Focus more on asking questions throughout the rehearsal instead of showing or telling the students how to play." Jacob leaves the meeting feeling misunderstood and frustrated.

QUESTIONING IS A common pedagogical technique that dates back to at least the ancient Greek philosopher Socrates, who famously walked the streets of Athens questioning the beliefs of the citizens he encountered. His process gave birth to the Socratic method of asking questions, which is used to help students learn new material. Like Socrates, today's effective teachers ask questions in order to find out what students know, guide their thinking, aid them in recall, and increase engagement. Because of the effectiveness of questioning as a pedagogical strategy, teacher evaluation systems regularly require its use. While questioning might be a sound pedagogical approach, as Jacob's story suggests, music teachers are often skeptical of asking too many questions and often differ with their evaluators about the role of questioning in the music classroom (Bernard, 2015). Jacob contends that music must focus on the skills required to create, perform, and listen to music; questions, for him, take away valuable instructional time from these learning processes, which are unique and essential to music teaching and learning. However, Jacob's evaluator suggested that questions can improve students' playing, taking the place of telling students what to do. How, then, can music teachers effectively implement questioning strategies to succeed in teacher evaluation systems and improve practice, while retaining other effective instructional strategies unique to music?

In this chapter we look at questioning strategies and the ways music teachers can integrate requirements of evaluation systems to improve student participation, learning, and understanding while still preserving music making, skill building, and maintain effective rehearsal strategies. First we describe the connection between questioning and teacher evaluation. Next we discuss the importance of asking questions and address some concerns music teachers often have about asking questions. We then describe the different types of questions and how to word them and provide a way to respond to students' answers. Finally, we offer strategies to implement and sequence questioning strategies in lesson plans, including ways to "layer" questions, as Jacob's supervisor described.

APPLYING TO PRACTICE 3.1

- What is your initial reaction to Jacob's story? Have you found yourself in a similar situation? If so, how did you respond to your evaluator's comments?
- Do you find any merit in Jacob's evaluator's comments about asking questions instead of telling students?

QUESTIONING STRATEGIES IN TEACHER EVALUATION

Jacob's story might be familiar to music teachers. Jacob and his evaluator disagreed about the types of questions asked in the rehearsal. Musical skill, Jacob argued, must be acquired before students can analyze or answer detailed and descriptive questions about repertoire. However, as Jacob's evaluator pointed out, it is necessary to examine closely how a teacher plans and executes this hierarchy of skill and knowledge, particularly within the context of teacher evaluation. Asking a variety of questions throughout the learning process is an effective teaching strategy, regardless of subject matter (Baxter & Allsup, 2004; Danielson, 2007, 2013; Lee, 2007; Nassaji & Wells, 2000). When a teacher asks students to solve problems, be creative, or make connections to their previous knowledge, even before students have acquired a skill, the likelihood of their gaining and mastering that skill increases (Vygotsky, 1978). Jacob's evaluator, then, does make a valuable point in asking him to explore different types of questions and strategies in teaching orchestra. Although the evaluator does not possess much content knowledge in music, her knowledge of teaching in general can benefit Jacob and his students.

Regardless of content, questioning is a component of teacher evaluation required of all teachers. Most teacher evaluation systems have a section related to questioning strategies. Table 3.1 outlines common teacher evaluation systems and the ways in which questioning may be construed or required.

The majority of evaluation systems describe characteristics and indicators of effective questioning strategies. These often include questions that have high cognitive challenge, which require students to answer beyond a one-word response of "yes" or "no"; multiple correct answers, even if there is a single correct response; and questions that honor, use, or apply student responses and ideas to questions in an active and meaningful way. Other indicators include questions that facilitate class discussion, in which the teacher takes on the role of mediator and allows the

TABLE 3.1.

Questioning in current teacher evaluation systems

Evaluation System	Questioning Requirement	Possible Evidence of Using Questioning Strategies
Danielson Framework for Teaching	Domain 3b, Instruction: Using Questioning and Discussion Techniques	• Maintain high quality of questioning and prompts, including questions with multiple or detailed answers. • Demonstrate discussion techniques, with teacher as facilitator. • Show high level of student participation.
Marzano Causal Teacher Evaluation Rubric	DQ3, Practice and Deepen New Knowledge; DQ9, Communicating High Expectations for All	• Review content with students to revise knowledge. • Examine errors with students. • Examine similarities and differences within content with students. • Ask questions of and probe low-expectancy students.
Strong Teacher and Leader Effectiveness Performance Evaluation System	Performance Standard 3, Instructional Delivery	• Build upon student knowledge. • Develop higher order thinking through questions. • Use multiple levels of questions to communicate clearly, adjust instruction, and check for understanding.
McREL	Standard IV, Teachers Facilitate Learning for their Students	• Incorporate a wide range of ways to communicate with students and help them make connections.
Marshall	Rubric C, Delivery of Instruction	• Ask questions and anticipate student responses. • Use questions to check for understanding and drive instruction.

students to lead themselves in discussion; then, using questions to prompt discussion, the teacher can see how students exhibit their reasoning through their responses. Finally, asking effective questions may yield high levels of student participation in discussion and application. These questions may encourage student participation through verbal responses, or perhaps even musical responses, in which students demonstrate a musical idea or musical changes through playing, connecting musical skill and knowledge.

Music teachers' abilities to implement questioning might be considered part of a teacher's general pedagogical knowledge. It is a general strategy that works in different educational settings, regardless of the content or subject matter. However, translating this general pedagogical knowledge into pedagogical content knowledge—the unique strategies and skills required of teaching music—is often difficult for music teachers. Rehearsals and music making in music classes require that teachers employ questions differently than teachers of discussion-based classes do. For example, the types of questions the teacher and students ask and when in a lesson the questions are asked will differ between, say, a choir and a math class. Knowing how and why to ask questions is an important step for music teachers as they speak with evaluators and deepen their professional practice.

> Questioning is typically a required observation component in teacher evaluation, often linked to communicating with students, responding to students' answers, and facilitating discussion.

APPLYING TO PRACTICE 3.2

- Scan your school's teacher evaluation system. Where, if at all, is questioning explicitly listed? Is there a dedicated component? What are the indicators of effective questioning strategies?
- If it is not listed explicitly, in what domains/components might questioning be observed?

MUSIC TEACHERS' CONCERNS ABOUT QUESTIONING STRATEGIES

Even though educators largely agree that questioning is a strong pedagogical device, and that is reflected in teacher evaluation systems, music teachers sometimes express concerns regarding questioning. A common issue music teachers often voice is that asking questions takes too much time. They might say, "Isn't it more efficient to just tell them?" or "I just cut to the chase and tell them the answers rather than ask them." However, simply telling students information does not help them retain or completely understand it, as Jacob's evaluator explained in the opening vignette. For example, we have often heard said, and to our chagrin have said ourselves, "No matter how many times I tell my ensemble to play *pianissimo*, they never do it!" When simply told something, students do not remember it, and repetition often is not efficient. However, when music teachers involve students in the process of figuring out this information, they are more apt to retain and understand the information and transfer it later on in learning new music. If students are led to understand why the composer would mark a certain passage *pianissimo* and why it is important to perform it quietly, they will more consciously remember to play with the correct dynamic. Questions are a powerful way to lead to this retention, participation, and understanding.

Music teachers are often concerned that asking questions takes up too much time and will slow down the learning process. They may think "students will never get to the harder repertoire." Likewise, music teachers sometimes argue that beginner level students are "not ready for high-level questions because they are gaining the basic skills," and the majority of time should be spent making music, as we saw in Jacob's vignette. These concerns raise an important point for all instruction: spending too much time doing *any* activity—playing, singing, or talking—loses the attention and focus of students. Therefore questioning, like other strategies, cannot be the only process teachers use to help students. However, questioning can also help vary instruction in traditional rehearsals and other techniques commonly used in music classrooms.

In this aim to vary instruction, it is important for music teachers to recognize that questioning is not a separate strategy from other forms of music teaching. As we introduce the concept of questioning in instruction to our preservice students, they often think of "question time" and "music-making time" as two separate activities. They often stop rehearsals or lessons to have long conversations rather than smoothly integrate the process into the other instructional strategies they employ. As teachers become more comfortable with questioning strategies, they can begin to seamlessly blend them with other instructional procedures. A teacher who has command of questioning strategies can integrate music making, movement, and other activities with questions. This integration can allow students to gain the necessary musical skills and work toward more challenging repertoire in a deeper way. In sum, asking questions is a sound pedagogical strategy in all educational settings, including in music education.

APPLYING TO PRACTICE 3.3

- Assess your overall feelings toward asking questions. What concerns, if any, do you have about asking questions in your classroom?
- Do you purposefully use questions in your lessons? When and where in your lessons do you think you use questioning strategies most?

WHAT TO ASK: CLOSED, OPEN, AND GUIDED QUESTIONS

Although questioning is an effective pedagogical strategy, not all questions are of equal quality or usefulness. Different types of questions require different kinds of answers and types of thinking to answer them. Some questions have definite answers; some do not. Some require students to draw upon previous knowledge; others ask them to speculate or predict. Some questions require students to answer verbally, while others invite them to make music or move. Each of these types of questions has a different purpose. However, regardless of purpose, it is important for music teachers to consider asking a variety of questions.

How do music teachers begin to generate and sequence a variety of questions? Music educators Marsha Baxter and Randall Allsup (2004) provide a way to organize the different types of questions music teachers might ask. They suggest that questions in the classroom fall into three categories: open, guided, and closed. *Open* questions are broad and require divergent thinking and varied answers. Teachers often use open questions to assess what students already know, gather various ideas or solutions to problems, and seek students' opinions and views. *Guided* questions move students in a direction that a teacher wants to go. They push students toward a particular course that hints at information the teacher wants students to notice or figure out for themselves without telling them outright. These questions encourage students to effectively think through a problem in an outright way. Finally, *closed* questions seek to find unambiguous, convergent, specific answers. They often more pointedly ask students to recall information or content. Closed questions have one correct answer and often begin with *where*, *what*, or *who*. For example, "Where do the tenors hold their note on pg. 3?" or

> Questions can be categorized as *open*—to allow broad and varied responses; *guided*—leading students to information or an answer; or *closed*—looking for specific answers.

TABLE 3.2.

Examples of open, guided, and closed questions

Open: Broad questions with multiple answers used to assess students' perspectives or to think creatively.	**Guided:** Questions that lead students in the direction a teacher wants to go.	**Closed:** Pointed questions with one correct answer.
• What do you want to do today? • What did you hear? • What do you think of this recording? • What are some things that need improvement?	• What are some materials we need to accomplish our goals? • What are some ways we can categorize what we heard? • Why do you think this recording is lacking? • How can we improve our rhythmic accuracies? • What are some ways we can practice to improve our intonation?	• What is the transposition of a clarinet? • What do we call it when there are different melodies going on at the same time? • What could the producer do to make the balance better on this recording? • Were our eighth notes even? • Was that sharp or flat? • Who has the melody at measure 41?

"On what beat is the accent?" Table 3.2 lists some examples of open, guided, and closed questions in a music classroom.

Categorizing questions into open, guided, and closed can illuminate why and where music teachers have difficulty with questions in teacher evaluation. As Jacob's vignette suggests, music teachers often have difficulty with questions, but in particular open questions. When music teachers do employ questions, they often gravitate toward closed ones, which often have only one answer. However, as we discussed in the previous section, evaluators and teacher evaluation systems encourage and promote open-ended and guided questions, which have multiple answers, such as, "What do you think this phrase is trying to express?" In Jacob's vignette, his principal suggested that Jacob ask open questions based on discussion with students. Conversely, the questions Jacob reluctantly used were closed, such as, "What is the note in measure 12?" Guided and open questions tend to push students toward higher-level thinking by requiring them to draw upon their knowledge and ability more than closed questions do.

APPLYING TO PRACTICE 3.4

- If possible, video or audio record yourself teaching a lesson; otherwise, consult a recent lesson plan. As you watch or listen to the recording or read the lesson plan, tally how many questions you ask throughout the lesson. Categorize these questions into open, closed, and guided. Do you tend to ask questions in one category more than the others? If so, how can you incorporate more of the other categories?
- Return to your school's evaluation rubrics and guidelines. Note where they either explicitly or implicitly address use of questions. While consulting one of your lesson plans, create a list of the ways your lesson fulfills this requirements and ways you can improve it.
- Last, make a list of ways you can articulate to an evaluator the modifications you have made.

HOW TO WORD QUESTIONS

Once music teachers determine the types of open, guided, and closed questions that are worth asking, they may think about how to word the specific questions they will ask. *How* teachers ask a question can have a profound impact on how students process and respond to it. For example, compare these two questions that are seeking similar answers:

- Why are there staccatos over these notes?
- Why do you think the composer put staccatos over these notes?

Both these questions ask students to think about the meaning and reason for the staccatos in the music. But which one do you think is more inviting for students to answer? The first question might give students the impression that there is only one correct answer to the question. The second, by adding "do you think"—as we just did in the question we asked the reader—might convey that students should interpret and form an educated guess. This subtle change invites students to take a chance in answering. By adding phrases such as "do you think" to a question, music teachers can subtly invite more students to participate and take more chances in answering.

TABLE 3.3.

Techniques for wording questions differently

How should we play this phrase?	How do you think we should play this phrase?
What did we talk about last time?	Can someone tell me one idea we covered last class that they remember?
What does tenuto mean?	What are some words you might use to describe tenuto?

In addition to using words in questions such as "what do you think," there are other ways music teachers can subtly phrase questions to invite students to consider answering. Compare the questions in the left-hand column in table 3.3 with a similar question on the right. Just as the first question in the previous example was more inviting, the questions on the right in the table are more inviting than those on the left. When asking questions, it is important to word them in ways that invite students to make informed guesses, to take chances, and to speculate. Music teachers might word questions in such a way that they elicit what students "think" rather than "what the correct answer is," even when the question is closed, with one correct answer.

> Music teachers should consider wording questions in ways that invite students to share what they think rather than what they think the "correct answer" is, even if the question is closed with one correct answer.

Because wording is so important in subtly encouraging students to participate and answer, thinking about the ways music teachers ask questions provides many opportunities to make easy and effective tweaks to the words teachers use in the classroom. There are some quick word modifications that music teachers can immediately apply to become more comfortable with questions. Many commands in the music classroom can easily be modified into questions without sacrificing large amounts of playing time. Instead of saying, for example, "Violins, you played an F-sharp in measure 12. Please play an F-natural," a teacher might rephrase this as, "Violins, there was a wrong note in measure 12. Who can tell me what it was?" Or instead of saying, "We need to play this faster," music teachers might say, "I wonder how this would sound if we played it faster. Let's try it." Then, after the students have played it, the teacher can ask, "How did it sound?" or "What do you think we need to do to make that cleaner?" These small modifications do not seriously reorganize or shift the focus of lessons, but do actively include students through questions. Additionally, these modifications model a sense of inquisitiveness about the music, allowing students to make thoughtful decisions and critiques.

APPLYING TO PRACTICE 3.5

- Find places where you can turn your most commonly used commands and prompts into questions. What are some rephrased questions you can use?
- Record yourself in class and identify places where you give commands, such as, "Violins, in m. 8 you played an F-sharp, not F-natural—low third finger." Is there a place to change that to "Violins, there is something incorrect in m. 8; does anyone think they know what it is?" After a student answers correctly, you can follow up with, "Good, how do we play F-natural?"
- Find places in the music where students can suggest phrasing and dynamics. Instead of saying, "There's a crescendo there, make sure you play it," perhaps change it to "We missed something in that passage with our dynamics. What is it?" or "What's happening with our phrasing and dynamics here?"

RESPONDING TO STUDENTS' ANSWERS: THE "THIRD TURN"

We have discussed using a variety of open, guided, and closed questions, as well as subtle ways teachers can word questions to invite students to answer and take chances. However, as we mentioned at the beginning of this chapter, although questions are necessary, alone they are insufficient in instruction. One of the most difficult but crucial aspects of asking questions is how to respond when students answer. How a teacher responds to a student's answer is just as important as the question the teacher initially asks. The way in which teachers use student responses is a major factor in teacher effectiveness in the evaluation systems, as we mentioned in an earlier section. Students give varied responses to questions and prompts, including insightful answers—both anticipated and unanticipated by the teacher—right and wrong answers, and responses that are irrelevant to the original prompt.

Consider these teacher questions, followed by student answers and then teacher responses. (As you read them, you might want to cover up the last line of each example and imagine how you would respond to the student answer.)

T: What is the note in measure 5?
S: An E (the correct answer is Eb)
T: Ok. Let's look at our key signature. Which notes are flat?

T: In what ways do you think it is best to play this note?
S: (silence).
T: Ok, let me ask this: What articulation do you think would fit best for this note?

T: What dynamic should we sing at mm. 49–52?
S: Piano, because it is a contemplative part of the song.
T: Great, how do we know that?
S: Because the text at this part talks about a person remembering and reflecting.
T: So singing piano makes sense at this point. What do we need to do with our breath to sing piano, but still have a full sound?

T: How should we count the rhythm on the board?
S: I have to pee. (Other kids laugh.)
T: Take the pass and go to the bathroom. OK, eyes on me and let me ask the question again: How should we count this rhythm?

In these moments, music teachers must make immediate, in-the-moment decisions about how to respond to the students. As seen in the examples, teachers might give feedback on the accuracy and quality of the response, ask another question, build upon the student's response, move in a different direction, redirect the class, ask students to sing or perform, or make another choice. Making these responses to students' answers is what some educators call the "third turn" (Lee, 2007; Nassaji & Wells, 2000).

Some researchers have categorized the different responses that teachers use in the third turn. Nassaji and Wells (2000) and Lee (2007), for example, suggest that teachers' responses in the third turn can help rephrase a question, break down a question to focus on a particular part, or lead students in a new direction. Teachers may also use the third turn to incorporate ideas not previously anticipated, redirect unrelated answers or classroom management issues, or guide answers toward the lesson objectives. The third turn need not always be verbal, and responses can be extended for music teachers, because a third turn is often asking students to play, sing, or move. Consider the following scenario:

T: The composer repeats "Kyrie Eleison" three times on the same pitches. Each one should be different. How can we perform them?

S: Each time we could get louder.

T: Let's hear that (and cues the ensemble to sing). (After the students sing:) Is there another way we could perform them?

In this moment, the music teacher responded to a student by prompting the class to sing. This allows students to apply their responses to music making and gives them the opportunity to see if the response—in this case, getting louder with each "Kyrie"—worked. Following the singing prompt, the teacher may respond again, asking for an alternative way to sing the repeated text.

This example also demonstrates the need for music teachers to recognize and advocate for nonverbal answers. Students' nonverbal answers to teacher questions, as in the example, are an important component in music education. Playing or moving is an added way that students answer in the music classroom. Music teachers' abilities to create situations in which students answer nonverbally constitutes pedagogical content knowledge. While they are important, evaluators can sometimes overlook these nonverbal responses in an observation. A common nonverbal response in music is following a conductor's gesture. Evaluators from other subjects might not recognize these techniques because they lack this knowledge. Evaluators who are not music teachers might miss that these types of nonverbal responses are responses at all. The evaluator might be, say, a former English teacher who used dialogue primarily or exclusively for students to respond to questions. Because of this, it is important for music teachers to articulate clearly to an evaluator that these are indeed responses or answers to questions. As we discuss in more detail in chapter 7, when talking to evaluators it is useful for music teachers to inform them about specific pedagogical content knowledge and how they employ it in the lesson.

In summary, students respond in varying ways to music teachers' questions, and music educators have a never-ending variety of ways to respond to those student answers. In the third turn, music teaching is more of an art than a science. Music teachers cannot anticipate every twist and turn in a lesson. The third turn is a way to embrace a level of uncertainty but respond with flexibility and adaptiveness to

> The "third turn" is the way a teacher may respond to students' answers and responses.

that uncertainty. However, music teachers can think deeply ahead of time about possible answers students might give to questions, how they might respond to students' possible answers, and their objectives and where they want the lesson to lead.

APPLYING TO PRACTICE 3.6

- Take some questions that you have either generated in the previous Applying to Practice exercises or used in other lessons. Look at these questions and anticipate some answers students might provide. What is your "third turn" going to be if the answer is
  - No answer—silence?
  - Incorrect?
  - An answer that is unrelated (as often happens in early elementary grades)?
  - Not useful?
  - Correct but answered hesitantly?
  - An interesting and insightful answer that you did not anticipate?
  - An answer you're looking for?
- Based on these potential answers, how will you respond? How will you
  - Rephrase unclear questions?
  - Narrow the question down, focusing on a particular aspect?
  - Redirect for unrelated answers and classroom management issues?
  - Incorporate ideas you did not anticipate?
  - Push anticipated correct answers toward the objectives of your lesson?

STRATEGIES TO IMPLEMENT AND SEQUENCE QUESTIONS

We have discussed the importance of asking open, guided, and closed questions that direct students to be inquisitive. These questions signal that students are reviewing content, using higher-level thinking, and applying their knowledge. We have also noted that music teachers should word questions in open ways that aim for students to share their ideas and interpretations rather than seek out the answer they think the teacher wants, and should consider how to respond to students' answers in the "third turn." How can music teachers effectively formulate, word, and sequence questions to create an effective lesson plan and succeed in teacher evaluation?

In this section we provide strategies for music teachers to implement and sequence questions in a lesson plan. We look at structuring lessons from open to closed questions as well as the opposite sequence—from closed to open. Knowing how to utilize and sequence questions can help music teachers consider the role of questions in their instruction. This can aid in speaking with evaluators about the types of questions used or the ways in which questions guide students' learning.

FROM OPEN, TO GUIDED, TO CLOSED QUESTIONS

Here we return to Baxter and Allsup's (2004) categories of open, guided, and closed questions and how to order them for optimal learning. Baxter and Allsup (2004) suggest that music teachers should structure their teaching beginning with open questions, followed by guided questions, then end with closed ones. This sequence leads students through a thinking process of taking in information and then focusing that information to look for specific answers to answer those initial questions of wonderment. In this way, questions that become more specific and narrow comprise the third (and fourth, and fifth, etc.) turn. Table 3.4 shows some examples of how proceeding from open to closed questions might look in a lesson.

TABLE 3.4.

Sequencing questions from open, to guided, to closed

	Open→	Guided→	Closed
Composition	What do you want to do today?	What are some materials we need to accomplish our goals?	What is the transposition of a clarinet?
Listening for Concepts	What did you hear?	What are some ways we can categorize what we heard?	What do we call it when there are different melodies going on at the same time?
Listening for Audio Production	What do you think of this recording?	Why do you think this recording is lacking?	What could the producer do to make the balance better on this recording?
Rehearsal	What are some things that need improvement?	How can we improve our rhythmic accuracies?	Were our eighth notes even?

These questions start by soliciting students' initial thoughts and their perspectives. By starting with students' perspectives, music teachers can easily see what information the students know and they need to begin the lesson. Open questions at the beginning of a lesson are a sort of informal pre-assessment. They allow students the freedom to explore and then slowly lead to information that the teacher wants to cover. Open questions at the beginning of a lesson also signal to students that their opinions matter and that the classroom is an open space where they are welcome to share ideas. Then, guided questions can be pivotal in leading students to identify, name, and fix problems on their own before the teacher does it for them. Finally, closed questions can provide the specific content that teachers want the students to understand.

Music teachers may benefit from using the specific elements of a score to help move questions from open to closed. Table 3.5 provides a list of musical elements to draw upon when leading students through open to closed questions. Using these musical elements, music teachers may better plan the questions they will ask, moving from open to closed. When music teachers look at a piece of music, their first inclination might be to pick out the musical terms or skills to be taught, such as naming the key, locating where the score calls for *forte*, navigating

TABLE 3.5.

Musical elements to structure open, guided, and closed questions

- Score structure
- Form
- Pitch
- Rhythm
- Lyrics
- Diction
- Articulation
- Tempo
- Phrasing
- Composer's intentions
- Circumstance/story
- Character
- Student personal connection
- Body movement

the *D.C. al Coda*, or selecting which scales and exercises to use to best warm up the group when rehearsing a specific composition. Of course students must know aspects of the score to properly perform the composition; however, focusing on these aspects alone can easily lead to closed questions. Instead, music teachers might think of how these musical aspects relate to how the piece is put together and generate questions from there. The background of the piece, such as the historical period or composer's life, or the meaning and purpose of the piece may inform these questions. Music teachers may ask open questions about the construction or theory of the work. Additionally, the more artistic components surrounding a piece—such as lyrics, composer's intentions, circumstance/story, and character—can allow space for students to answer questions differently in a more open and descriptive way. The musical content is an avenue toward creating rich, open-ended questions.

It may be helpful to consider and identify some broad, more open questions in specific contexts when looking at a particular section in a piece. For example, in chorus, a teacher may draw attention to the first two pages of *The Road Not Taken*, by Randall Thompson. In this four-part, SATB piece, the beginning is entirely in unison. A teacher may begin by asking: "What do you *see*?" This open question can lead students to notice that all parts are in unison. Students may notice the only dynamic marking at the beginning of the vocal line is *pianissimo*. They may also notice the lack of phrase markings. Perhaps students are drawn to the text, the poetry of Robert Frost. After looking at the score, the teacher may have students sing these first two pages, then ask the guiding question, "Now, what do you *hear*?" Depending on students' answers, the teacher may respond, "Though there are no phrase markings, we sang some phrasing. What type of phrasing did we lean toward?" This question guides the students toward identifying a more legato, smooth phrase. The teacher may finish by asking, "What musical terms do we know that describe 'smooth'?" to lead students to recall and name legato as the phrase marking of choice. These questions guide students to consider the built-in musical elements surrounding this unison section and begin to refine students' analysis of the melody.

Likewise, in elementary general music, the teacher might have students move to a recording such as Tchaikovsky's 4th Symphony, third movement (which is entirely pizzicato strings) or while singing (say) the folksong "Chicken on a Fencepost." The excerpts from both of these pieces include a short, staccato pattern. The teacher may say, "I'm interested in the part that goes [sings or hums short musical excerpt]. How could we show this part on our bodies?" This open question invites students to put the sounds anywhere on their bodies. The students and teacher sing or can then listen again and create their own movements individually.

Because the teacher wants students to focus on the staccato aspect, she might then ask: "When we hear/sing this part, would we use a paintbrush or a hammer to match the sound?" This guiding question provides the students with two choices without giving them an answer, but creates a sense of imagery of what a paintbrush and hammer look and sound like in motion. If a student answers "paintbrush," the teacher can lead the students through the singing/listening activity while painting on their imaginary canvas in front of them. Then students can repeat this process by imitating a hammer. The teacher may end this section by asking, "Which one do we think worked better?" and then, "Why?" to guide students to differentiate between short and long sounds. The teacher may use the words *short* and *long* at this point after students experience these concepts in their bodies.

Finally, organizing these musical elements on a word wall for students may aid in reminding them of important aspects of the piece of music and can help them with their responses to questions. Through questioning, music teachers can guide students to look or listen for certain things in the repertoire and recall them from the word wall. Once this is established, open questions can elicit a myriad of student responses, allowing students to look and listen inquisitively and analytically at their voice parts, the piano part, and the score as a whole.

APPLYING TO PRACTICE 3.7

Look at a piece of music you are currently teaching. Consider what your lesson might look like using the open-guided-closed sequence. What questions will you ask? Use the musical elements from table 3.5 to guide you.

FROM CLOSED, TO GUIDED, TO OPEN QUESTIONS

While Baxter and Allsup (2004) recommend a lesson plan sequence that moves from open to closed, we suggest that the opposite order—from closed to open questions—can also be an effective way to structure a lesson. Framing a lesson around closed questions and then moving to open questions can allow students to gather information and then use that information in different ways. Students and teachers may begin looking at something by determining the information they already know and then figuring out new information, skills, or applications.

To move from closed to open questions, a K-W-L chart might prove useful as an organizational tool. In a K-W-L chart, the students and teacher fill in three columns that list (a) what the students *Know*, (b) what they *Want* or need to know, and (c) what they *Learned* by going through a process. For example, a teacher might devise a listening lesson on the second movement of the divertimento *Ein musikalischer Spaß* (translated as "A Musical Joke," K. 522) by W. A. Mozart.

In this piece, Mozart creates a humorous composition by adding in unusual and unidiomatic aspects, such as dissonances and phrases of irregular length. After having students listen to a recording and look at a score, traditional or iconic (even if they cannot read music), the teacher can then ask some questions that the students can answer. Closed questions might be: "Who is the composer?," "What is the title of the piece?," or "What do you know about this piece?" Students might even write down some of their more subjective observations, like it sounds "odd." From that list, the teacher can then lead students to notice what information is not there and what they want or need to find out to better understand the piece. Finally, students can seek out that information via websites, books, other sources, or even the teacher just telling them, to answer those questions. Table 3.6 shows what a K-W-L using this Mozart divertimento might look like.

Three aspects of this K-W-L chart in relation to questions are worth pointing out. First, the teacher needs to guide this process by asking the right questions at the right time. In the beginning, the teacher asks the students to explore the information in front of them (the recording and the score) and to determine the facts that they "know." By looking at the score, students know who wrote the piece and what

TABLE 3.6.

A K-W-L chart for *Ein musikalischer Spaß*, K. 522, by Mozart

What I *Know*	What I *Want* (or *Need*) to know	What I *Learned*
(from looking at the score and listening)	• When did Mozart live?	• Mozart lived from 1756 to 1791.
• It was written by (someone named) Mozart.	• Who is Mozart?	• He is a composer of the "classical" era.
• It is titled *Divertimento.*	• When did he or she write this piece?	• He composed this in 1787.
• It is written for strings and two French horns.	• For what purpose did he or she write this piece?	• It was written as background music for social gatherings.
• It sounds odd.	• Why did he or she write it this way?	• It appears that Mozart intended this work to be humorous.
	• Why does it sound odd?	• There are dissonances in the French horns.

it is called, and from the recording, what it sounds like. Typically, the students will not do this type of investigation automatically. The teacher more likely will need to ask key questions, such as: "By looking at the score, who do you think wrote this?"; "What is the title?"; and "What instruments are used? Does this sound odd in any way?" After this fact-gathering stage (done using closed questions), the teacher might need to propel the questions forward by asking: "Do we know when Mozart lived?" and "What might that information tell us about this piece?" Beginning with closed questions such as "Who wrote this?" and "What is the title of this composition?" is important to figure out what information is missing and for (a) the students to seek out this information, (b) the teacher to provide the information either verbally or in written form, (c) the class as a whole to speculate about the answers, or (d) the teacher to use a combination of these strategies.

By creating a lesson that sequences from closed to open questions, students can begin by investigating what they know through observation or listening to music and then ask broader questions that help give meaning to the answers of those closed questions. In stringing questions in this way to create the third turn, music teachers can effectively use them to guide students toward discovering music through questions and inquiry.

FROM THEORY TO PRACTICE OF SEQUENCE

We have just presented two mirrored sequences in a lesson plan: moving from open to closed and from closed to open. While it is helpful to think this way, many lesson plans will use a combination of these two processes. Music teachers will often move back and forth between these sequences. They may combine these two sequences in the same lesson, first moving from closed to open and then for the second part of the lesson, moving back from open to closed, as a way to help students summarize the lesson. Based on students' understanding, teachers may need to backtrack, returning to previous questions in order to reinforce ideas. So, like many educational theories, these distinct categories are heuristics, or useful tools for thinking about sequences of questions, but are not doctrine. Instead, music teachers might be flexible in sequencing and blending different approaches.

APPLYING TO PRACTICE 3.8

- Modify a lesson plan that is not as effective as it could be. What are some ways you can sequence questions and activities so that students can achieve the objectives? Is it better to start with open questions and move to closed, or vice versa? How might you anticipate your students'

responses to both the open and closed questions? Are they stronger answering open or closed questions? How will these responses drive or shift your instruction?
- Find a piece or idea you would like to teach and generate a new lesson plan or use one generated in previous Applying to Practice exercises. How will you sequence the questions in the lesson?

WHO ANSWERS: MAKING SURE EVERY STUDENT CONTRIBUTES

Finally, a component of the Marzano (2013) teacher evaluation rubric, as well as others, requires that teachers make sure all students contribute to a lesson. For that reason, music teachers might ensure that all students answer questions. As we noted previously, wording questions in inviting ways encourages all students to participate. However, the teacher also must not repeatedly call upon the same students. One strategy to aid in encouraging every student to participate is to fill a cup with popsicle sticks, each of which has a student's name on it. When music teachers ask a question, they can pull out a popsicle stick and ask the student whose name is on it, then put that stick to the side or in a different cup, so as not to call on the student again until all others have answered questions. This quick process can ensure that teachers reach all students and help them be involved.

Even when teachers use this popsicle stick strategy, some students still may be reluctant to answer. Wait time is important in asking questions. As we described in the third turn section, rewording questions when they are confusing may help all students participate. Looking around the room to see if any students seem confused by the question will help encourage them all to participate. Typically, waiting a minimum of five seconds after asking a question allows time for all students to form an answer in their minds.

Some students may not feel comfortable answering questions out loud. Questions, of course, need not always be answered verbally, and this might encourage all students to participate. Asking the students to answer questions by performing or moving is a quick, low-pressure way to invite all of them participate. For example, a teacher might play a legato passage and then say, "Everyone show me how you think this sounds by moving your scarves." This encourages every student to respond, and the teacher receives all students' responses immediately. The teacher might follow up by asking some students, "I like how you moved your scarf smoothly back and forth. What in the music made you move it that way?" This question can allow teachers to delve deeper into observing students' knowledge and understanding.

APPLYING TO PRACTICE 3.9

- Record yourself teaching a lesson. Are there some students who answer more often than others? If so, why? What are some aspects of student participation that you can control by making small changes to your teaching? Can you ask questions differently or vary the questions so that all students can answer simultaneously?
- Devise some questions that all students can answer. This might mean some answers may extend beyond verbal responses. Create or modify some questions so that students can answer by moving, making music, showing the answer visually through gestures, drawing pictures or other graphic devices, using technology, writing, or by another means.

SUMMARY

Music teachers often struggle with the teacher evaluation requirements of incorporating questions into classrooms, and they sometimes feel that questions are inefficient or not germane to music teaching. However, questions prove to be an effective way for students to retain information, regardless of the content taught. Because of this, teacher evaluation systems explicitly and implicitly focus on incorporating them into lesson plans. In order to incorporate questions effectively, music teachers might ask open, guided, and closed questions. In asking these questions, the wording is important. To encourage participation, music teachers might word questions in ways that invite students to interpret and take chances rather than feel they have to search for the right answer or the answer the teacher wants. Also, just as important as what questions to ask and how to ask them is how to respond to students in the third turn. In this third turn teachers must make in-the-moment decisions to redirect students, review material, or build upon students' responses by transitioning to new material. One way of responding is for teachers to sequence questions and responses in either open to closed or closed to open order. Finally, music teachers can use strategies such as having students respond through music or motion, which encourages all students to answer, to quickly ascertain all students' responses. Using these strategies, Jacob the orchestra teacher, who struggled with using questioning strategies, can begin to incorporate strategies that both reach a desired musical quality and invite student participation and learning. By understanding the nuanced and varied uses of questioning, and the unique aspects educators must attend to when using it in the music classroom, music teachers like Jacob can have more productive conversations with their evaluators:

High school orchestra teacher Jacob is observed by his evaluator, an assistant principal who taught social studies. In the observation, Jacob keeps a brisk rehearsal pace, addresses musical ideas and issues as he heard them, and polishes a section of Alshin's arrangement of "Danny Boy," focusing on the movement of the melodic lines. As students play through a phrase, Jacob tells them, "Something doesn't sound quite right in this phrase. I think it's a tuning issue. Which notes did we have issues with?," leading students to identify the out-of-tune F-sharp in the passage. He then asks, "Where's the note going?" One student answers, "up to the G." Jacob responds, "Exactly. We want this F-sharp to be in tune as we have an ascending melody, going up in pitch. So, think higher to tune that note as you bow through the phrase." In Jacob's post-observation discussion, his evaluator shares, "I noticed that you stopped and started a lot to fix spots. I liked the way you had the students figure out they had a tuning issue in that one section. You asked students to identify the problem, and put the problem in a larger context of the piece—saying the notes go up so they have to 'think high.' Students were able to immediately fix their issue and move on with their playing." Jacob responds, "I notice that when I ask many questions that pertain to their playing or directly to the music, they think differently about their playing. They listen better and actually tend to play more expressively." Jacob's evaluator thanks him for his reflection and gives him an "effective" rating for his questioning strategies, saying she looks forward to seeing Jacob develop his questions further in the next observation.

ADDITIONAL RESOURCES TO AID WITH QUESTIONING STRATEGIES

Music teachers interested in thinking more about questioning strategies may want to consult the following resources, which discuss the role of questions in larger curricular work, both in music and in general education.

Barrett, J. R., McCoy, C. W., & Veblen, K. K. (1997). *Sound ways of knowing: Music in the interdisciplinary curriculum.* New York, NY: Schirmer Books.

The facet model of exploring a musical work also can be a starting place to generate a variety of questions. Barrett, McCoy, and Veblen suggest that in looking at a musical composition, eight questions might drive the study of a piece of music. They suggest using a series of open questions to help students answer specific questions related to the repertoire, such as: "What does it sound or look like?" and "What kind of structure or form does it have?" They can ask questions about its meaning, such as: "What is its subject?" and

"What is being expressed?" Questions might pertain to the historic context and social function of a piece, such as: "Who created it?," "When and where was it created?," and "Why and for whom was it created?" Finally, a question can be used that ties these all together: "What techniques did its creator use to help us understand what is being expressed?" While these questions are of varying degrees of openness, they include areas or categories that teachers can use to begin to generate open questions. Teachers and students may use the musical elements to guide their questions and responses.

National Coalition for Core Arts Standards. (2014). *National core arts standards*. Dover, DE: State Education Agency Directors of Arts Education. Retrieved from www.nationalartsstandards.org

The *National Core Arts Standards* in music are based on the *Understanding by Design* (2005) curriculum. Each area has essential questions. The questions in this document might be starting places for thinking about open questions.

O'Toole, P. A. (2003). *Shaping sound musicians: An innovative approach to teaching comprehensive musicianship through performance*. Chicago, IL: GIA Publications.

Shaping Sound Musicians asks teachers to identify the "heart" of the musical works they want to teach. In other words, why is this piece worth teaching, and why do people listen to this work again and again? It is not because the piece demonstrates a music concept well or develops a technique or reading ability, but because it speaks to those who perform and listen to it. Trying to answer those questions may spark areas of interest and avenues of open questions to ask your students. For example, O'Toole suggests that Handel's "Hallelujah Chorus" from the *Messiah* is worth performing, not because it improves vocal technique or reading ability, or even because it is a famous piece, but because it masterfully uses tension and release and an unrelenting drive. How does Handel create this tension and release and drive through compositional techniques? How can young musicians effectively perform these aspects of the piece through dynamics, tone, rhythmic precision, diction, and other performance aspects? These questions can inform the questions teachers may use to guide their students in the study and performance of this work.

Wiggins, G. P., & McTighe, J. (2005). *Understanding by design*. Alexandria, VA: Association for Supervision and Curriculum Development.

Wiggins & McTighe structure curriculum around "essential questions." These do not have definitive answers, but are the big questions of the academic subject being taught. In music, essential questions might be, "How is music expressive?" or "What is music?" These questions are starting points that structure teaching and aim toward exploration and wonder.

EXAMPLE LESSON PLANS

Middle School or High School Band

Composition: *Air for Band*, by Frank Erickson.
Behavioral Objective:
   • Students will perform mm. 1–16 of *Air for Band* with correct phrasing.
Conceptual Objective:
   • Students will experience musical phrasing, including tension and release.
US Core Arts Standards: MU:Pr4.2.E.5a; MU:Pr4.2.E.IIa; MU:Re8.1.E.Ia;
   MU:Re8.1.E.IIa
Essential Question:
   • How do musicians make musical melodies and harmonies expressive?
Enduring Understanding:
   • A musical phrase is the shaping of a musical idea.
Materials: score, parts, recording
Procedure:

1. Have students play mm. 1–16. This is the A section of the work. Ask the
   students: *Do you see or hear any patterns in the melody of the section we just
   played?* Students might give several answers. Aim for students to observe that
   it is the repeat of a main melody twice. If students do not provide answers,
   then playing a recording might be useful as well. As a follow-up, the teacher
   may also ask: *If it's the melody two times, what's different the first and second
   time?* Possible answers include that the instrumentation is different and
   that the phrases end differently. The first statement ends on a half cadence,
   and the second on a full cadence. Repeat the playing of the section (either by
   performance or recording) so that students can listen to it multiple times.
   The teacher may also ask: *If you don't play the main melody, how do you think the
   nonmelodic lines support the melody expressively?*

2. Have students play one of the iterations of the melody (e.g., mm. 8–16).
   Then ask: *Do you think you can divide the melody up into smaller musical parts?
   How would you describe the first four measures of the melody in contrast to the
   second four?* By doing this, the teacher is trying to lead students to discover
   an antecedent (mm. 8–11) and consequent (mm. 12–16), even if he or she
   does not use that specific vocabulary. Students can also hum the melody
   together in its entirety or four measures at a time. If it makes them feel
   more comfortable, ask them to hum along with a recording or have half the
   ensemble play while half hums (and then switch).

3. Play a recording of mm. 1–8. Have students stand and move/conduct how
   they think the music should go. Several options, based on the ability and
   maturity of the group are available: The teacher can allow students more
   autonomy to move around the room. If the teacher does not feel this will be
   conducive, he or she may ask the students to start crouched and move up

and down as they feel the music moving. To further modify, the students might simply move their hands. Alternatively, if movement is not an option, students can draw what they hear. If it appears students may be self-conscious about this, have them close their eyes for their movement while standing by their chairs or move to the perimeter of the room.

4. Have some students demonstrate their movements. Discuss with the class those movements. Ask the students who watched: *What did this student just show us?* Ask the student who presented: *Why did you move that way? What were you trying to show?* As the teacher and student come up with ideas, record some of the important ones on the board. Ask all students: *Are the movements and interpretation of the melody the first time different from the melody's repetition? If so, how?*

5. Have students perform mm 1–16. This is done mostly to regather and refocus them, as a classroom management procedure. Review the ideas that were placed on the board. Ask the students: *What are some things the composer put in your part to show he wanted it to be played this way?* If no answers arise, point out the tenuto markings at mm. 5, 6, and 7 and ask: *What do those markings mean?* (Have students answer.) *Why do you think the composer put these marking over those notes?*

6. Next, ask students: *What are some things we want to add that the composer did not put in the music?* Relate this question to what the movements from the previous part of the lesson showed. Undoubtedly nuances occurred that are absent in the score. Some answers might include writing crescendos and decrescendos or adding more tenuto marks. Direct students to put those markings in their parts. Students can turn to one person next to them to discuss their marking decisions.

7. Next ask: *What are some movements I can do as the conductor to help remind you to do these things?* Some answers may be to make your movements bigger as the ensemble should get louder or to emphasize notes with tenuto markings over them. Alternatively, percussion does not play during mm. 1–16, so percussion students can come up to conduct the ensemble.

8. Perform mm. 1–16. Remind students of the phrasing they decided to do and what they need to do to make it happen.

9. Ask students: *Was our performance effective?*

10. Introduce the term *phrasing: what we did was phrase.*

11. Ask students: *How can you translate the movement and nuance of the phrase we have discussed to your performance on your instrument?* Ask percussionists to evaluate the execution of the musical ideas that are being suggested and provide feedback.

Assessment:
- Performance of the piece.
- Movement and conducting by the students.

- Feedback given by percussionists.
- Students talking with one another about their phrase-marking decisions.

Possible Next Steps and Extensions:
- Remind students the next day of the phrasing they decided on.
- Do a similar lesson with other sections of *Air for Band.*
- Do a similar lesson with other compositions.
- Create a chart or other visual representation of the phrasing.
- Connect the idea of breathing, air support, and air speed to phrasing, allowing students to draw connections between their conducting and phrasing markings and their breathing in mm. 1–16.

Anticipated Areas of Difficulty or Student Misunderstanding:
- It may be necessary to make accommodations for students with limited mobility.
- Numbers 5, 6, and 7 in the procedure will be difficult for students to do. Many follow-up questions and wait time after asking questions will probably be required.

MIDDLE SCHOOL OR HIGH SCHOOL CHORUS

Composition: *Oye*, by Jim Papoulis, ed. Francisco J. Núñez.

Behavioral Objective:
- Students will sing mm. 1–15 (verse 1) with correct dynamics and diction.

Conceptual Objective:
- Students will interpret text and musical sequences through dynamics and textual analysis.

US Core Arts Standards: MU:Pr4.1.E.IIa; MU:Pr4.2.E.8a; MU:Pr4.3.E.IIa; MU:Re7.1.E.8a; MU:Re9.1.E.8a; MU:Cn10.0.E.Ia

Essential Question:
- How do musicians convey and express a message through song?

Enduring Understanding:
- Similar or repeated musical ideas can be communicated differently through phrasing and dynamics.

Materials: score, piano, conga drum

Procedure:
1. Ask: *If there was something—some message—you as a group really wanted people outside our chorus to know, what would it be? What would you want to tell them as a group of young adults?* Have students discuss. Possible responses are that kids have knowledge and ideas to contribute to the world or that sometimes people don't think we know anything because we're young or we don't know how to communicate, but we do. The teacher might follow up (third turn) their responses with questions: *Why? How come?*
2. Have students speak through the Spanish text beginning at m. 4. Picking out keywords, speak the text with the students repeating. Lead students to

translate (if there is a Spanish speaker, he or she may help as well)—and fill in the remaining text.

Verse 1

Está solo, llorando en silencio, en la oscuridad.
[Alone, crying in silence, in the darkness]
Está soñando, deseando con esperanza, por l'oportunidad.
[It is sounding, desiring with hope, for opportunity]
Escúchalos, escúchalos, ellos te llaman.
[Listen to them, listen to them, they're calling you]
Oye, are you listening?

3. Ask: *What do you think* solo *means?* Llorando? *En silencio?* Students may interpret many of these words as alone, crying, in silence, or in darkness.

4. Continue picking keywords for students to identify—*soñando, deseando, esperanza, l'oportunidad* (dreaming, wishing, hoping, for the opportunity).

5. Ask questions such as: *What do you think is the overall tone or feeling here? To whom do you think the character is singing? Why do we think he or she is singing about being alone? How do you think the composer shows this in his writing?* (unison singing). *If the singer is alone, what dynamic level should we begin with?* (soft, *piano*).

6. Have students speak the text in rhythm. The teacher should play a basic rhythmic pattern on the conga (setting a moving accompaniment or groove) to establish the style of the piece immediately. Draw attention to trouble spots (such as quarter note rests at the beginning of measures). Students should walk to a steady beat to anticipate these rests and to begin to feel a pulse in their bodies. Remind students to tell the story they just discussed: *We just picked out some important words, perhaps we need to emphasize them as we speak.* Have students speak in rhythm again.

7. Have students sing from verse 1, m. 4 with pitches. Play part 2 on the piano when the vocal line divides for assistance and reinforcement.

8. Ask: *Escúchalos—escuchar—what is that*? (To listen, are you listening?) *Ellos te llaman?* (Can you hear their cries?) *How many times do we say escúchalos?* (two). *Why do you think the composer would repeat that?* (for emphasis that we need the audience to listen). *Each time we sing this, what should we do to get our emphasis across?* (get louder).

9. At *escúchalos*, something different happens with the voices; ask students: *What do you notice?* (voicings move from 2-part to 3-part). *Why does that happen in this section?* (The sound is building as we sing listen, and then it moves to the chorus, which should be louder). *Notice the pitches at this part: What direction are they moving?* (up). *As the pitch rises, often we want to get louder. The composer gives us a clue by writing the ascending line, and he also writes in a dynamic for us: Where and what is it*? (crescendo).

10. Add pitches to *escúchalos* with crescendo. Have students show with their bodies the growth in sound as they sing. Ask one student to conduct this part with the group. Ask the student conductor: *What did you hear? Did they sing the growth in sound you wanted and showed?* After the student responds accordingly, have the group sing again. Ask for two more students to share their conducting.

11. Share that the text for this piece was written by children. Ask: *Knowing this, how might we want to sing this? How does this change the text for us? Who are the children singing to? What do they want the audience to do? How are we going to show this in our singing? Let's try that. There's a lot of sound building in this verse; show this with your hands while you sing. And keep moving your feet on the beat* [this is to begin feeling the groove of the piece].

12. Have students sing verse 1, m. 4. Play chords in some rhythmic pattern on the piano for a harmonic foundation. Have one student keep a beat or play an easy pattern on the drum.

13. Ask: *What did you hear? Did we like that? What did we like/not like about it? How did we do? Were we effective in communicating the children's message through our words and dynamics?*

Assessment:
- Student score navigation of verse 1, finding musical markings.
- Student singing of piece.
- Student interpretation of text in discussion and singing.
- Student movement to show dynamic growth.

Possible Next Steps and Extensions:
- Remind students of dynamic growth they tracked in verse 1 with movement.
- Repeat questions and process similarly for verse 2.
- Students, individually or in groups, can write their own message asking people to listen, Oye!
- Incorporate a written assessment in which students show a translation of the text or write what the text might mean.

Anticipated Areas of Difficulty or Student Misunderstanding:
- Students may have a difficult time with pronunciation of the text.
- Parallel thirds in the harmonies can be difficult. Be prepared to isolate one line at a time and build on it.
- There may be follow-up questions to some of the more interpretive questions, requiring wait time.

ELEMENTARY GENERAL MUSIC (GRADES 2–3)

Repertoire and Games: Missa-la, Massa-la; Rocky Mountain; Sansa Kroma; Liza Jane (numerous videos of how these games are played and sung are available online through web searches)

Behavioral Objectives:
- Students will sing and move in 2-beat, 4-beat, and 8-beat phrases.
- Students will identify, compose, and improvise in a 4-beat phrase.
- Students will derive the rhythm to a known song.

Conceptual Objective:
- Students will experience 2-, 4-, and 8-beat phrases in their bodies through structured and improvised activities.

US Core Arts Standards: MU:Cr1.1.2; MU:Pr4.2.2; MU:Pr6.1.2

Essential Question:
- How do musicians work together to create new musical ideas?

Enduring Understanding:
- Musical patterns are strung together to create a phrase, a musical idea.

Materials: large fabric elastic with ring attached; rhythm sticks; *Summertime* book (Gershwin, Heyward, Heyward, & Gershwin, 2002)

Procedure:

1. **Welcome:** Play "Missa-la Massa-la" (ring passing/guessing game with "It").
   Key of C, 1st pitch = E (7–10 mins.)

   Activity: A close standing game of players with hands behind their backs who pass a ring (sometimes attached to a long cord or string around the entire circle). A player in the middle tries to guess who has the ring. Outside singers can help the inside player by singing loudly when the ring is nearby and softly when the ring is far away. Questions to ask while setting up the game: *How do you think we will be able to pick out who has the ring? What are some things we can do with our faces to pretend we don't have the ring, even if we do have it? How will we make sure the guesser can't see if we have the ring? What can we do? Let's practice passing our rings.*

   Transition: Collect the elastic/ring prop, simultaneously singing directions to sit in a circle to the melody of "Missa-la," then start singing "Rocky Mountain" while tapping a steady beat.

2. **Song:** "Rocky Mountain"
   Key: do = C (2–3 mins.)

   Activity: Sing the song while tapping a steady beat; move the beat-tapping into 2-beat patterns, then 4-beat patterns on the body.

   Concepts: steady beat; prep 4-beat patterns.

   Transition: Tap a steady beat with the 4-beat pattern used in "Sansa Kroma" passing game.

3. **Game:** "Sansa Kroma"
   Key/Timing: do = C (7–10 mins.)

   Activity: Start by modeling and saying "pick-up, click, tap, pass" (or some 4-beat movement) without sticks. Students join and add movement. Gradually add sticks. Sing the song only after most students master the passing pattern.

Transition: Ask: *How many different movements are involved in our passing pattern? Let's do it and count them* (answer: four). *Each time we have these four movements—or beats—they make up a phrase, or a musical idea.*

4. **Group Work:** "Sansa Kroma"
    Key of C (10–12 mins.)
    Activity: Ask: *How can we make sure that we do all four steps on the beat?* Possible responses are don't lift our arms so high; keep the body in self-control; and listen to each other/watch each other's movements, just like musicians in an orchestra.

    In groups of four (or five), students create their own 4-beat (4-movement) passing pattern. If there are ten minutes left in the lesson, groups can share with one another (if not, they can simply perform simultaneously). The teacher may make observations or ask questions about particular movements.
    Transition: Have two volunteers collect sticks while the rest make a circle for the next game (standing for Liza Jane).

5. **Movement (if Time Allows):** "Liza Jane"
    Key of D or E (3–5 mins.)
    Activity: Students put the beat in their feet; then the rhythm in their feet. They clap the rhythm or the way the words go. Ask: *Does the beat move faster than the rhythm, or vice versa?* Students derive the rhythm from the first phrase. Ask: *How many beats do we have in this first part, or phrase?* (The teacher may write beats as numbers or as hearts on the board to help students derive them more quickly.) Have students write the derived rhythm on the board. Ask: *Is there anywhere else in this song where we have the same phrase? The same rhythm?*

    Ask students for other ways to keep the beat, showing the high note by using movements from various sports (bouncing an imaginary basketball and shooting it for the high note, cradling with a lacrosse stick and then throwing the lacrosse ball, spinning the line of a fishing pole and then throwing the hook back out to sea, etc.). Ask: *Which of the three movements gave the class the best sound? I noticed your singing was quite good. Why do you think that motion helped your singing?*

6. **Story:** "Summertime" (Gershwin et al., 2002) (3–5 mins)
    Activity: Ask: *What are you looking forward to (or maybe not looking forward to!) about summertime? What's different about your community/where we live in winter and summer?*
    Sing the song and read the story to students.

Possible Next Steps and Extensions:
- Review and practice a 4-beat phrase—recalling the word *phrase*—using another song or game using movement.

- Begin composing and notating rhythms within a 4-beat phrase. Possibly use "Summertime" as a basis. Possibly add dynamics of *forte* and *piano*. Students may string their phrases together.

Anticipated Areas of Difficulty or Student Misunderstanding:

- Students may need another model of what a 4-beat movement could look like.
- Students may confuse putting the beat versus rhythm in their feet for "Liza Jane."
- Students may not agree on a 4-beat movement/phrase in their groups.

4

DIFFERENTIATION

Terrence is preparing for his formal observation by his principal. He composes his lesson plan for rehearsing Frank Ticheli's arrangement of "Amazing Grace," one that Terrence is proud of because he feels he is able to get students to play long, expressive lines. Terrence's principal also asks him to fill out a form to accompany the lesson plan. One of the questions on the form is, "How does this lesson incorporate differentiation?" To answer, Terrence writes, "The different parts differentiate. For example, the third clarinet part is easier than the first clarinet part." Feeling satisfied, Terrence hands in the lesson plan and form. The following week in his pre-observation meeting, the principal addresses Terrence's differentiation: "Different parts aren't differentiation; that's tracking. How are you going to make this a meaningful, individualized lesson that reaches each student?" Terrence cannot think of any strategies and is at a loss for words.

DIFFERENTIATION IS A word often used in educational jargon that music teachers, along with teachers in other disciplines, may have difficulty grasping. As the vignette above depicts, evaluators—particularly those with teaching experience outside of music—may have definitions of differentiated instruction that do not match those of music teachers. This might create situations in which evaluators miss how music teachers differentiate, but it also provides opportunities for music educators to improve their teaching. How do music teachers discover where they already differentiate but could refine their teaching to create instruction that is sensitive to each student's individual needs, desires, and strengths while meeting curricular objectives?

In this chapter we look at differentiation and its relation to teacher evaluation. First, we describe the need for differentiated instruction and how it is expressed in teacher evaluation. Second, we discuss the qualities of differentiation. In this section, we address some concerns that music teachers might have with the concept of differentiation. Next, we provide some strategies for how music teachers might differentiate their instruction and curriculum. Finally, we apply the concept to teacher evaluation so that music teachers may successfully complete this aspect in their evaluations.

APPLYING TO PRACTICE 4.1

Conduct an initial evaluation of your attitudes about and experiences with differentiation:

- What is your reaction to Terrence's evaluator's comment in the vignette that using different parts in an ensemble is *not* differentiation? How would you respond?
- What constitutes differentiation? Can you come up with your own definition?
- Do you have concerns about implementing differentiation as you understand it?
- Have you used differentiation in your classroom before? If so, how? Write down a list to compare with the strategies discussed in this chapter.

DIFFERENTIATION IN TEACHER EVALUATION

Why should teachers differentiate instruction? Differentiation as a practice and educational philosophy has emerged because there is evidence that it has an effect on student learning and achievement. Research suggests that students tend to favor classrooms that are differentiated (Kanevsky, 2011; McAdamis, 2001). Some studies have shown gains in students' test scores and outcomes (Hodge, 1997; McAdamis, 2001). Other research points to the need for differentiation for gifted students (Baum, Cooper, & Neu, 2001; Hertberg-Davis, 2009). One study found that early career teachers who were encouraged and supported to use differentiation found the process more enjoyable than nondifferentiated teaching (Johnsen, 2003). Affolder (2003) suggests that when teachers adopt differentiated instructional approaches, their perception of students' individual differences and their responsibility for achieving student growth increases. Despite these positive aspects for teachers, earlier studies have suggested that teachers with more experience can find the process of differentiating difficult (Tomlinson, Moon, & Callahan, 1998), especially if they do not have administrative support (Tomlinson, 1995).

Because there is evidence that it has effects on students' learning, differentiation is often found in teacher evaluation protocols. For example, the Danielson framework requires that materials be "appropriately differentiated" and that "assessment methodologies have been adapted for individual students as the need has arisen" (Danielson, 2013, p. 2). The framework also requires that a teacher "successfully adjusts and differentiates instruction to address individual student misunderstandings" (p. 4). Differentiation, however, also appears in places where the term is not used. For example, although it is not stated

> Differentiation is not always explicit in teacher evaluation, but may be understood in ways that teachers help students learn and interact with new knowledge and use choice to assess students' learning.

directly, in Marzano (2013), domain 2, number 48, "planning and preparing for the needs of students receiving special education," calls for teachers to be evaluated in differentiation. In Danielson, the Distinguished criteria for 1F, devoted to assessment, include this criterion: "Assessments provide opportunities for student choice." Although it does not use the word differentiation, this criterion calls for that approach.

Teacher evaluation systems are trying to encourage teachers to understand their students' individual needs and characteristics and then act upon that understanding. Each student is unique, and a "one-size-fits-all" approach is not an effective strategy. Instead, being sensitive to students' differences within the class and adapting instruction to those differences is valued as an important component. Teacher evaluation encourages a teacher's disposition toward being curious about students' individual profiles, experiences, and interests, then creating ways to seek out those differences. Once these differences have been discovered, teachers can create lesson plans that respond to the information gathered. If a teacher can demonstrate the ability to modify curriculum and instruction to students' unique attributes, then he or she will likely prove successful in the differentiation component in teacher evaluation.

APPLYING TO PRACTICE 4.2

Look at your teacher evaluation system. Are there places where differentiation is asked for explicitly? Are there other places where differentiation is not explicitly named, but differentiating in the classroom might fulfill some of the requirements?

WHAT DIFFERENTIATION IS (AND IS NOT)

While educators generally agree that differentiation is a strong pedagogical practice and is therefore included in teacher evaluation requirements, *differentiation* and *differentiated instruction* are frequently ill defined. Like many terms in education, their meaning has become distorted and watered down over time. Teachers and administrators often use *differentiation* to describe any time teachers treat students in the same class differently. While that is certainly one aspect of differentiation, the concept is a more specific way of creating instruction that will reach each student. What, then, is this term that is so often used in teacher evaluation systems and elsewhere? In this section we describe some qualities of differentiation and some characteristics that educators often label as differentiation but that according to research are not inherently differentiation strategies.

QUALITIES OF DIFFERENTIATION

A definition by Tomlinson et al. (2003) serves as a starting place for discussing differentiation: "*Differentiation* can be defined as an approach to teaching in which teachers proactively modify curricula, teaching methods, resources, learning activities, and student products to address the diverse needs of individual students and small groups of students to maximize the learning opportunity for each student in a classroom" (p. 121). Essentially, differentiation consists of modifying teaching to meet the needs of students to maximize learning opportunities. However, Tomlinson et al. (2003) elaborate on this straightforward definition. They suggest that differentiation (1) meets the needs of diverse students; (2) modifies curricula, teaching methods, resources, learning activities, and student products; and (3) is proactive. Each of these qualifications merits further description.

Differentiation aims to meet the diverse needs of students. Students in classrooms are, indeed, diverse. They might have different cultural backgrounds and experiences in previous years of schooling. They might also prefer to learn in different ways, and they each have their own interests. Because of these different profiles, students learn differently, and a "one-size-fits-all" approach will not reach all the students in equally effective ways (Tomlinson et al., 2003). Differentiation is a varied approach to students in which teachers modify curriculum and assignments.

Differentiation modifies curricula, teaching methods, resources, learning activities, and student products. There are many types of differentiation. It can occur within *what* is taught, *how* it is taught, and what students are asked to *do* and *produce*. In a differentiated classroom, any one, some, or all of these might vary among the students based on their needs, strengths, and preferences. Later in the chapter we expand on this crucial aspect.

Differentiation is proactive. Teachers plan ahead of time how they will differentiate and anticipate how they will modify materials for students. This might mean that teachers pre- and post-assess students to gather information on how to best tailor the curriculum to their unique profiles. However, while they plan ahead, perhaps paradoxically, teachers who differentiate are also flexible. They look for students' interests and areas that they are struggling with and consider opportunities to differentiate yet again. Teachers who differentiate balance planning of material with adapting the material based on assessments and new evidence.

> Differentiation addresses student needs and diversity; it is proactive and flexible, allowing teachers to modify curriculum, instruction, resources, and outcomes.

Tomlinson et al. (2003) provide a neat and precise definition that highlights the aims of differentiation as meeting students' diverse needs, modifying in a variety of ways, and being proactive. In contrast, Wormeli (2006) provides a more aspirational description that adds to the first definition:

Differentiated instruction is doing what is fair for students. It's a collection of best practices strategically employed to maximize students' learning at every turn, including giving them the tools to handle anything that is undifferentiated. It requires us to do different things for different students some, or a lot, of the time in order for them to learn when the general classroom approach does not meet students' needs. It is not individualized instruction, thought that may happen from time to time as warranted. It's whatever works to advance the students. It's highly effective teaching. (p. 3)

Like Tomlinson et al. (2003), Wormeli describes differentiation as modifying the curriculum with the aim of meeting the needs of students. Again, there are some qualifiers that give more direction to that modification, including that differentiation (1) is fair, (2) occurs for individual students and small groups, and (3) includes giving students the tools to cater their learning to their needs.

Differentiation is fair. Wormeli's (2006) definition asserts that differentiation is "doing what is fair for students"; it is giving students whatever they need to learn the content and grow. However, some teachers might disagree and think that differentiation is the opposite, that it is unfair and inequitable. This is perhaps the most common objection to differentiation. As the argument goes, if John receives different materials, more support, or different objectives than Emily, that is not fair to Emily.

Differentiation is not about equality in the sense that everyone receives the same thing. Such a conception of students and learning is perhaps too narrow. Instead, differentiation is about equity and fairness in that, when done properly, it provides every student with needed support so that equality occurs in the end goal. In this way, the conception of differentiation requires teachers to shift their conception of equity and fairness from the *inputs* to the *outcomes*. In other words, differentiation is indeed about equality, but that equality is focused and measured in the outcomes—what students are able to do and know at the end—rather than on the inputs—what the teacher provides them. Equality, then, lies in the outcome of each student becoming successful and learning. While even the end product might look different and even the concept of success might vary from student to student, the goal is for every student to receive what he or she needs to be successful. From this perspective, differentiation is fairer than an "equal" treatment of students. The fairness and equality reside in the more important outcomes than in the inputs or the means to achieve those outcomes.

Differentiation occurs for individual students and small groups. A common concern of teachers is that differentiation is a great theory, but in practice it simply is too much to handle. Catering to every student's individual need, devising individual assignments, and delivering instruction aimed at each individual student's learning style is too much of a workload for teachers. When it comes to grading, devising different criteria for grading students is too difficult, cumbersome, and unfair. Similarly, teachers might argue that differentiation creates chaos in the classroom; students are running around and there is no order to the classroom.

This is why both Tomlinson et al. (2003) and Wormeli (2006) state that differentiation is not only individual instruction. Differentiation may include some individual work, but there is simply not enough time to provide individualized instruction all the time. The management of different criteria and standards for each student will quickly overwhelm teachers. Also, individualized instruction does not allow students to collaborate and learn from one another. This often means that teachers may group similar students together. A music teacher, for example, might modify a lesson so that there are three entry points. He or she may notice that when identifying the sections of sonata form in a music theory class, students fall into three broad categories: those who struggle identifying key centers, those who have trouble identifying the different melodic sections, and those who understand the concept and need a challenge. The teacher can then pick three different composition excerpts that target what these three groups of students need in order to improve their learning. There is no need, in this case, to choose a different work for each student.

Instead of only thinking of differentiation as individualized instruction, Wormeli and Tomlinson et al. both suggest that differentiation could take on a *whole group/small group/whole group* structure. In this structure, differentiation usually begins with some whole group instruction by the teacher as an introduction, then the class breaks up into smaller differentiated groups, and finally the class comes together again for whole group instruction, using their work in small groups to inform the whole class. Teachers might consider this process a cycle that can be repeated any number of times. While differentiation need not always function in this way, it is a useful pattern to follow when constructing differentiated lessons. It eases grading and makes classroom procedures more manageable.

Differentiation includes giving students the tools to adapt learning to their needs. Wormeli notes that differentiation is also giving students the tools to modify their learning and understand that their processes and products might look different than other students'. Some music educators might object to differentiation because they believe it serves as a crutch. "In the real world," the argument might go, "no one is going to differentiate for you. As we, the authors, even suggest, the outcomes are what count. Differentiation merely enables and sets students up for failure in the future."

This is an interesting critique of differentiation. Certainly educators do not want to rely only on students' strengths and never provide opportunities for them to grow and be prepared for life outside of schools. However, if one looks for it, differentiation can be found everywhere in the "real world." Take music teaching as a profession, for example. While it might not be entirely apparent at first, music teachers differentiate for themselves quite often. They play on their strengths to support their weaknesses. General music teachers, for example, might gravitate toward piano or guitar to accompany students when they sing, based on their strengths. In recitals, professional musicians pick music that highlights their strengths as performers rather than their weaknesses. Differentiation in the workplace, however, is not always about displaying strengths. In these examples as well, sometimes teachers and musicians purposefully pick specific challenges to improve their practice. A teacher might challenge himself or herself to become better at accompanying on the piano rather than always relying on the guitar. A performer might pick a composition that stretches her technique. Differentiation also entails picking materials that help to improve areas that need improvement. Rather than a crutch, then, differentiation is an essential part of success in the workplace and learning outside of school. Helping students learn how to differentiate through example helps them prepare for the "real world" rather than protecting them from it.

WHAT DIFFERENTIATION IS *NOT*

In addition to the difference between individual instruction and differentiation, there are some other areas in which teachers confuse the idea of differentiation. Differentiation is not tracking. Differentiation was created in part to deal with the negative consequences of tracking students into different classes of abilities. Tracking of students into abilities has a number of negative consequences, including that it tends to segregate them along racial and class boundaries, it disadvantages students with disabilities, and it widens the gaps among "high-," "average-," and "lower-" performing students (George, 2005; Wormeli, 2006). A nontracked classroom in which students of differing abilities and makeups learn together is beneficial for all students. Differentiation is in part a strategy to exercise the democratic desire to not privilege some students over others, while more closely tailoring students' education. This same concept holds true for intra-class tracking, like consistently assigning the clarinet 1, 2, 3 parts to students based on ability, as Terrence did in the vignette at the beginning of this chapter. Similarly, assigning students to reading groups based on ability in elementary school is not considered a form of differentiation (Tomlinson et al., 2003; Wormeli, 2006).

> Differentiation is not tracking. It should be both group based and individual and take on a whole group-small group-whole group structure, not dividing students into "tracked" groups.

Instead, differentiation is looking at ability in a nuanced way that does not simply divide students into oversimplified categories of high, average, and low achievers at the beginning of the course and keep them in place all year.

Differentiation is looking at strengths in more nuanced and fine-grained ways. For example, rather than defining a student as a "low achiever" or "not talented" in music, differentiation allows the teacher to see where a student is performing well and where she is not, then use her strengths to mitigate the areas needing improvement.

For example, rather than creating different recorder groups based on ability, a teacher might modify parts based on the students' abilities and needs for improvement. All students might perform "Hot Cross Buns"; however, those who struggle with the notation could be given additional materials to help them decipher the notation. It might be written with iconic notation, for example. Those who struggle with technique—the fingerings—might play long notes as the others play the melody. Finally, those who excel in these areas could be given a variation that is more challenging. Likewise, when playing ukulele, students could have different strumming patterns. Some students might strum only on the downbeat of 1 to practice moving from chord to chord, some might strum with palm mutes, and some might make up their own strumming pattern. What is important is that this happens simultaneously as students play together. All this results in "flexible grouping," meaning that instead of assigning students by ability level or tracking at the beginning of the year, teachers find ways to group students in various configurations that change based on the students' strengths and areas in need of improvement (Heacox, 2012).

This aspect of differentiation is important for music teachers to acknowledge, particularly secondary ensemble directors. By this definition, creating "select" and "regular" ensembles or devising homogeneous, small-group lessons or sectionals based on technique or notation-reading ability is *not* necessarily a form of differentiation. Similarly, as we saw in the vignette on Terrence, providing different parts is a form of intra-class tracking and is not necessarily differentiation. Often, ensemble directors like Terrence believe that since ensembles have different instrument parts, such as trumpet 1, 2, and 3, instruction in these settings is inherently differentiated. According to the qualities discussed here, for different parts to be considered a form of differentiation, the teacher would need to consider students' *specific* strengths and areas of improvement, then the different parts would need to address those areas.

Many music teachers, of course, do tend to target students' specific strengths. However, it is important to continually and regularly look for ways that will help students succeed, not simply to track. This might mean adjusting parts as music teachers determine student needs, rather than just planning who gets what part at the beginning of the year. Second, teachers might need to point out these forms of differentiation to evaluators. It is important for music teachers to understand this as they converse with evaluators, particularly those outside of music.

Another important aspect is that differentiation is about quality, character, or type of work—not quantity. Providing students with more or less homework—or in the case of music education, more or fewer pieces of music to practice based on ability—is not a form of differentiation. Instead, differentiation is about changing the quality or character of the work required of students. This might mean all students receive one piece of music to learn, but each piece addresses each student's areas in need of improvement. Students could also choose their own music. It might also mean that some students perform while others compose, or record music, or do a research project. It might mean giving students the same assignment, but providing more information and materials for students who struggle and allowing greater uncertainty for more advanced students. In all these cases, the quantity does not change; there is not "more of the same." Instead, in each of these examples the quality or type of the work changes.

> Differentiation is about quality, character, or type of work—not quantity.

THE CHARACTERISTICS OF DIFFERENTIATION

Table 4.1 summarizes the characteristics and provides strategies that are examples of differentiated instruction, as well as ones commonly employed in music education that are not inherently differentiated instruction.

These characteristics may allow teachers to create and refine practices so that they better meet the needs of students. For communication purposes, it might help music teachers realize that an evaluator's definition of differentiation might be more in line with the characteristics from Tomlinson et al. (2003) and Wormeli (2006) and might vary from music teachers' definition. Understanding this perspective on differentiation can help teachers better engage in dialogue and improve practice.

TABLE 4.1.

Qualities of differentiation and examples of what differentiation is and is not

Qualities of Differentiation (compiled from Tomlinson et al. [2003] and Wormeli [2006])

- Meets the needs of diverse students.
- Modifies curricula, teaching methods, resources, learning activities, and student products.
- Is proactive.
- Is fair.
- Occurs for individual students and small groups.
- Includes giving students the tools to adjust their learning to their needs.

Examples of strategies commonly employed in music that are *not* inherently differentiated instruction	**Examples of differentiated instruction in music**
Ensembles tracked by ability or different sections (first violin vs. second violin).	Flexible grouping of students based on areas in which they need improvement.
Additional work (more pieces to learn, more worksheets to complete).	Tailored work (choosing pieces or other work that help students work on specific areas in need of improvement).

APPLYING TO PRACTICE 4.3

- What are the varying needs of your students? Similarly, what are their strengths? How can you use those strengths to support learning in the areas where they need improvement?
- Talk to one or two students in a class who struggle and list where they specifically need help. This might be specific concepts; it might be following procedures. Aim to be as specific as possible. Next, list what their strengths and interests are. If you cannot list any strengths, talk to other teachers, call home, and/or talk to the students to find out their strengths and interests.

- Throughout this section we have mentioned some common concerns teachers have with differentiation. Do you have other concerns about differentiation? If so, do advocates of differentiation have a response to this critique? Do a search on the web to see if there are any responses to your concerns. In addition to the resources cited in this chapter, the following are good sources to consult:
  - Chapman, C. & King, R. (2005). *Differentiated assessment strategies: One tool doesn't fit all*. Thousand Oaks, CA: Corwin Press.
  - Educational leadership website and publications from ASCD (formerly the Association for Supervision & Curriculum Development).
  - *Gifted Education* (journal).
  - *Journal for the Education of the Gifted*.
  - Strickland, C. A. (2007). *Tools for high quality differentiated instruction*. Alexandria, VA: Association for Supervision and Curriculum Development.
  - Tomlinson, C. A. (2001). *How to differentiate instruction in mixed-ability classrooms* (2nd ed.). Alexandria, VA: Association for Supervision and Curriculum Development.
  - Tomlinson, C. A. (2003). *Fulfilling the promise of the differentiated classroom: Strategies and tools for responsive teaching*. Alexandria, VA: Association for Supervision and Curriculum Development.

DIFFERENTIATION STRATEGIES IN THE MUSIC CLASSROOM

While clearly defining differentiation can be useful, music teachers may want to know how to employ differentiation as a pedagogical strategy. Despite its inclusion in teacher evaluation systems and the research that suggests differentiation positively affects students' learning, music teachers—like teachers in other academic subjects—might have concerns about applying it to practice. How do music teachers employ differentiation in a fair and manageable way to help students grow rather than enabling them? In this section we provide specific ways music teachers can differentiate curricula and instruction. First, music educators might consider differentiating the *products, content*, and *process* in their curriculum and instruction (Tomlinson, 2001). Furthermore, the content, process, and products may be differentiated for individual students or groups of students based on the students' *readiness, interests, learner profiles* (Tomlinson, 2001), and *cultural backgrounds* (Ginsberg, 2005; Santamaria, 2009). Looking for places to modify the curriculum in these areas and using this language in teacher evaluation systems may provide music teachers with opportunities to differentiate effectively in their classrooms. Table 4.2 presents these parameters for differentiating and the ways to differentiate based on student characteristics. By looking at these in detail, music educators could begin to devise numerous ways to differentiate their instruction as well as provide vocabulary for how they talk to evaluators and other educators.

DIFFERENTIATING THE CURRICULUM: PRODUCTS, CONTENT, AND PROCESSES

Music educators might begin differentiating by considering how they could modify the curriculum. Three parameters that they can differentiate are products, content, and process.

Products. Differentiation of products can be defined as the teacher allowing the students to demonstrate their learning through a variety of means. Products, or what students are expected to produce, are the easiest parameter to differentiate in a classroom, and this is particularly easy in classrooms where creativity is a central focus. Obviously student-created compositions are a form of differentiation. However, use of compositions alone is not sufficient for teacher evaluation systems, and more important, for reaching students. Teachers who regularly require students to compose might examine whether the differentiation supplies enough variability among acceptable products. How many parameters or requirements are specified? Are they absolutely necessary?

TABLE 4.2.

Parameters of curricula that can be differentiated and ways to differentiate those parameters

Parameters	Ways to Differentiate Based on Student Characteristics
• Products: what students are required to produce. • Content: what students learn. • Process: how students learn.	• Readiness: students' ability based on previous knowledge and experience to learn the material. • Interests: students' desires, hobbies, and areas of fascination. • Learner profiles: students' preferred ways of learning and receiving information. • Cultural backgrounds: students' racial, ethnic, socioeconomic, and religious background, among other identities.

For example, a teacher might specify required instrumentation, number of measures, time signature, meter, harmonies, rhythms, and so forth. As a teacher aims to differentiate, he or she might ask: Are the given requirements absolutely necessary for the student to be successful? Providing as few parameters as possible increases the likelihood that students will incorporate their own interests or creative ideas. The second question is whether the requirements are necessary for *every* student. Some students may need structure and thrive under the guidelines, while others will not; differentiating the number of parameters each student receives allows for greater likelihood of success.

Differentiation in ensembles is more difficult than in classes that use composition. In some sense, ensembles are about people coming together and sharing a collective goal; however, even while working towards this collective goal there are many opportunities for differentiation. One way to think about this is to consider the role of a method book in ensembles. Must everyone play from the same method book? Must students play the method book material in order or play from the same page at the same time? Providing differing materials to work on is a form of differentiation. This means that students receive some materials to help them work on their individual areas in need of improvement. Ensemble directors often do this, and it is important to articulate this practice to evaluators.

Content. There are times when it is appropriate for students to learn different content. Content differentiating can benefit students who excel at content as well as those who learn the material at a slower pace. For students who learn the material quickly, "curriculum compacting" (Reis, Burns, & Renzulli, 1993) is an option. This is a form of differentiation in which the teacher finds places where more advanced students already know the material and then provides them with opportunities to learn new material. In this process, the teacher first performs a pre-assessment to see whether any students already understand the material. Second, the teacher determines what skills or knowledge related to the topic those students would benefit from learning. Third, the teacher devises projects or homework assignments appropriate for learning the new material. For example, in ensembles, if a student has learned her part quickly, she may take time away from rehearsal to learn a more difficult piece or complete a research project on the composition the ensemble is performing. Importantly, differentiation is not "piling on more work" but rather is creating different work that is enriching and interesting. Linking the new piece to the repertoire being performed by the whole band might be beneficial.

On the other hand, there are students who may take more time to learn the content of a class. In these cases, it might be appropriate for the teacher to distill the content down to its essential components. For example, as many ensemble teachers know, it seems unreasonable to expect a student who recently began to learn an instrument to perform with the same ability as a student who has received private instruction for many years. While one student might be able to play all twelve major scales, it might be appropriate to allow the other to learn just three. Similarly, there are times when students need their parts further differentiated by simplifying the rhythm or range. In solo work, the teacher might transpose the work into an easier key or range. These modifications are a key component of music education; students continue to play music alone and with others and experience the process of preparing and studying music. They have retained that overarching goal even though the content has been slightly modified to ensure their success.

Some teachers might be uncomfortable with the scenario of modifying parts for students who struggle. There is, indeed, an ethical consideration to weigh as a teacher differentiates for content. If a teacher is modifying content simply by leaving out some information, he or she must make that decision carefully. There is a potential to create inequity for students if they are not allowed access to that key information. However, if a teacher remembers the essential information or experiences that she wants all students to gain, modifying the content to suit that larger goal will be ethical and beneficial for the students.

Process. Adults and children have different ways of thinking through a problem. Differentiation around process acknowledges the idea that people have a variety of ways of completing a task. As teachers look to differentiate, they might ask themselves: Do I allow a variety of ways for students to work through problems and assignments? For example, a teacher might provide students with three or four ways to count a rhythm. Teachers often adhere to a methodology when counting rhythms, such as Kodály, Gordon's Music Learning Theory, traditional counting, or assigning familiar words to rhythms. Differentiation the process suggests that teachers might use these and many other ways of learning rhythms. Sometimes it might be appropriate to use du-de and other times, ta and ti-ti. Other times it might be better to learn a triplet by saying cho-co-late. More important, there might be other ways that students could decipher rhythms. They might use manipulatives, such as Legos or popsicle sticks, to depict a rhythm.

Music teachers may be familiar with many or all of these strategies. However, what might be new for some music teachers is that differentiation can encourage educators to use them all at once, employing different strategies with different students. Teachers who differentiate around process acknowledge that one process is not the best for every student. Instead, they realize that some processes suit some students, while different processes suit others. This might be an uncomfortable way to think about teaching music for some educators. Some people might identify with one particular method or have been focused on one teaching strategy in their teacher education and professional development. Some school districts might require all teachers to use one teaching technique for learning pitch or rhythm, such as Orff or Kodály. It is important to acknowledge that the strict adherence to a method, uniformly applied to all students, is not compatible with the research and practice of differentiation. Differentiation, by its nature, is an eclectic, pragmatic approach that utilizes a variety of teaching strategies based on what will be most effective with each student. Teachers must keep these views in mind as they experience teacher evaluation and discuss these ideas with evaluators. In order to be successful, music teachers must be open to a variety of approaches if they want to fulfill the differentiation component in teacher evaluation, even if this conflicts with teaching approaches they have always used or were taught are superior pedagogies. We return to adopting this open stance of trying new strategies in the final chapter on talking to evaluators.

APPLYING TO PRACTICE 4.4

- Allowing students to use a variety of processes for learning may be in conflict with certain philosophies of music learning that require a consistent, uniform approach to learning rhythm and pitch in singing, playing, reading notation, or other aspects of music. How do you feel about this? Are you comfortable adopting different approaches, or does this conflict with your beliefs about learning or what you were taught in professional development and teacher education?
- If they do conflict, how will you reconcile your beliefs and the requirement to differentiate in teacher evaluation?

FOUR WAYS TO DIFFERENTIATE: READINESS, LEARNER PROFILES, INTERESTS, AND CULTURAL BACKGROUNDS

As we just reviewed, music educators can differentiate their curriculum by modifying the products, content, or process. These three parameters may be differentiated based on the students' readiness, learner profiles, interests, and cultural backgrounds.

Readiness. One of the most difficult aspects of teaching is that students come to the classroom with differing abilities. Some high school students who have taken private lessons for several years may sit next to students who began playing an instrument at the start of the school year. A kindergartner, through rich experiences at home, may come to the first day of music class already keeping a beat and singing in tune, while another student has never experienced these activities and is struggling. Another student who did not receive the same education as the other students might join the school and the music class in the middle of the year. Effective teachers take this information into account and adjust their teaching to students' *readiness* to learn content. Readiness varies from students' previous knowledge, to their ability to direct their own learning, to their ability to learn new information quickly.

An important aspect of all differentiation, but particularly differentiating for readiness, is the need to assess in order to gauge students' abilities (Wormeli, 2006). Teachers must collect information on their students' strengths and areas that need improvement in order to differentiate instruction. This is done through pre-assessing students and then continual assessing. It is important to note that readiness is determined not through hunches or "feel," but by carefully gathering information on students in ways that are valid and reliable. While this need not mean that a teacher provides a formal test, it does mean that teachers think carefully about how they gain that information. We cover aspects of assessment in chapter 6, and readers can look there to find more information on how to create a variety of assessments that may gather information on students' readiness.

Once music teachers determine students' readiness, they can begin to think about differentiating instruction. According to Tomlinson (2001), teachers can adjust for each student or group of students by using the following parameters: (1) setting a slow or quick pace, (2) providing greater or less independence, (3) using more or open structure for assignments, (4) focusing on the big picture of a concept or providing more details, and (5) focusing on many facets of an idea at once or narrowing to one facet. Each of these areas is a continuum, and depending on groups of students' readiness, the teacher can adjust each of these parameters.

> Music teachers may differentiate by making modifications to products/materials, content, and learning processes; using student interests; and assessing student readiness levels and cultural backgrounds.

These strategies for differentiating student readiness could be useful for music educators. In choir, for example, while preparing a piece, the teacher might use each of these areas to adjust how the students prepare their parts. The teacher might instruct the whole class in a way that keeps a quick pace and provides much information; this might be done by focusing on different aspects all at once. For some students, the first part of the instruction might be enough, and because they are able to work independently, they can do much work on their own, with the teacher checking in with them periodically. So, the teacher might provide a cursory amount of information about the dynamics, pitch, diction, and phrasing all at once, then let the students find ways to apply it themselves in sectionals or small groups. Meanwhile, there might be other students who need to have each of these aspects of performing the work addressed individually, at a slower pace. They need more teacher-directed guidance as they apply those concepts to the piece. While the other students work more independently, the teacher can provide the extra instruction and guided practice that these students need.

The difficult part of this configuration is to not neglect the students who work well independently, because they, too, need and deserve guidance. The teacher must find appropriate time when the students who need more guidance can work without direct teacher guidance and use that time to work with the other students. Regardless of how a teacher might differentiate for readiness, the concept suggests that teachers are aware that students have different levels of ability and that the teacher adjusts the teaching to meet the needs of each of those students.

APPLYING TO PRACTICE 4.5

Consult a lesson plan that has not been as successful as you would have liked in improving students' learning. What was the aim of the lesson? What do you want students to learn? Is it a process, about learning specific content, or designed to create a specific product? How many different ways did you differentiate in the other areas and still retain the lesson's goal?

Learner profiles. There is a common view in education and in society at large that there are different types of learners (Pashler, McDaniel, Rohrer, & Bjork, 2008). Some are auditory learners; they learn best by hearing information. Others are visual learners, and still others are kinesthetic oriented: they process information best through bodily movements. Differentiation based on learner profiles acknowledges that we all have different preferences for learning. Many music teachers may be quite familiar with the theories that can help to differentiate using learner profiles. Howard Gardner's (2006) multiple intelligences theory, for example, provides a way of thinking about students as different learners. Educators might rely on students' spatial, interpersonal, or linguistic intelligences to teach music.

These theories suggest that music teachers could find different ways of introducing materials to students. For example, when teaching notation in elementary general music or in beginning instrumental ensembles, the teacher could make sure to vary the experiences that students have regarding the concept. Instead of only engaging with notation visually by putting it on the board, the teacher might also ask students to use manipulatives to experiment with it. They could use Legos to create iconic representations of both pitch and rhythm. Or they might move their bodies. The teacher could paint a giant staff on the floor and ask students to move to the correct line or space. These differing activities, the theory of multiple learning styles suggests, access students' learning preferences in different ways.

Though the idea of learner profiles or visual, auditory, and kinesthetic learners is a widely held conception, we would like to caution against uncritically adopting this language and approach to differentiation. There is little or no evidence that using learner profiles is an effective strategy for differentiation (Geake, 2008; Landrum & McDuffie, 2010). For example, after conducting a literature review of research on learner profiles and multiple intelligences, Geake (2008) concluded that they "do not reflect how our brains actually learn, nor the individual differences we observe in classrooms" (p. 123). Instead, he concludes that learning is more holistic and multisensory than these theories suggest.

Music educators might choose to react to this information in several ways. Having students engage in lessons in which they see, move, write, and hear will strengthen their knowledge of the content of the lessons. A more radical approach would be simply to not use learner profiles as a way to generate differentiation. This seems reasonable considering the lack of evidence that it benefits students. However, this stance may lead to a further problem in teacher evaluation. Because of this concept's widespread use in public schools, an evaluator could conceivably recommend a music teacher use learner profiles as a strategy. What then does a music educator do when an evaluator recommends a strategy that the teacher has legitimate and well-researched reasons to question or reject? We address difficult situations like this in the final chapter on talking to evaluators. Despite the controversy, the concept of learner profiles could be a strategy for teachers to think about ways to differentiate their lessons so that they include multisensory experiences.

Interests. It is common sense to acknowledge that when someone is interested in an idea or project, that person is more likely to invest more time and effort in it. Differentiation for interest acknowledges this by allowing students the freedom to tailor assignments to their preferences and to direct them into areas that are personally meaningful to them. Music teachers might be particularly lucky in this area, because many people find music inherently enjoyable and interesting. However, it is not true for everyone. How can music educators incorporate each individual student's interests into the classroom to increase motivation?

The easiest way is to allow students to include the music they prefer in the classroom. Using popular music can be an interesting way for students to explore different aspects of music. Studying music theory and the elements of music or learning to sing or play an instrument can be approached through popular music. However, as many music teachers can attest, students have strong opinions about the music they like and do not like, making achieving consensus by an entire class on one song or artist difficult or impossible. That is why it is important for teachers to allow flexibility in their instruction for students to choose the music. However, we caution that incorporating popular music should not be used as a "reward" or "carrot" for students in addition to the other, or "real" repertoire they perform, as this is not truly honoring students' interests.

Besides using popular music, music teachers can differentiate for interests in other ways. In composing, students can write about topics that are interesting to them, such as shopping or their favorite sports team. Students can write a programmatic piece that depicts their favorite superhero or write music with lyrics about their favorite sports team. All of these interests can be incorporated while the teacher continues to include aspects that will help students achieve the lesson objectives. In addition, teachers might also slightly alter the lesson objectives so that they incorporate each student's interests. For example, if a student or group of students are scientifically minded, a teacher might have them study acoustics. Important in differentiating for interest is making sure that assignments and activities have enough flexibility so that students can complete what is required of them while incorporating aspect that are appealing to them.

Cultural backgrounds. Finally, music educators might look at students' various cultural backgrounds to differentiate instruction. While some educators do talk about differentiation around cultural background (Ginsberg, 2005; Santamaria, 2009), a more robust—both qualitatively and quantitatively— description of modifying teaching to include students' cultural backgrounds is found in the research on the concepts "culturally relevant pedagogy" (Ladson-Billings, 2009) and "culturally responsive teaching" (Gay, 2010). In these areas, educators suggest that teachers purposefully take students' cultural backgrounds into consideration to alter pedagogy and incorporate, celebrate, and build upon them. Gay (2002) defines culturally responsive teaching as "using the cultural characteristics, experiences, and perspectives of ethnically diverse students as conduits for teaching them more effectively. [. . .] when academic knowledge and skills are situated within the lived experiences and frames of reference of students, they are more personally meaningful, have higher interest appeal, and are learned more easily and thoroughly" (p. 106). Research suggests that acknowledging and celebrating students' cultural backgrounds, including how race influences them, can have positive effects on students' education (Aronson & Laughter, 2016; Morrison, Robbins, & Rose, 2008). In reference to differentiation, music teachers might seek to understand students' cultural lives outside of school. Are there cultural practices in their families—such as making music together, celebrating certain holidays, or other rituals and activities—that the students participate in at home? Are there community organizations, local music scenes, or other community events that the students and their neighbors participate in? Answers to these questions can be gathered by talking to students. At first, students might be apprehensive about sharing their cultural backgrounds, but if a teacher builds relationships, they may begin to share their heritage. A teacher might also elect to send a survey home to parents to learn more about students' families. All these efforts, it might be added, can also contribute to contact with parents, which is frequently a parameter included in teacher evaluation systems.

After asking and answering these questions, if a teacher finds that many or all students have an activity or characteristic in common, he or she might directly incorporate it into whole group instruction. For example, if a community has a vibrant music scene around a particular genre—such as hip-hop or folk music—a teacher might use that cultural background as a way to teach about a variety of aspects of music, from composition, to the elements of music, to how music functions as a social activity in people's lives. However, in areas where there is greater diversity, a teacher might differentiate instruction by allowing and even encouraging students to incorporate aspects of their cultural identity. Students might be encouraged to learn a piece of music in a style and manner that are personally and culturally meaningful to them. A teacher could ask students to form arrangements of, say, "Für Elise" in the styles of their choosing, including mariachi, country-pop, folk music, and hip-hop. Important in processes like this is that the teacher allows them to choose, rather than imposing specific styles, and to make music in ways that are authentic to that music genre. A common element of the genres we have mentioned is playing by ear—some of them partially, some exclusively. When inviting students to include these genres, it is important to include the types of music making that accompany these genres, not just the sound of the music. If, after examining a lesson plan or assignment, a teacher confidently sees ways students can incorporate their cultural experiences, perspectives, and identities, then the lesson has been differentiated around cultural background. For more strategies and rationales for culturally responsive teaching in music, see Lind and McKoy (2016).

PUTTING IT TOGETHER: DIFFERENTIATING INSTRUCTION AND COMMUNICATING
WITH EVALUATORS

Table 4.3 summarizes the strategies of differentiation covered in this section. Each cell provides an example of how the products, content, and process might be differentiated for readiness, learner profiles, interests, and cultural backgrounds. For example, the first cell shows how products might be differentiated for readiness.

Thinking about differentiation strategies through the categories of products, content, process, readiness, interests, and cultural backgrounds provides some benefits in teaching in general and, more specifically, within teacher evaluation systems. First, it provides teachers with language to discuss with evaluators how they approach differentiation. Second, it provides a way to diversify and increase differentiation strategies. Third, it provides teachers with ways of thinking about differentiation while maintaining those aspects they want all students to experience. For example, a teacher might decide that certain content is absolutely necessary; she might want all students to learn scales or the district curriculum requires them to learn this content. The teacher can then look to different products and processes, and consider readiness, interests, and cultural backgrounds as she finds ways to differentiate for students. Similarly, a teacher might be interested in having all students engage in the experience of performing, which is a process. The teacher then can differentiate the products and content and consider readiness, interests, and cultural backgrounds. Differentiation allows teachers to think about what they want all students to experience or learn, then find strategies for varying the other aspects of instruction and assignments.

Thinking about a variety of ways to differentiate instruction can put music educators in a position to address areas of teacher evaluation. As we discussed in chapter 2, music teachers can openly advocate and educate evaluators about their goals and thinking processes in each of the categories of teacher evaluation. This can help evaluators better observe music teachers. By coming to the conversation with clearly articulated differentiation strategies and theories, music teachers will better guide evaluators in observations in terms of differentiation. However, as we also argued in chapter 2, understanding and communication work both ways. It is just as important for music teachers to understand an evaluator's perspectives. If the evaluator thinks of differentiation as, say, tailoring content, but the teacher will only stubbornly consider differentiation as product because he or she lacks a strong knowledge of the various ways to differentiate, then the teacher misses an opportunity to listen to feedback to improve practice and succeed in teacher evaluation systems. Knowledge about the

TABLE 4.3.

Differentiation strategies in music

	Readiness	Learner Profiles	Interests	Cultural Backgrounds
Products	Modifying what students are asked to produce based on previous knowledge and abilities. For example, ask a student who is excelling to produce a more in-depth assignment.	Inviting students to use their learning preferences to create a unique product. To demonstrate their learning of form, some students might compose a song, others make a graph depicting the form of a song, and others choreograph a dance that represents the form of a song.	Inviting students to use interests in other areas outside of music to do an assignment. For example, a student who is interested in video games might transcribe and perform the music from his or her favorite game.	Inviting students to create music that they find in their community or home. For example, a student could pick a piece learned from his or her family and find out more information about that song.
Content	Simplifying content for a student with a learning disability, while a student who appears bored is given material that goes deeper into the chosen subject.	Targeting specific content to address either students' strengths or areas in need of improvement. For example, students who have trouble with the spatial aspects of playing the piano might receive more instruction in that specific area.	Inviting students to find topics or pieces of music they find interesting and conduct a research project.	Inviting students to seek out content and topics that are meaningful to their community or family. For example, allowing students in Appalachia to learn how to read and perform shape music.

(continued)

TABLE 4.3.

Continued

	Readiness	Learner Profiles	Interests	Cultural Backgrounds
Process	Providing more parameters of a composition for a student who struggles with the content covered or has difficulty planning out and executing long-term projects, while allowing a more advanced student more freedom to choose parameters.	Inviting students to engage in the material in a variety of modalities around their strengths. To perform a work of music, some students might rely on notation, others on listening to recordings, and others on reading materials to help with their interpretations.	Inviting students to pursue different avenues to learn a topic. For example, a student interested in science might run an experiment while another student interested in guitar learns a solo.	Inviting students to make music in ways they experience outside of school. For example, allowing students to create a reggaeton arrangement of a classical piece using the processes that musicians in that genre employ to make music.

theories of differentiation, and other educational theories for that matter, aids music teachers in both advocating and listening to feedback to improve practice.

APPLYING TO PRACTICE 4.6

- Return to the lesson plan referenced in Applying to Practice 4.5 or any other lesson. Look at all aspects of the plan. Are the objectives flexible enough for a variety of processes, products, content, interests, readiness, and cultural backgrounds? Do the instruction activities and style in the procedure section favor certain types of processes, products, interests, learner profiles, or cultural backgrounds? Does the lesson help students at differing levels of readiness? Does your assessment allow students to demonstrate their knowledge in multiple ways? Does the assessment require only one process to complete it?
- Think of a specific student or group of students who often struggle in class. Why do they struggle: Are they bored with the content, or do they find different content, processes, or products difficult to engage in? Differentiate for that student or students.
- Can you find ways of differentiating using the approaches outlined in this chapter? For example, create a lesson on the content of dotted-quarter, eighth-note rhythms in beginner band by differentiating the following:
  - Content
  - Cultural backgrounds
  - Interests
  - Process
  - Product
  - Readiness

SUMMARY

Differentiation is a strategy and philosophy of tailoring student learning to each individual student or groups of students. Employing differentiated instruction does not mean that the teacher must use individual instruction, in which each student receives his or her own individual curriculum. Instead, it entails teachers' continued efforts to create flexible assignments and activities that build upon students' strengths and backgrounds in order to address their areas that need improvement and to increase the likelihood of students' achieving growth and success. Because of its effectiveness as a best practice, differentiation is often included in teacher evaluation systems. Music teachers might engage in differentiation in their teaching and teacher evaluation by differentiating the products, content, and process. Furthermore, music teachers might choose to differentiate these areas by considering students' readiness, learner profiles, interests, and cultural backgrounds. These areas and characteristics give music teachers the strategies and the vocabulary to successfully differentiate instruction and to communicate with evaluators in teacher evaluation.

With this information, the teacher Terrence, who appeared in the vignette at the beginning of this chapter, might be in a better position to demonstrate his ability to differentiate.

Terrence is preparing for his formal observation by his principal. He composes his lesson plan on the phrasing of Frank Ticheli's arrangement of "Amazing Grace," one that Terrence is proud of because he feels he is able to get students to play long, expressive lines. His principal asks him to fill out a form to accompany the lesson plan. One of the questions on the form is, "How does this lesson incorporate differentiation?" For this question, Terrence thinks about the learners in his room. He then writes: "I am differentiating for content: I know that Kelly, the principal flutist, has accomplished the objectives and is bored in rehearsal, so I am allowing her to compose a variation on 'Amazing Grace' for instruments of her choice. As she gets closer to the concert, she can ask other instrumentalists who have learned the piece sufficiently to join her to perform it. I am differentiating for readiness. One of the saxophonists just joined band this year. I rewrote some of the parts so that it stretches his range a little, but does not overwhelm him. I am also differentiating for learner profile and process. For the class you will observe, I am dividing up the ensemble in to groups based on learner profiles. One group is deciding how to phrase by looking at the score and analyzing the harmonies. Another group is listening to the piece and moving their bodies. A third group is color-coding their parts based on where they think the most and least intense parts of the composition are. Finally, there is another group working on long tones to increase the time they can play." Feeling satisfied, he hands in the lesson plan. The following week in his pre-observation meeting, the principal addresses differentiation. "These are really good," she says. "I'm wondering, are there other ways you can improve upon your differentiated instruction?" Terrence thinks about it and realizes he hasn't overtly differentiated for interest and cultural backgrounds. He says, "Well, I could have the groups then find a song they like and do similar activities to discover the phrasing of that song. They can pick a song on the radio or choose other music they like or experience at home. They might also be able to make music in different ways. Perhaps they will choose to use folk music practices like playing by ear and peer learning to apply phrasing to new contexts." "Excellent," says the evaluator. Terrence feels confident in his differentiating ability after leaving the meeting.

APPLYING TO PRACTICE 4.7

Now that you have seen lesson plans in which differentiation is specifically identified, look at other lesson plans and do the same to them:

- Go through the lesson plans in the other chapters in this book. Are there places where there is differentiation? How would you label that differentiation?
- Are there places in these lesson plans that could be modified to further differentiate?
- Complete this process with your lesson plans. Label the types of differentiation you already use. Find places where you can modify to further differentiate.

EXAMPLE LESSON PLANS

In each of the lessons, we have identified in parentheses the types of differentiation used.

Middle School or High School Orchestra

Composition: *Water Music*, G. F. Handel
Behavioral Objectives:
- Students will decide and then write in the correct bowings for mm. 1–8.
- Students will perform the correct bowings for mm. 1–8.

Conceptual Objective:
- Students will make interpretive decisions on bowing and then perform those bowings. They will understand how expressive and technical considerations inform bowing choices.

US Core Arts Standards: MU:Pr4.2.6; MU:Pr4.3.6; MU:Pr5.1.8; MU:Re8.1.6
Essential Question:
- How do the interpretive and technical decisions a musician makes change the expression of a musical work?

Enduring Understanding:
- Musicians perform musical works differently for interpretive and technical reasons.

Materials: score and parts (including some or all of the following: original urtext score, midi files, commercially available arrangements, teacher-generated modifications and arrangements, and copies of score for students to draw on), computers, recordings, and pencils

Procedure:
1. Listen to a recording of *Water Music*. Ask the students some open, guided, and closed questions about the recording to focus them on the interpretation and bowing. Questions might include: *Do you think this is difficult or easy to perform?*

Why? Are there some ways to make the performance of it easier? How do you think it was bowed?

2. As a possible extension, the teacher can play different recordings: some that are slower or faster, or others that have different bowings, in which one is shorter and more detached and another more legato. Ask or prompt: *How does the tempo of the piece impact what bowing might be best for these measures? Do you think a musician should decide on the bowing first (the technical aspect) or the musical aspect? Why?*

3. Give students a pre-assessment. Ask them to write in the bowings for the first eight measures of the *Water Music*. To ease the anxiety of performing a pre-assessment, the teacher might say to the students: *I'm curious to see how you'd bow this if you were given the music. I am going to give you the first eight bars and I want you to write down how you would play it.* If the teacher wants to go into a greater degree of detail, he or she can ask students to discuss bow speed as part of this lesson. Students can also discuss what part of the bow they propose for the passage. The teacher has options for how to use this pre-assessment. A teacher might choose to (1) give all students an urtext (the original score written by Handel, with minimal articulations); (2) give some students the urtext and others an edition with the articulations written in, either by the teacher or from a commercially available arrangement; or (3) give all students an edition with the articulations written in. A teacher's choice among these is contingent on how well he or she knows the students and what degree of difficulty they can handle. Also, some teacher evaluations might include a uniform pre-assessment, requiring the teacher to provide all students with the same assessment (readiness).

4. Have the class move on to other objectives or other pieces to rehearse. After class, review the pre-assessments. Based on their answers, prepare lessons that match each student's needs and strengths (some examples follow) (readiness).

5. Remind students of their discussion and play the recording of *Water Music* again. Tell students: *We are going to work in groups to figure out the best way to bow the first eight bars, more, or the bowings for another piece entirely.*

6. Break the class up into small groups based on various configurations and on previous knowledge of the students and/or results of the pre-assessment (potentially differentiation in all ways). Throughout this process, it is important for the teacher to circulate among the groups, help them, and ask them questions that help them articulate and reflect on the decisions they make. In addition, it might be possible to add excerpts for students who complete the task earlier. Some options could include some or all of the following:

    a. *Readiness:* Students who successfully completed the pre-assessment might be "compacted out" by giving them work on a different piece with bowings that are more difficult. Depending on how many students and the instrumentation, the teacher might choose to have the students perform chamber group or solo works.

    b. *Interests, content, and cultural background:* Allow students to choose the music, including music in styles other than classical, such as popular music or music that is culturally significant to them.

   c. *Learner profile and process:* some groups, perhaps visually oriented, might mark up an enlarged score to learn the bowings, while others learn by ear and experimentation, while others watch video recordings of professional groups to compare bowings.

   d. *Readiness, process, and content:* Some groups might be given the more difficult urtext without articulations, others might be given an edition that has the articulations written in, others might be given a part with the bowings and articulations written in, and finally, others might be given a modified part that has simplified rhythms and pitches. Furthermore, the teacher might scaffold the process to varying degrees. Some groups might be given specific exercises that work up to the ability to write in the bowings. The students might first figure out the bowings of smaller excerpts, roughly a measure at a time, then be asked to put them together. This could be organized in a packet.

7. After students have worked on the bowings, they could present their interpretations to the class. They can perform (live or video recorded) and explain their interpretation. They might show their interpretations by presenting the score or parts with the bowings written in. (products)

8. After each group has presented its interpretation, come to consensus in the group about the best way to bow the first eight measures. The teacher has two options: (1) Find some common interpretations and discuss where the groups vary, then as a group organically decide which is the best. This might include discussing how they want the piece to sound: more legato and smooth or detached and rhythmic. (2) Show the students the edition that the teacher has chosen and see how their decisions compare with those of the editor. Important in this process is not to present the edition as the "right" answer and the students' answers as incorrect, but rather as one option. The teacher can point out both the strengths and weaknesses of the editor's choice of bowings.

9. Rehearse the composition. The teacher might choose to mix and match different editions. For some, the students might play the urtext, others might play a simplified arrangement, and others might play further modified parts. The teacher might need to do additional modifications to make sure that these different editions will work together (readiness).

Assessment:
- Pre-assessment.
- Products students create in small group work.
- Discussions with students during small group work.
- Performance during the rehearsals.

Possible Next Steps and Extensions:
- Repeat this lesson using other parts of *Water Music* or other compositions.
- Ask a local professional or collegiate group to come in and talk about their interpretations of the work. It might be possible to ask a group in another musical style to perform the work and discuss their interpretations. For example, how might a mariachi band or a bluegrass group play this piece (cultural backgrounds)?

Anticipated Areas of Difficulty or Student Misunderstanding:
- Classroom management and planning is crucial for the small group work. Providing students with enough tasks that are targeted, while also making sure

they are flexible enough for students to solve the problems in ways that work best for them, is important. Also, making sure to circulate often and help all groups is important.

- Take care to discuss your expectations for group work: how to work respectfully with one another and listen to each other. Consider assigning a group leader (this position can rotate) and perhaps also a group secretary to write down ideas. Perhaps do a self-reflection/group reflection so students can comment on the nature of their productivity and respectfulness.

MIDDLE SCHOOL OR HIGH SCHOOL CHORUS

Composition: "Sesere Eeye," folk song from Torres Strait Islands
Behavioral Objectives:
- Students will learn "Sesere Eeye" by ear with harmonies.
- Students will decide on the conducting gesture, movement, and visual representation appropriate for piece.
- Students will perform the piece with new musical and interpretive decisions.

Conceptual Objective:
- Students will make musical decisions about folk songs in small groups and perform them in large group. They will discuss and begin to understand how these decisions influence the performance.

US Core Arts Standards: MU:Cr1.1.7; MU:Cr3.2.8; MU:Re7.1.7; MU:Cn10.0.8
Essential Question:
- How do musical decisions influence an authentic performance?

Enduring Understanding:
- Musicians make different interpretation decisions based on style and creative vision.

Materials: paper; markers
Procedure
1. Introduce a new song, "Sesere Eeye," a folk song in three parts from the Torres Strait Islands, by ear. Students keep the downbeat in their feet. (There may be movements written into the score. These can be introduced later.)
2. Introduce harmonies (either one or two part harmony depending on how quickly students learn; can teach second harmony in the following lesson).
3. Share with students that the song is about the wind and the sounds the wind makes when it blows in the mountains. Ask: *What might that sound like? What can we add to make this piece more effective, so that an audience might be able to guess that we are singing about a specific place? What are some important musical elements we can add to this piece?* (dynamics, tempo, phrasing)
4. Break students into groups, choosing one element to enhance the musical performance. Write the elements on the board to help students. They may choose to work on solidifying their voice part (products, readiness); conducting, adding choreography/movement, or creating rhythmic ostinato (percussion

instruments are common for this culture), or to draw a visual representation of the score to help others learn (learner profiles, process). If students would like a visual copy of the score to help in their work, the teacher will provide it.

5. Students come back together and present their performance enhancements. Ask the class after each group performs: *How did this work change based on our knowledge of the song? Using your work in your groups, what can we incorporate into our large ensemble performance of this song?*

Assessment:
- Products students produce in small group work.
- Discussions with students after small group work.
- Small group and large ensemble performance during rehearsal.

Possible Next Steps and Extensions:
- Teach harmonies to the piece, or students can create their own harmonies in groups.
- Solidify phrasing as a group and make decisions about percussion and movement.

Anticipated Areas of Difficulty or Student Misunderstanding:
- The teacher should circulate in the room to provide assistance to all groups. Some groups may need help getting their work started, particularly the visual score group.
- Take care to discuss your expectations for group work: how to work respectfully with one another and listen to each other. Consider assigning a group leader (this position can rotate) and perhaps also a group secretary to write down ideas. Perhaps do a self-reflection/group reflection so students can comment on the nature of their productivity and respectfulness.

SECONDARY GENERAL MUSIC

Behavioral Objectives:
- Students will represent musical form through charts and other visual representations.
- Students will evaluate and analyze elements of contrast in musical works.
- Students have the option to compose a musical work with identifiable form.

Conceptual Objectives:
- Students will manipulate (musically, visually, etc.) elements of musical contrast, timbre, texture, dynamics, and tempo.
- Students will understand that balance between repetition and contrast is an essential structural principle in artistic work across styles and genres.

US Core Arts Standards: AC1; AC7

Essential Question:
- Why is there contrast in music?

Enduring Understanding:
- Contrast is a component of music that keeps the listener interested.

Materials: recordings, computers, additional reading sources, instruments for performance; other materials: paper, markers, room for students to move around.

Procedure:

1. The teacher plays a recording of a song that has an easily recognizable form. As an example, the teacher might pick "Let it Be," by the Beatles. Provide the students with a chart to write down whether each part of the song is an A (verse), B (chorus), or C (bridge). As the musical except proceeds, the teacher can call out numbers to prompt the students to write A, B, or C. Give some students the opportunity to demonstrate their knowledge by moving. They could perform different movements with their arms or go to different parts of the room to show their knowledge of the form (learner profiles, process).

2. After filling out the chart, ask the students: *Why do you think there are different parts to a song?* The students might answer that it keeps the music interesting. Write down on the board the different answers students come up with (learner profiles).

3. Ask students to pick a song or composition that they like. As a class, listen to a recording of it and analyze the form (interests).

4. Have students complete an assessment in which they listen to a short excerpt and have them identify the form.

5. For those who have successfully identified the form, provide an opportunity to do independent work on form (readiness). They might do an analysis of another song (interests), read an interview with an artist on how he or she writes music and uses contrast (interests, content), read a music theory text on form (content), and/or watch videos of musicians in different cultures of the students' choosing, using form (interests, cultural backgrounds). While those students work individually, review the original material with the rest of the class. Listen to more excerpts and as the class labels the form (readiness, content). Use a variety of material, from simple songs like "Twinkle, Twinkle, Little Star" (readiness), to songs that they identify (interests) and music that is familiar to them (cultural backgrounds). Continue to use a variety of ways for students to express their understanding of form: creating charts, moving around the room, or calling out the different formal sections (learner profiles, process).

6. As a whole group or in small groups, perform music with a particular emphasis on creating contrast on form. Allow students to choose the song (interests) and the style and genre they use (process and cultural backgrounds). Use open, guided, and closed questions in this part, such as, *What are the different parts of this song, how do we create contrast between these parts, and what instruments should we use?* (See chapter 3 for more guidance on creating questions.)

7. Give students the assessment assignment below.

Assessment:
Give the students a series of options to demonstrate their knowledge of form. The assessment has two components: (1) an activity that is differentiated in a variety of ways (the musical contrast project) and (2) a self-assessment and reflection. (See below)

Musical Contrast Project

Instructions: Choose a project from the list below to complete as a way to demonstrate your understanding and knowledge of musical contrast. For any option you may work alone or in a pair. If you are interested in a group larger than two, talk to the teacher to get your idea approved. The Musical Contrast Chart discussed in class is included below for your reference. [These options differentiate for content, process, and products. Furthermore, music teachers might choose to differentiate these areas by considering students' readiness, interests, learner profiles, and cultural backgrounds.]

Option 1: Musical Composition with Preset Loops
Create a musical composition in GarageBand using preset digital loops. Choose either the ABA or "beginning, middle, end" structure to organize your composition and include at least two elements of musical contrast. Complete the self-assessment and reflection at the end of creating the composition. Share and discuss your final project with the whole class or with the teacher.

Option 2: Original Musical Composition
Create an original musical composition using digital or live (or a combination) instruments that represent a balance between repetition and contrast. Utilize the elements of musical contrast as well as musical material to generate contrast within your composition. Complete the self-assessment and reflection at the end of creating the composition. Share and discuss your final project with the whole class or with the teacher.

Option 3: Song Analysis and Diagram
Choose a song that you enjoy listening to that has clear sections that are easy to identify (e.g., verse, chorus, introduction). For each section create a list of musical qualities, then determine what elements of musical contrast change between sections. Create a visual representation (this could be a picture, chart, or digital drawing) that explains the structure of the song as well as the musical contrast. Complete the self-assessment and reflection at the end of creating the analysis. Share and discuss your final project with the whole class or with the teacher.

Option 4: Song Analysis Presentation
Choose a song that you enjoy listening to that is a good example of balancing repetition and contrast. Create a presentation (using Google Slides, Prezi, or iMovie video) that identifies the elements of musical contrast in the song and explain how

the balance of repetition and contrast is used successfully in the song. Complete the self-assessment and reflection at the end of creating the presentation. Share and discuss your final project with the whole class or with the teacher.

[After completing one of the four options, all students will complete the self-assessment and reflection.]

Student Self-Assessment and Reflection
[This is to be completed by each student individually, even if students worked with others.]

1. Reread the instructions for the option you chose. Did you include everything required? Revise your work if you did not complete all aspects of the project. If you purposely chose to leave out something, explain why you did not revise or include that requirement.
2. What elements of contrast did you either create (options 1, 2) or discover (options 3, 4) in your piece of music?
3. What elements of contrast were easier to create or identify? Explain why.
4. What elements of contrast were more difficult to create or identify? Describe what was challenging about those elements.
5. Describe the relationship of repetition and contrast in your composition (options 1, 2) or chosen song (options 3, 4).
6. What are you most proud of about your final product?
7. What would you improve or change if you were to create the project again?
8. What resource(s) did you find most helpful in completing your project?

Possible Next Steps and Extensions:
- Perform the songs and demonstrate them for the whole class in a concert.
- Create a podcast in which the students interview each other about their assignments.
- Analyze a classical work, looking at the first movement of a sonata and learning about sonata form.
- Build vocabulary to label different parts of form in many different styles: verse, chorus, bridge, primary theme, secondary theme, transition, etc.

Anticipated Areas of Difficulty or Student Misunderstanding:
- Extra attention must be paid to the classroom management during item 5 in the procedures list. Make sure students who are working individually have a clear idea what they are working on.

5

LITERACY

Maria has prepared for her observation of a fourth-grade general music class by her principal by selecting one of her favorite lessons. In this lesson, students sing and play "Circle Round the Zero" and then use similar rhythms and intervals to create their own melodies. In the post-observation, Maria's principal says, "I'm evaluating you on literacy teaching. I saw the students really enjoying themselves and working nicely together, but I didn't see students engaging in discourse like they did in my English classroom. Instead, I saw them doing a lot of singing, playing, and using manipulatives on the rug." Maria is somewhat confused by the comment. "Why are you talking about discourse? I thought we were talking about literacy." "How do I know if students are literate unless they are talking?" her principal responds. "I need to see them talk about music to be sure I know what they know about music. I need to see them more engaged and using discourse. Why don't you incorporate more literacy by having students read and write? Perhaps they can read an essay on Mozart and then write a paragraph about him." Somewhat offended by the suggestion, Maria responds, "But I am teaching literacy; I'm teaching them music literacy. The students are using their rhythmic and melodic knowledge to derive the rhythms and pitches for the songs. They then apply them to a new situation, writing their own melodies. They are reading and writing. It's just that it's music notation, not language." The principal responds with a nod. "I see, but that's not what the system means by literacy. For the next observation, I need you to incorporate more discourse and literacy."

LITERACY AND ITS application to music education and teacher evaluation is often a contentious issue. As the vignette suggests, disagreements about what literacy is and how it applies to music sometimes occur between evaluators and music teachers. Maria understands music literacy as reading notation, while her principal thinks it is reading, writing, and talking about language. What are the different ways educators can approach literacy so that they can begin to have conversations about what counts as literacy in the music classroom? How do teachers incorporate literacy in an "authentic" way that contributes to the teaching of music rather than as an added burden of teaching literacy next to or on top of music in a way that is divorced from or ancillary to music?

In this chapter we describe ways music educators might conceive of literacy. This might help them implement a variety of literacy strategies in their classrooms and better articulate their literacy practices to evaluators. First, we briefly describe the relationship between literacy and teacher evaluation. Second, we introduce "disciplinary literacy" and "artistic literacy" as frameworks for thinking about implementing literacy in music classrooms. We then outline ways in which disciplinary literacy and artistic literacy may be used to improve communication with an evaluator. Finally, we describe different ways teachers are asked to implement literacy and then provide strategies for incorporating these various approaches into the music classroom.

APPLYING TO PRACTICE 5.1

- Can you relate to Maria's situation? Do you agree with the way Maria responded to her evaluator?
- How might you have responded to the evaluator's suggestion that students write about Mozart to incorporate more literacy?

LITERACY AND TEACHER EVALUATION

Maria and her principal miscommunicated with one another because they had differing definitions of literacy. What might cause these types of miscommunications? In this section we look at the relationship between literacy and teacher evaluation, focusing specifically on the lack of a definition shared by music teachers and evaluators.

COMPETING DEFINITIONS AND AIMS OF "LITERACY"

Literacy is often not an explicit requirement of teacher evaluation; however, evaluators may interject literacy into teacher evaluation (Bernard, 2015; Gabriel

& Woulfin, 2017). While doing so, they might not effectively communicate their motives and rationales to teachers. There may be times, as in Maria's case, when evaluators ask for "more literacy," but are unclear about what that means or assume that the teacher has an agreed-upon definition. For Maria's principal, "more literacy" means she wants to see students talking about music and demonstrating a verbal command of vocabulary. However, she has not articulated any of this to Maria. Conversely, Maria is using a definition of literacy common to music teachers: reading music notation. These two educators are using different definitions and talking past each other, resulting in miscommunication.

> While evaluators often highlight literacy as a large component of the evaluation observation, it is not often an explicit requirement of the evaluation rubrics and systems.

A broad definition of *literacy* might be helpful to begin to close the gap between these perceptions. As Coiro, Knobel, Lankshear, and Leu (2014) note, literacy "has now come to mean a rapid and continuous process of change in the ways in which we read, write, view, listen, compose, and communicate information" (p. 5). In other words, in the classroom, literacy constitutes the many ways in which people demonstrate and use their knowledge; this moves beyond just reading and writing. This view of literacy stems from the Common Core State Standards (CCSS) (National Governors Association for Best Practices, 2010) initiatives prevalent in most school districts. The standards require that students demonstrate their knowledge beyond defining, summarizing, and initial response, through synthesis, discussion, prediction, interpretation, and independent application and skill.

Like Maria's principal, many evaluators want to see evidence of literacy—of applying knowledge and skill—through reading comprehension and written composition. For evaluators, this is an evident indicator of student understanding and knowledge of content as well as critical ways of thinking. When the students write, they respond to what they read. So, evaluators are not necessarily looking to see *if* students are reading and writing, but *how* they're reading and writing. Reading and writing signal to the evaluator that students are summarizing, predicting, drawing connections, and communicating effectively about the

> Evaluators look for strategies that allow students to become literate and that exercise higher-level thinking, synthesis, and application.

learning material. This supports the preceding description of literacy as a process of reading, communicating, listening, writing, and observing. Students communicate and demonstrate their understanding of learning material. In other words, evaluators look for strategies that allow students to become literate and exercise higher-level thinking, synthesis, and application.

While evaluators might look for higher-order thinking through reading and writing, for music teachers, incorporating literacy through reading and writing can be difficult, given the aims and functions of music classes. Cara found in her research (Bernard, 2015) that, conversely to evaluators' definition of literacy as fluency through language, music teachers often view literacy as the ability to read and play notation. Music teachers feel that "literacy [as defined by reading and writing] isn't about music," or that it isn't their job to "teach literacy." Many music teachers do not see a place for a literacy of reading and writing in the music classroom and instead want to focus on musical content and skill, in particular reading notation.

Music teachers are not alone in their criticism of literacy defined and implemented this way. Moje (2008) notes that teachers in many subjects have this perspective on literacy integration. Teachers do not want to take time out of class to write when students should be solving equations in math or performing a lab procedure in science. Teachers want to engage in the heart of their discipline. Additionally, music teachers struggle with knowing why literacy as reading and writing needs to be present in a music class. As one music teacher argued: "We're not a writing subject unless you're into composition. We don't write, it's not what we do, so why would you take a class that's not designed for that and have them do it? So, it's trying to find that balance of understanding what the intent is and then how do you fulfill the intent" (Bernard, 2015, p. 141). When evaluators do not communicate how reading and writing demonstrates levels of student learning, music teachers often cannot articulate to an evaluator how reading and playing notation can be a form of literacy in the sense of synthesizing and predicting, similar to reading and writing. Herein lies the difficulty in finding a common ground between what the evaluator and the music teacher conceive of as literacy.

INTERJECTING LITERACY INTO TEACHER EVALUATION

Evaluators' and music teachers' different goals for and definitions of literacy might suggest that the miscommunication between Maria and her principal is not completely their fault. While literacy might be a central focus for evaluators, in the most commonly used teacher evaluation systems the term *literacy* is not used, nor is there guidance on what literacy should look like. In the Marzano (Marzano & Toth, 2013) and Danielson (2013) systems, for example, literacy is not a requirement in their components, nor do they use the term. Similar to Maria's principal, evaluators might understand literacy as being displayed only through written or spoken dialogue and communication. Table 5.1 outlines the ways in which evaluators might construe literacy through the Danielson and Marzano domains.

Based on the description of literacy as outlined by Coiro et al. (2014) and the CCSS (National Governors Association for Best Practices, 2010), literacy may be encompassed within each of these evaluation domains in the ways teachers and students identify, summarize, predict, and make connections through the learning material. However, since literacy is not required in the rubrics, it might be miscommunicated or communicated in an arbitrary way by both evaluators and teachers. Because of the lack of specificity about literacy within the evaluation systems, literacy, as evaluators may implement it, often becomes a tacit, hidden requirement that is left to the evaluator's assumptions and biases about what constitutes it (Bernard, 2015).

APPLYING TO PRACTICE 5.2

- In your evaluation system, what components might your evaluator use to observe literacy?
- In conversations with your evaluator, how have you discussed literacy in relation to the evaluation requirements? Has your evaluator linked literacy to specific components of the rubrics or given examples of what literacy can or should look like in your instruction?
- Do you incorporate literacy in ways that an evaluator might interpret as fulfilling the requirements in Danielson and Marzano mentioned here? Do you think these ways are observable?

DEFINING LITERACY: DISCIPLINARY AND ARTISTIC LITERACIES

As we have described, music teachers and evaluators have varying definitions of literacy, and the term is not explicitly defined in teacher evaluation. Music teachers and evaluators can strive to achieve a consensus on defining the term to better understand and more productively communicate with one another. This consensus is imperative for teaching in the discipline without the incorporation of literacy as ancillary or "on top of" teaching and learning music. In this section we provide and explain literacy defined as "disciplinary literacy." This definition can

TABLE 5.1.

Ways literacy may be interpreted in the Danielson and Marzano evaluation systems

Danielson Domain	How Literacy May Be Construed
Domain 3a, Communicates with students.	• Teacher facilitates discussion with and for students. • The way the teacher asks for follow-ups to what a student said helps to make connections between two students' ideas. • Students draw upon their knowledge to use vocabulary when they talk about an idea, book, or person. • Students draw upon their knowledge to use vocabulary when they talk about an idea, book, or person.
Domain 3c, Engaging students in learning.	• Student engagement includes enthusiasm, interest, thinking, and problem solving. • Students talk and demonstrate their ideas outwardly with their peers.
Domain 2b, Establishing a culture for learning.	• Students actively participate with learning material and use it to demonstrate their understanding, interpretation, and skill level.
Marzano Domain	**How Literacy May Be Construed**
Domain 1 DQ 3.19, Practice skills, strategies, and processes. Domain 1 DQ 3.20, Revise knowledge.	• Students engage in discussion, looking for ways to "revise their knowledge" through refining their ideas and words. • Students display how they can apply their skills and the ways in which they gather or synthesize new information into knowledge. • When students synthesize content or ideas in their own words, they display their understanding of the content.
Domain 1 DQ 2.6, Identify critical information.	• Students identify critical information on their own, including vocabulary, or draw connections between ideas or materials.
Domain 1 DQ 2.7, Deepen knowledge and engage in complex tasks.	• Students use their knowledge of the material through application.

help teachers approach literacy in the music classroom "authentically" and not as forced or added onto music teaching.

As we mentioned in the previous section, literacy might be defined as the ability to read, write, speak, think critically, listen, respond, and perform in different ways and for different purposes. Yest as we saw in the opening vignette, students need specialized literacy and reading practices in order to understand, analyze, and interpret important ideas in discipline-specific settings, like in music classrooms. Music teachers can develop the ability to communicate these discipline-specific practices to their evaluators. To accommodate these specialized practices, music educators can benefit from a definition that embraces both reading and writing and music notation as literacy. This

> Disciplinary literacy focuses on subject-specific practices, vocabulary, and text for students to better understand, interpret, and apply their knowledge within a discipline.

literacy includes vocabulary that is subject specific, different ways to demonstrate and communicate ideas, and subject-specific practices. In other words, students build vocabulary and skill and use them to summarize, predict, make connections, and ask questions, all to demonstrate their understanding of the subject-specific material. This literacy is called *disciplinary literacy*, and it focuses on *specialized* reading practices required for comprehension and critical analysis within a specific subject.

To think more deeply about subject-specific reading practices, consider what characteristics these four snapshots of classrooms have in common:

In a high school English class, students debate whether Holden Caulfield is phony as he criticizes others in The Catcher in the Rye.

In a middle school choir, students perform Dona Nobis Pacem *from a score. As they work, they discuss how to create a clear tone.*

Students in a high school general music class create songs in GarageBand. One student creates a beat and another student raps. They discuss if the verse should be 32 bars or 16.

In elementary school, students play and sing the Ghanaian song and passing game "Sansa Kroma." The students need to sing and keep a steady beat in order to participate in the activity.

What do these four scenarios have in common? Many things. However, in reference to literacy, they have four characteristics in common: (1) students focus on an object or "text"; (2) students take on a particular role as they focus on that text; (3) students take on that role with other students to forge dialogue; and (4) students use knowledge of the subject to solve problems. We describe each of these in the following sections.

> Disciplinary literacy encompasses different types of texts; students take on different identities and identifications and discourses and practices; and they gain knowledge specific to the discipline.

TEXT

In each of these classroom scenarios, students focus on some sort of object or content. For example, the students in these scenarios are learning about music or English using *The Catcher in the Rye*, the sheet music for *Dona Nobis Pacem*, GarageBand, or the oral tradition around "Sansa Kroma." The students and teacher are not talking about music or English in the abstract, but they are tending to a "thing" that exists in order to talk about larger concepts. This thing need not be physical; as students sing and dance to "Sansa Kroma," they are not focusing on a literal object, but there is still a process or idea to focus on. In education, learning is focused on something, rather than discussed purely in the abstract.

In literacy, this something that is the focus of learning is often called a *text* (Moje, 2008). Usually, teachers consider texts to be printed matter, including textbooks, novels, essays, and other written materials. However, more recently literacy educators have applied the term *text* to a wider array of materials. Text in this case should not be understood literally as simply words or written documents. Rather than thinking of text narrowly as, say, a paragraph, an essay, or other written matter, a text can be a beaker, a newspaper, a piece of music, a person's facial expressions, or the layout of a softball diamond. In music, text encompasses music notation, of course, but other musical materials and situations as well. For example, a text can be a work of art, piece of music, music video, photograph, painting, sculpture, collage, song, or symphony (Moje, 2008; Shanahan & Shanahan, 2008). Texts, then, are the focus of learning that students "read" in a sense that is broader than reading written language. Music teachers' ability to name the different types of texts they use and why they use them when talking with evaluators about literacy can help them in teacher evaluation.

IDENTITIES AND IDENTIFICATIONS

While students are attending to texts, they take on a role, or what is often called *identities and identifications* (Moje, 2008). These are the ways in which we enact a particular identity within a discipline. In each of the four snapshots, students take on the roles of literary critics, performers, producers, rappers, and dancers. As students try on these roles, hopefully they begin to see themselves in a new identity. Through this identity, they see themselves in particular roles where they learn, use, and value the knowledge, rather than as students who memorize information. As the examples show, multiple identities, or roles, exist within a subject area. In music, for example, students may begin to identify as a composer. They may compose a short musical composition, then work with performers on conveying the piece as they intended. By taking on this identity, students engage authentically as a composer would. Similarly, students may experience the role of a critic by providing feedback on a fellow student's composition. Both of these identities use knowledge to engage actively in discourse and music-specific practices in different ways based on role.

DISCOURSES AND PRACTICES

Students use those texts and identities to engage with others. They have discussions and make music with others. For example, as the students compose on GarageBand, they debate how long their verses should be. Through this dialogue, the students take on the role and identity of a musician. By taking on this role, they are doing the work of musicians and artists together. In turn, this allows students to communicate with the larger community. They are also preparing themselves to engage in conversations and musical practices outside of school, so that they may become competent musical citizens. In dialogue with other students in the classroom and while preparing for music making outside of school, the students are engaged in what is called *discourses and practices* (Moje, 2008). They are in dialogue with others and participate in established practices. These dialogues and practices are not limited to the immediate community of the classroom, but may extend to the wider community and in preparation for future action. The dialogue and practices signal that students are becoming different types of artists and musicians and using their skills in a hands-on way.

DISCIPLINARY KNOWLEDGE

Students use the vast knowledge known to the general public about music to accomplish their roles. The students and teacher do not make up how they talk about or make music completely on the spot. They use the collective knowledge of music history, theory, performance, and other areas of music to accomplish their roles. In the snapshots, the teacher and students use what others say about good vocal technique to improve practice. The high school students listen to recordings of hip-hop artists to begin to create their own style and complete the GarageBand composition. The elementary students copy the movements of the Ghanaian people, where the song originated, to embody the music. They are using what is called *disciplinary knowledge*—the vast body of knowledge about music—to help them complete their tasks (Moje, 2008; Shanahan & Shanahan, 2008).

PUTTING THEM TOGETHER: DISCIPLINARY LITERACY DEFINED

Table 5.2 summarizes these four components: texts, identities and identifications, discourses and practices, and disciplinary knowledge. Together, these components constitute what literacy educators call *disciplinary literacy* (Moje, 2008). It is a process of reading texts in a role with others, using the knowledge and practices established in the discipline. To return to the four snapshots, students are engaging in disciplinary literacy. They do this in an authentic way specific to the subject. Students use a text (*Catcher in the Rye, Dona Nobis Pacem,* GarageBand, and "Sansa Kroma"). They take on a role (literary critic, performer, or producer). They engage in practices and discourses (they debate interpretations and create music with others). Finally, they use disciplinary knowledge (vocabulary, common practices, and other established knowledge) to engage with the texts, practices, and others. These students are "disciplinarily literate" in these different domains (including literary criticism, singing, and producing).

Literacy defined as disciplinary literacy is a broader conception of the term than just the act of reading and writing. It encompasses the larger view of literacy as described by Coiro et al. (2014) and the CCSS (National Governors Association for Best Practices, 2010), in which students are communicating, listening, identifying, and making connections, applying their knowledge and understanding of the content. As mentioned previously in the chapter, evaluators look for strategies of students demonstrating their knowledge—or showing their learning process. In other words, this broader conception of literacy includes a shift from products to process.

In summary, then, rather than simply considering that students are literate if they can read or write language or music notation, disciplinary literacy requires that students use knowledge to understand texts alone and with others. Students use the text to delve deep into larger ideas to interpret and evaluate them (Fisher & Frey, 2014; Lapp, Moss, Johnson, & Grant, 2012). This expanded conception of

TABLE 5.2.

Three components of disciplinary literacy

	Description	Example
Text	Any object or content that someone can "read."	• Musical scores, novels, recordings, artwork, facial expressions.
Roles and Identities	Specific artistic roles and identities, through which students view themselves as artists.	• Composer, arranger, critic, musicologist, performer, historian, conductor.
Discourses and Practices	Engaging in the practices specific to a role and discipline, gaining and applying knowledge.	• A conductor uses knowledge of music theory, history, and performance to analyze a score and applies this to communicate with musicians. • A critic listens to and evaluates a performance.
Disciplinary Knowledge	Knowledge gained through engaging with texts and arts-specific practices (not merely information that is told).	• An arranger uses previous recordings of a folk song as "text" to decide on instrumentation in a new arrangement of a piece. • A performer learns the skills needed to practice and improvise in the pentatonic scale.

literacy aims toward literacy as "independence." In other words, it seeks to help students develop the skills and knowledge to engage with and use texts and information on their own in ways that are useful and authentic to them inside and outside of school. In this way, students take on different musical roles to engage deeply with a text, identifying, making connections, and showing their musical knowledge through specific practices. Disciplinary literacy, then, includes reading, writing, talking about text, and acting/

> Disciplinary literacy defines literacy as reading "texts" in "a role" with others, using the knowledge and practices established in the discipline.

performing the text specific to a domain or subject area. So, in the music class-room students will interact with text as they develop strategies and skills to "read like musicians."

Disciplinary literacy—in which students read like musicians—can be used as a common basis to alleviate the miscommunication between Maria and her principal. Disciplinary literacy incorporates reading and writing practices and strategies, which include synthesis and making connections, debating interpretations, and applying knowledge, but in a subject-specific way. When music teachers can articulate the specialized literacy and reading practices needed to understand, analyze, and interpret important ideas in and through music, they can better communicate with their evaluators about the ways in which students read and write. We discuss this further in the following section on using disciplinary literacy to communicate with evaluators.

DISCIPLINARY LITERACY IN MUSIC: ARTISTIC LITERACY

How might music teachers incorporate disciplinary literacy in music instruction in order to improve practice and communicate with evaluators? In the arts, disciplinary literacy is sometimes called *artistic literacy*. Again, artistic literacy takes on the spirit of the Common Core Standards, in which students display their knowledge through reading, writing, communicating, listening, and doing. As David Coleman (2011), one of the creators of the CCSS in English, wrote, there is much alignment between arts education and the CCSS: "Meaningful appreciation and study of works of art begins with close observation. The Core Standards in Literacy similarly describe reading as the product of sustained observation and attention to detail. The arts reward sustained inquiry and provide a perfect opportunity for students to practice the discipline of close observation whether looking at a painting or lithograph, watching a drama or a dance, or attending to a piece of music" (p. 1).

The National Core Arts Standards (NCAS), which have been adopted by many states as their standards for music and the other arts, require that students become "artistically literate" as a result of their arts education. The National Coalition for Core Arts Standards (NCCAS, 2014) defines artistic literacy as, "fluency in the language(s) of the arts is the ability to create, perform/produce/present, respond, and connect through symbolic and metaphoric forms that are unique to the arts. It

> Disciplinary literacy in music may be called artistic literacy.

is embodied in specific philosophical foundations and lifelong goals that enable an artistically literate person to transfer arts knowledge, skills, and capacities to other subjects, settings, and contexts." By this definition, making, playing, discussing, and responding to music are discourses and practices. In other words, it is doing the work that musicians do using tools and texts specific to music. An artistically literate person may engage with—or read—artistic material alone or with others. He or she may actively participate in the artistic process and gain fluency by speaking about art or using language in an artistic way. These processes might not always be performance based, depending on the role. The way the NCCAS defines artistic literacy can be understood as a musical form of disciplinary literacy. Music teachers might use these two terms interchangeably when speaking with evaluators or colleagues.

This description of disciplinary—or artistic—literacy in music requires that students delve deeply into musical content. When teachers use artistic literacy as a framework, students are asked to make more inferences from the learning material, draw more conclusions, employ evaluative skills, and debate meanings. From an artistic literacy perspective, this requires a careful attentiveness whereby students become different types of artists to do detailed observations or close "readings" of text.

Different disciplines require close readings of texts differently. How musicians "read" and interact with texts is different than how a mathematician or scientist does (Shanahan & Shanahan, 2008). As Coleman (2011) suggests, the process of closely observing and engaging with a piece of music or art has the potential to mirror CCSS thinking processes, depending upon how students are asked to interact with the learning content. Understanding the connections between how students process knowledge and understanding and disciplinary—or artistic—literacy might help music teachers bridge the language gap between music and other disciplines. It might be helpful to reexamine table 5.2 to review the four key aspects of disciplinary and artistic literacy.

APPLYING TO PRACTICE 5.3

- Look at a recent concert program or think of a recent lesson. What repertoire, or texts, were chosen? What roles did students take on? What practices did they work on in these roles? What knowledge did they learn or apply in practice?
- Choose one piece and consider, if you were to teach this piece again, what would be some new entry points to develop artistic literacy and independence? How could students "read like musicians"? What are some opportunities for students to be in roles other than performer (researcher, historian, actor)?

DISCIPLINARY LITERACY AND ARTISTIC LITERACY AS A WAY TO IMPROVE PRACTICE AND COMMUNICATE WITH EVALUATORS

Conceiving of literacy as disciplinary literacy and artistic literacy may help music teachers and evaluators find common ground and ease communication. Recall the opening vignette with Maria and her principal; they had different definitions of literacy. These competing definitions were based on their differing concerns and experiences. Maria defined literacy as notation reading because it was one of her curricular goals for students to read notation. Maria's principal defined literacy as "discourse" or how students were reading, writing, and talking. Music teachers might bridge the gap between the definitions of disciplinary and artistic literacy to communicate more effectively with others; they can begin to name the texts used, the identities and roles students take on using the text, and the strategies they employ to improve their skill, gain knowledge, and make connections.

> Talking about literacy through disciplinary and artistic literacy might bridge the gap between definitions of literacy for music teachers and evaluators to communicate more effectively.

DISCIPLINARY AND ARTISTIC LITERACIES TO IMPROVE PRACTICE

Music teachers might use artistic literacy as a framework to improve and reflect on their practice. As a start, they might consider where their current literacy practices—either reading and writing or music notation—or activities occur. As music teachers review individual lessons, they might ask at what point students:

- Read most often (music, written excerpts)?
- Write most often (composer, arrange, respond, critique)?
- Talk about the work or concept being explored/examined?

These questions can help music teachers realize that there is designated reading and writing time in the class. Also, this may help them focus on the purpose of the reading and writing and notation (students synthesize, predict, apply knowledge) and the types of reading and writing that occur. Then music teachers can begin to articulate this understanding aloud in conversation. Once music teachers can locate where students read, write, or discuss, they may further discuss *how* students read, write, and talk. Again, the "how" encompasses the strategies for students to learn and "read like musicians," the ways in which students are engaging in higher-level thinking and problem solving, making connections. These questions allow music teachers to assess and expand the types of texts currently used, what roles students become during class, and what practices students engage in these roles. In this sense, music teachers may exercise their pedagogical content knowledge to converse with evaluators about what happens in the classroom.

Responding to these questions can provide context for what and how music teachers plan and integrate artistic literacy. For example, if students are reading solely during a designated sight-reading time, this is only one view of "reading." But when a disciplinary/artistic approach in which students "read like musicians" is taken, the sight-reading exercise may connect more authentically to the repertoire material. Students may use the sight-reading exercise as a basis to compose, arrange, conduct, or sing. These actions demonstrate students' knowledge and ability to apply their knowledge and skill.

For example, after sight-reading a four-measure rhythm in 4/4 time with dotted quarter-eighth patterns, students may arrange their own four-measure example using the dotted rhythm. They can switch arrangements with their peers and sight-read one another's work. Students can then locate the dotted rhythm in their repertoire and discuss how the composer uses this pattern throughout the piece or how it changes as the piece develops. Here, students are outwardly displaying how they talk about a text. So music teachers might tell the evaluator that students are reading an excerpt and identifying the different parts of the rhythms. Then they apply the content in the excerpt to arrange their own rhythms and discuss their choices for creating their rhythms. Students then will apply their rhythms to a piece of repertoire, where they will compare and contrast the ways in which the rhythms were used in the sight-reading example and in the repertoire. We discuss more artistic literacy strategies in detail in the following section.

DISCIPLINARY AND ARTISTIC LITERACIES TO COMMUNICATE WITH EVALUATORS

As we discussed in the previous section, locating where in the lesson reading, writing, and discussion occur—and in what ways—can help music teachers improve and reflect upon their practice. These reflective practices may also help them when they speak with evaluators, as they articulate the literacy practices aloud in conversation. This can be a form of advocacy as well. As a first step toward communicating with evaluators about literacy, it might be useful for music teachers to ask their evaluators what they mean by literacy, or by reading and writing. As we mentioned, evaluators do not always communicate why they want to see elements of literacy and reading or writing. If evaluators do not always communicate what reading and writing or literacy is for—strategies for showing student thinking and learning processes—the music teacher must help them establish this definition.

Once music teachers have an evaluator's working definition of literacy, they may draw upon the four components of disciplinary and artistic literacy to discuss these literacy practices with an evaluator more specifically. They may do this in conjunction with their literacy reflective practice, noting where students read most often (music, written excerpts), write most often (composer, arrange, respond, critique), and talk about the work or concept being explored/examined. Table 5.3 outlines a series of questions to help describe music teachers' artistic literacy practices and how they might use these questions to reflect upon practice and articulate their goals and decisions with evaluators.

By asking themselves the questions in table 5.3, music teachers may realize that they favor particular texts, roles, and practices over others, or that they vary them quite regularly. For example, when asking these questions, music teachers might realize that students took on the role solely of performer, following the conductor for the forty-five-minute rehearsal. Or students may have "read" throughout the rehearsal, following the conductor's gestures and interpreting them on their own through nonverbal responses like playing/singing or through discussion. As students "read," they changed their playing and discussed how their playing changed as they read the gesture. At the same time, these questions might help teachers rationalize why they chose a particular text over another, such as "Sansa Kroma" over "Kye Kye Kule" for a listening experience. A teacher may discuss the ways in which students "read" different texts and through what roles. This exercise helps teachers identify their literacy practices and form a rationale for why and how they have students reading, writing, listening, playing, and discussing. This rationale can then be communicated to evaluators using a common language of literacy that they understand, but in a subject-specific way.

If we return to the opening vignette, Maria can use the description and practice of artistic literacy as a way to talk with her evaluator about what she did in the classroom. She could use the terms of reading, writing, and discussing to share that her students took on the role of arranger and built upon their knowledge of reading particular rhythms to create an arrangement. Students were reading and communicating as they derived a rhythm; they needed to listen carefully and communicate what they heard effectively by writing down the appropriate rhythm. Then they applied their disciplinary knowledge of these rhythms as arrangers to write their own rhythm. Students made decisions about how they wanted

TABLE 5.3.

Ways to pinpoint artistic literacy in the music classroom

Question	Components	Reflecting on Practice	Communicating to Evaluators
What texts did I use?	Text	Helps teachers realize types of texts chosen/used.	Justify why the teacher chose specific texts.
How did the students read the texts?	Text; Discourses and practices;	Helps teachers consider different ways of reading and using text (playing, discussing, reading, listening, etc.).	Justify the different strategies and practices for reading the chosen texts.
What roles did the students read the texts as?	Identities and identifications	Helps teachers realize how many roles students take on in the class (composer, performer, arranger, etc.).	Justify the different roles and identities involved in learning about, making, listening, and responding to music.
Using these texts and roles, in what practices did students engage?	Discourses and practices; Identities and identifications	Helps teachers consider a variety of music/arts-specific practices that musicians and artists do.	Justify the work that students are doing pertinent to their roles.

to structure their composition and justify their decision, in the same ways that musicians write compositions or arrangements; it is the work that musicians do. Finally, Maria might say that the students did this on their own, independently, with little guidance from the teacher, which demonstrated their knowledge of the rhythms and of arranging. Using the literacy terminology of reading, writing, communicating, and listening to demonstrate how students learn through musical materials and practices can draw an evaluator's attention to the nuanced practices that occur in the music classroom, which can often be overlooked.

APPLYING TO PRACTICE 5.4

- Locate your current literacy practices. At what point of your lesson do the students read, write, or talk most? Would you say you are consistent with this structure? Do you have a designated time for sight-reading? Do the students make connections between the sight-reading and the repertoire material?
- How might you answer the questions in table 5.3 for yourself and for your evaluator: What were the texts? How did the students read the texts? What roles did the students read the texts as? Using these texts and roles, in what practices did students engage?

STRATEGIES FOR APPLYING DISCIPLINARY AND ARTISTIC LITERACIES

We have just described disciplinary literacy and artistic literacy as ways to frame literacy in music education. We have also presented disciplinary literacy as a way to frame discussions with evaluators and help come to agreement on terms. However, as the vignette that began this chapter demonstrates, sometimes evaluators or evaluation systems have specific, sometimes inflexible, definitions of literacy and a narrow list of what counts as evidence of a teacher addressing literacy. In these cases, how might music teachers use disciplinary literacy and artistic literacy to fulfill these requirements while also using those requirements to further students' education in music?

In the following sections we return to the two common ways evaluators and music teachers define literacy: as reading and writing language and as reading music notation. For each of these definitions, we provide strategies for how music teachers might use disciplinary and artistic literacy to improve practice and address evaluation requirements that might accompany each of these definitions. We provide different roles and practices students may take on within these views of literacy. We illustrate these definitions and strategies within a text, "Shenandoah," a well-known American folk song, used in various settings. There are numerous arrangements of "Shenandoah" for chorus, band, orchestra, and general music; as a text, it provides a versatile palette to consider disciplinary and artistic literacy strategies with multiple grades, levels, and abilities. These literacy strategies are intended to be small shifts, which allow students to become more independent in the discipline, gaining the ability to make decisions and to use tools, terms, and techniques in new ways.

LITERACY AS READING AND WRITING LANGUAGE

Both disciplinary and artistic literacy define literacy as a dynamic process in which people are able to use texts and knowledge in important ways to engage in roles with others. In an effort to improve students' reading ability defined this way, evaluators and administrators might require all teachers to incorporate some reading and writing in their lessons. On a surface level, this might include reading essays about music or writing about music; in younger grades, this might include incorporating vocabulary into lessons.

Music teachers might approach implementing reading and writing from a disciplinary literacy perspective. Incorporating disciplinary literacy may allow teachers to consider the ways musicians and artists read and write. By thinking of the roles and identities musicians take on, music teachers might find ways to incorporate reading and writing that are more akin to how musicians use language.

Identities, practices, and disciplinary knowledge. Artists engage in different roles and identities while reading and writing. They may read and write like musicologists, reading a historical letter written by a composer or the composer's notes for a piece. When students become musicologists, they take on certain discourses and practices. For example, they may write a letter to the composer. In order to engage in this manner, students need to have knowledge about the chosen text, using historical letters or composers' notes to gain information. So, students think like musicologists and have knowledge of the salient aspects of the text and how each part may work. Likewise, when students take on the roles of performers, they not only engage in the practice of performing, but also research pieces they are singing or playing, including the historical background and performance practices, interpretations, and past performances. They gain knowledge about the piece, what works or does not work for it, and how to work through it technically and interpretively. Finally, critics base their entire careers on evaluating musical works and performances. When students become the role of critic, they practice "reading" a performance. This practice allows them to consider the musical information critics must know and how they apply it in their critiques. Table 5.4 outlines some examples of incorporating reading and writing through a disciplinary literacy lens.

Identities, practices, and disciplinary knowledge in a text. A teacher might use roles and identities, practices, and disciplinary knowledge to introduce reading and writing in the piece "Shenandoah." Students may take on the identity of performers to research the text by reading the lyrics to inform their interpretation. With help from the teacher, as the students read, they might identify the

TABLE 5.4.

Strategies for incorporating disciplinary literacy in reading and writing

Roles and Identities	Discourses and Practices	Disciplinary Knowledge
Musicologist	• Read historical letters, documents, interviews, program notes, and documentaries/videos about composers and pieces. • Listen to other repertoire by the composer/artist/group.	• Information about composers, scores, and cultural and performance practices for the genre/style of music.
Performer	• Listen to recordings/watch performances of texts. • Compare and contrast performances. • Interpret text/lyrics.	• Technical ability (singing/playing leaps, legato, staccato, martellato, etc.). • Diction/lyrics (if any). • Vocabulary/musical terms.
Critic	• Watch/listen to performances of texts. • Respond to performances with constructive feedback.	• Vocabulary pertinent to the text/style/genre.

ascending melodic line on the lyrics "I long to hear you" as a form of text painting. Similarly, they might decide to decrescendo on the words "away you rolling river," because that appropriately sets the text as descending away into the distance. Through this process, students are using reading to take on the roles and practices of performers.

Students can take on the roles of poets and create their own poetry. "Shenandoah" might tell the story of the love of "Shenandoah." However, what or who Shenandoah is, is unknown. Different interpretations of the song suggest that "Shenandoah" is a beloved home, person, or mighty river (Library of Congress, n.d.). Teachers can ask the following questions to help students make a more personal connection to a place, person, or object that they love: What are some words you would use to describe a person, place, or thing you love? What does *your*

"Shenandoah" look like? Based on the discussion that arises from these questions, students might write their own poems or lyrics, taking on the roles of poets and songwriters. Through these actions, students are writing and interpreting in artistic ways central to the text.

Students may become musicologists and research performances of the text. Given the vast number of arrangements of "Shenandoah," performances are both sung and played in many styles and genres. Students may compare and contrast pieces, noting what is similar among them, such as a legato melodic line. They may interpret the lyrics of the text, as just described. "Shenandoah" is a sea shanty, a type of work song sung by sailors as they labored on their boats. Students may evaluate other sea shanties, such as "John Kanaka," "Molly Malone," and "Cape Cod Girls," and identify the aspects of each piece that make it a sea shanty, including call and response, strong beat structure, unison singing, and variation on a theme.

Finally, students may become critics and evaluate their own performance of "Shenandoah." They may consider what they should listen for and make a list; this may include tone quality, balance, timbre, or rhythm, to name a few. As they listen, students may use these categories to drive their critiques. Students may write their narrative or may create a podcast of their critique, making sure they have addressed the musical material categories initially outlined in a way both musicians and those without extensive music backgrounds could understand. When students incorporate reading and writing in this manner, the work is authentic to the work artists do in their roles. The reading and writing are specific to the musical processes, but they also allow students the opportunity to synthesize their knowledge or ideas and apply them to new settings in their own way.

APPLYING TO PRACTICE 5.5

- How might you begin to implement strategies for reading and writing through disciplinary/artistic literacy?
- What texts, roles, and practices will you use?

LITERACY AS READING MUSIC NOTATION

Sometimes evaluators, administrators, and music teachers have a slightly different definition of literacy, describing music literacy as the ability to read music. As a result, music teachers might be required to focus on students' abilities to identify, sing, or perform rhythms, pitches, dynamics, and other parameters of standard notation. Incorporating strategies of artistic literacy using identities, practices, and disciplinary knowledge may provide a more realistic and authentic way for students to create, respond, and connect to music through notation.

Identities, practices, and disciplinary knowledge. Teachers may be asked by their evaluators and administrators to implement more music literacy. But as we have discussed, teachers think of this as reading and playing notation—work that many performers do. It is important to consider other roles, identities, and practices that people engage in using notation, beyond performance. Even within the role of performer there are different practices and identities: creating and improvising, researching a piece or its history, interpreting, or listening and evaluating recordings, to name a few. Performers should be able to derive or dictate a melody by ear, either sketching it out on paper or playing it back by ear. This is particularly true in the jazz, folk, and pop genres when notating a melody or rhythm. Composers build pieces of music around certain scales (major, minor, pentatonic), and arrangers create new harmonies and lines to accompany these melodies. Conductors need to be able to read a text, envision how it sounds, and interpret the musical material with an ensemble. They may listen to previous recordings to help with their preparation. Table 5.5 outlines the roles, practices,

TABLE 5.5.

Strategies for incorporating disciplinary literacy in music notation

Roles and Identities	Discourses and Practices	Disciplinary Knowledge
Arranger/composer	• Derive/dictate rhythm and melody. • Make decisions on expressive elements (phrasing, dynamics).	• Notes and rhythms, key/ time signatures. • Musical form. • Expressive elements (phrase and dynamic markings).
Performer	• Derive/dictate rhythm and melody. • Listen and respond through improvisation.	• Notes and rhythms, key/ time signatures. • Musical form. • Expressive elements (phrase and dynamic markings).
Conductor	• Derive/dictate rhythm and melody. • Score study. • Interpret and communicate through gesture.	• Notes and rhythms, key/ time signatures. • Conducting gestures. • Expressive elements (phrase and dynamic markings).

and knowledge needed to use notation in an authentic and musical way, where students actively use and demonstrate the musical learning material.

Identities, practices, and disciplinary knowledge in a text. Using "Shenandoah" as a text, students may work with notation to derive—or dictate—the melody or rhythm in a dictation. This is a common practice of performers, arrangers, and composers. So, students are "reading like musicians," synthesizing their knowledge, and applying it in an active way. This also fosters the independence of using the materials specific to the discipline without relying solely on the teacher.

"Shenandoah" contains many pentatonic-based melodies. During a sight-reading or designated "music literacy time" in rehearsal, students may improvise on a pentatonic scale using the rhythm of the main melody (or perhaps a countermelody). In order to do this, students need knowledge of the pentatonic scale, what time signature and key the melody is in, and how to play the rhythm correctly. Students can read the rhythm, clap it, and play/sing it on a neutral pitch (B-flat or C for instruments, G or A for singers), then locate it in their music. Students are engaging in score navigation, gaining knowledge of the piece and of musical concepts through the text. This is work that musicians do regularly when learning a piece of music or learning to improvise.

Or students may take on the role of arrangers and add their own expressive elements like phrasing and dynamics to the melody of "Shenandoah." Students may sing the melody line of "Shenandoah" or sing their own vocal or instrumental line. They then may identify the salient musical aspects of their line. For example, in Frank Ticheli's band arrangement of "Shenandoah," the brass begins the piece by taking the melody, with the winds playing a complementary melody with moving notes leading to longer held notes. Students can make judgments about why particular dynamics belong where they do. As a class or in small groups, students may quickly play through and discuss what they think works and what doesn't. Students can take on the role of conductors and conduct their phrasing of "Shenandoah" for the group. These are different means of hearing what they have chosen from another perspective than that of performer. In an ensemble class, after students take on the role of conductor and then return to performer, they should be able to follow the conductor more clearly and have a more intimate connection to the music. As students embrace different musical and artistic practices, they expand their ability to participate in the process beyond reading, playing, and following a conductor.

As a way to extend this activity for some students, they might choose to add another part to create a countermelody. They need a pre-knowledge of the melody to do this, including identifying ascending or descending lines. Or they can compose a countermelody for their part/instrument. They may think like arrangers about how this new melody works with their part and with the melody. They may consider if this new part needs a quick movement of eighth notes or long, sustained notes, or if the notes move stepwise or skipping, or all around. Finally, students could create an audio guide for their arrangement, discussing their decisions and sharing why they made their musical choices.

APPLYING TO PRACTICE 5.6

- Which of the literacy approaches does your evaluator tend to favor? Which do you favor?
- How might you begin to implement the strategies for music notation through disciplinary/artistic literacy?
- What texts, roles, and practices can you use in your classroom?

SUMMARY

In music education, literacy tends to have two definitions: being able to read and write language and reading and playing music notation. Disciplinary literacy is a way to encompass and expand these approaches, working with and looking deeply at "text" through a particular subject. In this sense, a text can be a book, a painting, a piece of music, a recording, or a live performance. Through texts, we gain knowledge on a subject, take on identities and roles specific to the subject, and participate in practices and discourses central to the subject. In music, one practice is the ability to "read a text" like musicians in order to learn more authentically about the material. In music, disciplinary literacy is called artistic literacy.

Regardless of the literacy approach, disciplinary literacy allows students to engage in artistically literate practices as artists and musicians do, through reading and writing, notation, and standards-based learning. Using a variety of texts to target different styles and abilities, students may participate authentically in musical experiences on their own and with others, gaining independence to make, create, or respond to music in and out of the classroom.

We return here to Maria's vignette and provide an alternate approach to her conversation about literacy with her evaluator. To remind yourself about her story, it might be useful to reread the vignette at the beginning of this chapter.

Maria has prepared for her observation of a fourth-grade general music class by her principal by selecting one of her favorite lessons. In this lesson students sing and play "Circle Round the Zero" and then use similar rhythms and intervals to create their own melodies. In the post-observation, Maria's principal says, "I'm evaluating you on literacy teaching. I saw the students really enjoying themselves and working nicely together, but I didn't see students engaging in discourse like they did in my English classroom. Instead, I saw them doing a lot of singing, playing, and using manipulatives on the rug." Maria responds, "The students are reading the song as a piece of text. They're doing the work musicians do, artistic literacy: listening and figuring out rhythms and melodies by ear. Then they become the role of composers to create a new text using that knowledge and material." Sensing by the puzzled look on her face that the principal is somewhat confused, Maria continues. "The students talked about how to make decisions and how to apply their tools to the composing and playing of a new text. This combined their musical knowledge and skills of reading, writing, listening, and playing Orff instruments." "I was unaware this level of sophistication was happening," responds Maria's principal. "It would be good to help the students articulate the many things they were doing in this exercise, so they better understand the process and then are able to repeat it." Maria answers, "Maybe a chart could help the students consider the different parts of the process." Her principal agrees, saying she would like to see something similar next time she visits Maria's classroom.

EXAMPLE LESSON PLANS

High School Orchestra

Composition: *Brandenburg Concerto* no. 3 (J. S. Bach)
Behavioral Objectives:
- Students will determine appropriate use of terraced dynamics and interpret, sing, and play new dynamics through score study.
- Students will arrange *Brandenburg Concerto*, adding their own dynamics.

Conceptual Objective:
- Students will understand the historical use of dynamics of music from this time period and will apply them to their own original arrangement of the piece.

US Core Arts Standards: MU:Cn11.0.8; MU:Re8.1.8; MU:Pr6.1.8
Essential Question: How do dynamics contribute to the affect of a composition?
Enduring Understanding: Dynamic changes are an essential part of expressive performances.
Materials: score, recording of *Brandenburg Concerto* no. 3
Vocabulary: terraced dynamics

Procedure:

1. **Warm-Ups**

   a. Students begin an ensemble warm-up with a G major scale, using a rhythm of 2 eighths/quarter. To practice the idea of terraced dynamics, selected students may choose ways to add dynamics to the scale warm-up (e.g., start *forte*, and on the note D move to *piano*, on E, move back to *forte*). A student can conduct the scale warm-up using gestures to indicate these dynamic changes as well. The scale can be played at various tempi as well to work on bow strokes (violins/violas moving toward the middle of the bow, celli/ bass at the lower half). With each repetition of the scale, students have the opportunity to begin with breathing (instead of the teacher conducting). This connotes a more chamber music–like atmosphere.

   b. On the final note of the scale, students watch each other for the cut-off (this will prepare for the last note of *Brandenburg*, which is held, but has no fermata). Then ask: *How long should we hold that last note?* Students listen to and watch one another for visual cues.

   c. Isolate a phrase of *Brandenburg* within the piece in order to examine possible dynamic choices. There are no dynamics written by the composer. Say: *Let's think like arrangers and examine this text. What should we add in? What sounds good to us? A jump from* mezzo forte *to* forte? *In Bach's time, there were no written crescendos, but more abrupt dynamic changes. As a class, let's decide our changes, our terraced dynamics (write on board).*

   d. Students sing/hum the musical line/phrase, then play it, try different ideas, and arrive at a consensus.

2. **Students become arrangers using terraced dynamics:** Students play mm. 1–4.

   a. Students sing their parts as a group and in individual sections.

   b. Guide a conversation about dynamics. Ask the following questions:

      i. *Do we want this to be all the same dynamic?*

      ii. *If we want to change dynamics and observe the idea of terracing, then where do we change from one to the next?*

      iii. *If we want to move outside of performance practice ideas, then we can consider adding crescendo and decrescendo. Are we interested in that? If so, where do these ideas fit?*

      iv. *What in the music is guiding these decisions? We did some singing/humming of the music. Were you influenced by the group singing? Did you notice that it sometimes informs your idea?*

   c. Students perform the section with the proposed dynamics. As a class, reflect on the sound and either accept the introduction of the chosen dynamic as part of the arrangement (where students mark the dynamic in their scores) or continue to find what works better for the class. Students may vote to decide or come up with another system of deciding (e.g., each section of the orchestra decides on dynamics for assigned measures).

   d. Either as a class activity or as an assignment, ask students to locate other sections of the music where dynamic changes might be appropriate. Those sections may be visited in subsequent class periods to inform a new "class arrangement" of the piece regarding dynamics.

Assessment:
- Students can articulate justification for their dynamic choices.
- Students show ability to perform these dynamic choices.
- Students use terminology (*mezzo forte, forte, piano, pianissimo,* terraced) appropriately.

Possible Next Steps and Extensions:
- Examine some other arrangements of the *Brandenburg Concerto*. Sight-read and rehearse different arrangements and discuss whether or not students agree with the arranger's interpretation. If they do agree with the arranger's interpretation, discuss why they agree and pose to the class the idea of borrowing the intent of the arranger. If they disagree, discuss why not, and pose alternatives to the dynamics that are expressed in the different arrangements.
- **Students become evaluators.** Elect a panel of student judges who are unaware of the decided dynamics. As evaluators of the ensemble's performance, the panel's members are charged with the task of writing into a blank score the dynamics they hear as performed by their peers. As an audience, they relay back to the ensemble what they have heard, reporting either that they have identified the dynamic choices that the ensemble was attempting to perform or something different.

Anticipated Areas of Difficulty or Student Misunderstanding:
- Individual parts can be difficult. Be prepared to isolate one line at a time and build on it.

HIGH SCHOOL CHORUS

Composition: *Sicut Cervus,* SATB (Palestrina)

Behavioral Objectives:
- Students will sing *Sicut Cervus,* mm. 1–14, focusing on phrasing.
- Students will analyze the stress/release of a phrase and the dynamic contour of their own voice parts, as well as comparing among other lines.

Conceptual Objective:
- Students will recognize how voice parts function separately and together; they will recognize that entrances of parts form an overlapping of sound and melodic lines.

US Core Arts Standards: MU:Cr3.1.7; MU:Pr4.2.7; MU:Pr5.1.7; MU:Re8.1.7

Essential Question:
- How do singers create musical lines while blending and balancing with other voice parts?

Enduring Understanding:
- Singers make individual and group phrasing decisions based on musical style and vocal lines.

Materials: 8½" x 14" paper, markers

Vocabulary: texture-layering, counterpoint, polyphony, stress/release, dynamic contour

The following experiences may be used at different points in the learning of this piece, depending on singers' needs and readiness levels.

Procedure:

1. *Warm-ups*: Ask for volunteers to conduct the piece. One student will be learning to start the group, one to keep time, one to show shape, etc. Singers will mirror conductor and conduct themselves throughout, showing differences in heavy/light, legato/staccato (facilitated by the teacher). In arpeggiated warm-ups, students will create an arc/rainbow with arms to connect the voice to the musical line, creating a legato phrase.

2. While rehearsing *Sicut Cervus*, have students stand when their voice part sings, then sit down when they do not sing (have a rest). This allows students to see when they sing in relation to others, who has entrances at what points in a phrase, etc. Since this piece is through-composed, students will stand for the majority of the piece, thus showing the number of parts that are working simultaneously. Say: *We are singing in multiple parts in this section, and each part comes in at their own time, not all together at once. Which part begins singing at measure 1? Which part comes in next? Introduce term polyphony as two or more individual parts.*

3. After students sing and conduct through mm. 1-14 once, have them practice breathing on their individual entrances. The breath supports the melodic line and also displays who is singing when. Students can conduct themselves or move as they breathe to show the motion of the breath. Students may whisper the first syllable ("Sic") or just breathe. Students will exhale the breath throughout the phrase until their next breath.

4. Have students pair up with a partner from another voice part. Facing each other and joining palms, they demonstrate the phrasing through stress release (mm. 1–14). As one voice part's melodic line enters and begins a new phrase, the singer will push forward against his or her partner's palm. This will show the stress and release among the phrases of the different voice parts. The forward movement—or stress—will usually occur on entrances with held notes or moving eighth notes heading to a static. This stress-release helps to see where the phrase of the voice parts is moving and at what times. It also allows students to feel entrances and experience *layering* of voices. Name *texture* as the layering of voices. (This can also be done by holding hands, where one voice part pulls on the other hand for stress and lessens for the release of the phrase.)

5. Have students analyze their line for dynamics (often decrescendo-crescendo in *Sicut Cervus*) and mark their part in the score with hairpins. Have students evaluate the inner voices and demonstrate dynamics at mm. 7 in the alto and tenor lines. Ask: *Who is getting louder when the alto and tenor are softer* (answer: bass)? *Why?* Teacher can then name this technique as *dynamic contour. The use of dynamics in this piece accompanies the phrases of the voice parts. The melodic lines often crescendo on long static notes or moving eighth notes.*

Ask: *How does this feel in the voice? How does it shape the musical phrase line alone? With another part?* In small groups, students find another voice part and work through dynamics in their part to shape the phrase. They compare the phrases and dynamics between the two parts and put them together. Ask: *What do you notice about your line when sung with another part?* It may be helpful to provide students with a pitch pipe or tuner for their starting notes.

6. Have students create groups of three within their voice part. On paper, they create a visual representation of their musical line. Provide suggestions that the visual may look like hills, may be coded by different colors for dynamics. Ask: *How are you showing your voice part's breaths for entrances? How are phrasing and stresses/release being shown visually?*

7. Once they complete a visual representation, have each voice part group team up with groups of other the other three voice parts to create a visual score out of all of their parts. Each voice part will share its interpretation; students in these groups will practice singing together, then share with the larger ensemble. Some guiding questions for students as they share can include: *What made you create your musical line this way? Did you pick particular colored markers for this section? How did you assign colors to the sounds? How does your voice part's line look in comparison to another (for example, alto against tenor)?* Compare two voice part groups (such as two soprano groups): *What differences do you see/hear in their phrasing? What did we need to know about the music in order to create this visual representation?*

Assessment:

- Students' movements demonstrate the musical phrase of their voice part, including a difference in their singing to demonstrate their knowledge of their voice part's phrasing and dynamic contour.
- Students work together to feel the stress/release of their individual voice parts in comparison with others.
- Performance at the end of small group and larger group voice part work.
- Performance during rehearsal.

Possible Next Steps and Extensions:

- Continuation with the next section of *Sicut Cervus*.
- Once students are comfortable with their voice part, similar rehearsal techniques may be employed to examine the phrasing and counterpoint among voice parts. Use and naming of counterpoint as a vocabulary word may be used more as students have developed and begun to demonstrate the feeling of the term in their singing.

Anticipated Areas of Difficulty or Student Misunderstanding:

- Students may have difficulty pronouncing the Latin text.
- Individual voice parts sung together in polyphony can be difficult. Be prepared to isolate one line at a time and build on it. Students might not be ready to be independent on their own and may need a partner in their voice part to complete the rehearsal work.
- It might be necessary to make accommodations for students who might have limited mobility, particularly in the standing portion of class.

Secondary General Music

Behavioral Objective:
- Students will create their own musical scores based on visual prompts; they will score their own short film.

Conceptual Objective:
- Students will begin to understand how a visual piece of art may be represented through music using specific compositional choices.

US Core Arts Standards: MU:Cr1.1.T.Ia; MU:Cr1.1.6; MU:Pr4.3.5; MU:Re9.1.5

Essential Question:
- How does music change one's understanding or prediction of a storyline?

Enduring Understanding:
- Music can enhance and heighten one's visual or emotional interpretation.

Materials: excerpt from the beginning of the movie *The Shining*, found instruments (keys, paper, anything in or around the classroom), visual and written prompts (see below),

Procedure:
1. Have students watch the beginning of the movie *The Shining* without sound (the scene depicts a car driving on a mountainous road). Students respond to the questions in column 1 of the chart:

	1.	2.
What is happening in this scene/story?		
Who are the characters? Where are they?		
What do you think will occur in this story?		
Anything else you think is important to note about this scene		

   Students turn and talk with their neighbors. The teacher guides a quick large group share out.
2. Have students watch the scene again, this time with audio. In column 2 of the chart, students log their new predictions. Ask: *What has changed? How did the music enhance the visual of what you just watched? What did you notice about this music that helped you to draw some conclusions about the story?*
3. Say: *A film scorer, or person who wrote the music for this movie, was an essential part in creating emotion and suspense for the watcher. The music for this section is called* Music for String Percussion and Celeste, *by a composer named Bela*

Bartok. What do you think we need to know to be a successful scorer? On the board or using a Word document and projector, one student writes student responses. The teacher might also point out that the director of the movie chose this specific music for the opening scene; it was not written specifically for the movie. Possible questions to ask: *Why do you think the director picked this specific piece for this view and scene? What mood do you think he was trying to create by choosing this music?*

4. Say: *"Just like in this movie, we are going to be film scorers and use this knowledge of writing for film to produce a score based on a visual prompt."* Using found instruments, provide a model for this exercise, showing the photo or video prompt used, giving a performance, and displaying the score. Ask: *What sounds did you notice in this composition? What were some compositional choices I made? How did I show these choices in my score?* Lead students in pointing these out and writing them on the board. Since students can choose how to visually organize their score, the teacher guides discussion about how certain compositional choices might look visually in a score. For example, showing what an ascending siren might look like when written out, giving performers a key or legend, etc.

5. **Students as film scorers.** Have students create groups of five to create their own scores based on a teacher-provided prompt. Prompts can be both written and visual. Examples may include:
   - "As I walked down the long, dark hallway and opened the creaky door, I saw . . ."
   - A photo of a lion roaring
   - Four symbols (zigzag, starburst, spiral, small dots)
   - Student-created prompts. Students may write a prompt for another group that is then approved by the teacher. Or they write the prompt for their own group.

6. Have students brainstorm, rehearse, and create a visual score for their composition. Groups share their performances for the class. Without seeing the visual or written prompt and based on the performance, the class has to guess what each group's prompt might be and provide evidence for their guess. Each group shares their creative decisions about the score. Ask guiding questions to aid in sharing, including: *Why did they choose those particular "instruments" and sounds? How or why did they layer the sounds on top of one another?*

7. Call attention to the idea that often a composer will write a piece with a scene already in mind, like Mendelssohn's *Hebrides Overture*. Play an excerpt. Teacher might say to the class: *The visual prompts and cues can really influence how we interpret a piece of music. But, the way we hear and use the piece in a soundtrack may be a totally different application of that composer's original intention.*

Assessment:
- Group composition performance.
- As film scorers, students work together to create and articulate their compositional strategies.

- The teacher may create a written reflection that has questions for each student to answer, which might include: How was your product a successful representation of your image/prompt? Why did your group choose those particular "instruments" and sounds? How or why did your group layer the sounds on top of one another? If you were to change this piece, what would you change?

Possible Next Steps and Extensions:

- In subsequent classes, students may choose their own visuals (either picture or video) and how they will notate their score. Depending on classroom resources, students may score using GarageBand, instruments, or found instruments.
- Students may write a prompt for another group that is then approved by the teacher. Or they may write the prompt for their own group.

Anticipated Areas of Difficulty or Student Misunderstanding:

- Classroom management and planning is crucial for the small group work. Provide students enough and targeted tasks, while also making sure they are flexible enough for students to solve the problems in ways that work best for them, is important. Teacher should make sure to circulate often and help all groups.
- Take care to discuss expectations for group work: how to work respectfully with one another and listen to each other. Consider assigning a group leader (this position can rotate) or a group secretary to write down ideas. Provide a self-reflection/group reflection sheet so students can comment on the nature of their productivity and respectfulness.

6

ASSESSMENT

Sarah the chorus director needs to meet with her principal to go over her evaluation scores for the year, but she is anxious about the meeting. All year he has urged her to administer more paper-and-pen tests. She has been frustrated by these disagreements and has continued to run her rehearsals as she thought best fit her students' learning and to best prepare for the concert. Sarah enters the principal's office, sits down, and looks over the scores her principal has given her. She sees that in the category for assessment she has received a 1, "in need of improvement." "Why did I get a 1 on assessment?" she asks him. "I did not see any evidence of your assessing students," the principal replies. "Well, music is different than math," says Sarah. "The concert is my test. If the students can sing and perform, then they learned. The proof is in the pudding." "OK," the principal says, "but when I taught math the final exam provided documented proof of how each student did in the course. How do you know how each student did?" The principal looks at the class roster for chorus and points to a student's name at random. "What about James, here, for example?" he asks. "Who, Jimmy?" Sarah replies. "He sings baritone, he's come a long way since September. What about him?" "How do you know how he performed at the concert? There were fifty other kids singing at the same time. He could have been lip-syncing for all you know," the principal says. "Well, he sang fine in lessons, too," Sarah replies. "And what proof do you have of that?" asks the principal. Sarah shrugs, "I don't know. He sounded good to me each week and his tone improved. Also, he brought in a practice log each week and it said he practiced." "What does the amount of time practicing have to do with whether he achieved the goals of the class? When I taught math I didn't care how long it took a student to do his homework, just whether he did it successfully or not," the principal responds. He then sighs and continues, "I gave you a 1 because your assessment strategy of the concert serving as a test doesn't provide the specificity of data that is required in our teacher evaluation system."

PERHAPS THE MOST controversial and frustrating aspects of the current teacher evaluation systems are the components that address assessment. Teachers often feel the assessment practices in teacher evaluation aim to evaluate teachers on aspects they cannot control. Like Sarah the chorus teacher, music educators often find themselves disagreeing with evaluators and administrators about what counts as acceptable assessment practices in music education. Once again, there is a discrepancy between the pedagogical knowledge of evaluators and the pedagogical content knowledge of music teachers. In this chapter we explore how music teachers may continue to assess in effective ways unique to music education while remaining open to using the components of teacher evaluation to improve their practices. First, we review some common ways assessment is part of teacher evaluation. Second, we briefly cover some critiques of the assessment aspects of teacher evaluation. Third, we define some common vocabulary and tenets used in assessment. This vocabulary may help music teachers work through these critiques of assessment. Finally, we describe specific ways music teachers might apply assessment vocabulary and tenets to the requirements of teacher evaluation. This includes some ways of approaching the creation of assessments, including the creation of assessments alone or in a group and when assessments are chosen or mandated by the district or state.

APPLYING TO PRACTICE 6.1

- What is your reaction to the opening vignette? Do you tend to agree more with Sarah or the principal? If you were in Sarah's position, how would you respond?
- What are your current assessment practices? Do you have systems or strategies in place for assessing students throughout the year?

ASSESSMENT IN TEACHER EVALUATION

As we discussed in chapter 1, many teacher evaluation systems include assessment in two ways. First, assessment is usually included as a criterion for observation by evaluators. In this component, evaluators look for, evaluate, and rate the assessment practices of teachers. Second, "student growth" is evaluated. This component is intended to assess the "results" of a teacher's instruction.

ASSESSMENT IN THE OBSERVATION COMPONENT

Assessment is often part of the observation portion of teacher evaluation. For example, in the Danielson (2013) framework, Domain 1f, "Planning and Preparation," requires teachers to design formative assessments in their instruction. Similarly, Domain 3d, "Using Assessment in Instruction," focuses exclusively on assessment. This area requires that teachers "create assessment criteria, monitor student learning, provide feedback to students, and have students self-assess and monitor." In Marzano (2011), although assessment is not focused on explicitly, many parts of the framework require strong assessment practices. For example, DQ1, number 2, "Tracking student progress," relies on successfully assessing students. Domain 3 focuses on "reflecting on teaching," specifically subareas "51. Evaluating the effectiveness of individual lessons and units" and "52. Evaluating the effectiveness of specific pedagogical strategies and behaviors" (Marzano, 2011, p. 1). Teachers' effectiveness in this system must be shown by evidence. This evidence is how the teacher affects students' learning, and the most effective way to gather this information is by assessing students' abilities, knowledge, and growth.

What the assessment component of observation in teacher evaluation—whether Danielson, Marzano, or any other system—is trying to capture is that teachers engage in good assessment practices. These practices require teachers to assess their students regularly to determine if their instruction is effective. Assessment practices also stress that it is important to make clear to students the requirements of how they are being assessed and that teachers must provide evidence of student learning. Based on these assessments, teachers then provide feedback to students and adjust their instruction to address any areas where students need improvement.

As we have tried to show in the vignette at the beginning of the chapter and as we will later show in the chapter, the assessment strategies music teachers employ often do not align well with these practices. Sometimes music teachers do not fulfill these requirements and sometimes they do, but this might not be immediately evident to evaluators. For example, ensembles are set up particularly well for teachers to provide immediate feedback on students' performance. The students play and then the director cuts them off and immediately gives feedback for improvement. While this can be effective and efficient, the process is not easily documented. Also, it might not provide students with specific criteria on how their performance is being assessed. Using some of the criteria outlined in teacher evaluation might help improve these types of assessment practices. As we have argued throughout this book, improving these often-used assessment practices in music education requires both advocating effective strategies and pedagogical content knowledge in music education while also remaining open to evaluators' pedagogical knowledge and suggestions.

ASSESSMENT OF STUDENT GROWTH

In addition to the observation and evaluation of teachers' assessment practices, teacher evaluation systems often include a component to assess student growth. In theory, this makes sense. This component aims to determine the results of a teacher's instruction. In some academic subjects standardized tests serve as an assessment of student growth. These tests are often created by private companies or by state governmental agencies.

While standardized tests are commonly used in other subjects to measure student growth in teacher evaluation systems, including math and English, and to a lesser degree in science and social studies, in music they are not commonly employed. Instead, the creation of assessments of student growth occurs on the local level. For example, in some teacher evaluation systems, particularly those that were established as part of R2T, student growth is measured through SLOs. For subjects where students are not required to take a standardized test—and music is usually one of them—in lieu of such a test, teachers or districts can create pre- and post-tests to measure student growth. These pinpoint a learning objective, test

> Assessment in teacher evaluation may be required through teacher observations and assessing student growth, through summative forms such as tests or by achieving student learning objectives.

at the beginning of the course to determine what students know to form a baseline, and then test the same or similar material at the end to determine students' growth. What makes up these SLOs and who designs them varies. Some districts allow teachers to form their own objectives and pre- and post-tests. Others create them on a district-wide level, still others may choose to purchase a commercially available test, and there are other practices.

CRITIQUES OF ASSESSMENT OF STUDENT GROWTH IN TEACHER EVALUATION

The assessment of the student growth component of teacher evaluation has come under considerable criticism for its usefulness and accuracy. There is good reason for there to be controversy around assessment as a measure of teacher effectiveness in teacher evaluation. First, understandably, teachers resent that these assessments potentially threaten their livelihood for seemingly arbitrary reasons. Second, some teachers feel that continual assessment can hinder their everyday work with students. Third, many teachers have little or no input into the creation of these assessments and to what degree they are part of teacher evaluation. Often they are mandated by state or national laws or by district policy.

Other frustrations arise because the assessments often measure parameters over which teachers have the least amount of control. Standardized tests, whether created by corporations, state governments, or school districts, are handed to teachers with little or no input on their part. In some cases, music teachers are evaluated on their students' scores in other academic subjects. For example, in states that received R2T funds in 2011, their systems allow for standardized tests to count for teachers' evaluations even in nontested subjects like music. This creates situations in which music teachers' scores are determined in part by, for example, their students' English scores. This of course says little about their quality as music educators.

Another common criticism of measuring student growth is the variability of students. Students are not widgets; they have varying backgrounds, abilities, interests, supports outside of school, and access to resources. To address this concern, many evaluation systems use "value-added" models (VAMs) to account for these differences. Supposedly, VAMs take into account students' performance on previous tests and base determinations of successful growth in reference to those previous scores (Konstantopoulos, 2014; Robinson, 2015; Wesolowski, 2014). In this way, they aim to use growth-based factors to adjust the standards-based criteria of tests. Some value-based models also claim to account for students' socioeconomic and racial backgrounds. The thinking behind VAMs is that they account for the differences among students and create a grading system that does not penalize teachers who take on teaching in more challenging environments. However, the issue with VAMs is that it has not been established that they accurately weigh and evaluate these differences between students (Darling-Hammond, 2013; Polikoff & Porter, 2014). Similarly, VAMs do not account for other factors, including student interest, commitment to school, educational background, and personality (Amrein-Beardsley, 2014). Any single VAM, it seems, would not be able to account for every one of these difference between students (David, 2010).

THE LANGUAGE OF ASSESSMENT IN TEACHER EVALUATION

The issues of VAMs, the role of corporations in devising tests and capturing public funds, teaching to the test, and the arbitrariness of some test measures are some of the criticisms of assessment. Because of these issues, teachers are often frustrated with the role of assessment in teacher evaluation. However, some of these frustrations occur because of misunderstandings of assessment by policymakers, evaluators, and even teachers. Understanding the language of assessment can help teachers make more informed decisions about how to address the assessment aspect of teacher evaluation. With the right knowledge and understanding of assessment, teachers might be able to deal with these critiques and weaknesses and use teacher evaluation to improve their assessment practices. By refining and understanding the language of assessment, music teachers can begin to form assessments, prepare for different types of assessment, and advocate for themselves and their programs.

In the following we discuss some terms and tenets that can help music educators engage in teacher evaluation: *assessment, evaluation, measurement, validity, triangulation, data*, and *formative and summative assessments*. In addition, we discuss a common way music teachers assess, by listening to students' performances, and some of the problems that arise with this strategy in teacher evaluation. This is not a complete list of terms in assessment, nor are these explanations full descriptions. However, they are targeted to areas that music teachers often struggle with and can help them improve practice and performance in teacher evaluation systems and engage in discussion with evaluators. Readers who are interested in gaining more information on these concepts in music education can consult the additional resources at the end of the chapter. Within each of these explanations, we provide ways teachers can apply these tenets to their teaching.

ASSESSMENT VERSUS EVALUATION VERSUS MEASUREMENT

Although they are sometimes used interchangeably, *assessment, evaluation*, and *measurement* have different meanings. Educators Oakes and Lipton (2003) make a distinction between assessment and evaluation. They define *assessment* as "gathering all the relevant information that can inform decisions about teaching, including information about the student and conditions for learning" (p. 244). They explain that in contrast to assessment, *evaluation* "includes judgment of the student's performance and involves some element of whether the performance is *good*" (p. 244). We would like to add a third distinction, *measurement*, which is taking evaluations or judgments and placing them on a scale or grading system or sorting them in reference to one another (Reynolds, Livingston, Willson, & Willson, 2010). Based on these definitions, assessment, evaluation, and measurement are more limited and narrow; measurement is a subdivision of evaluation, and evaluation is a subdivision of assessment. Figure 6.1 depicts the relationship of these terms.

An example of the differences among these terms is the various ways music educators assess students' musical performances. To *assess* a student's performance in a general sense requires that the teacher listen to the student perform. It might also include talking to the student about her performance, asking her

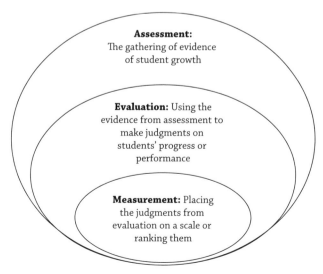

FIGURE 6.1. Relationship among assessment, evaluation, and measurement

to reflect on how she performed and how she prepared for the performance. It might also entail providing feedback to the student on how she might improve. *Evaluation* might narrow and focus the assessment toward making a judgment about the performance, for example, noting what was good and lacking in it. This evaluation might be guided by a rubric or other preestablished list of criteria to judge the student, or it may not. Evaluation guided by preestablised criteria might be used to provide feedback to the student in specific areas. Finally, *measurement* narrows even further. It uses this preestablished criteria to rank or grade the performance. For example, in state and ensemble festivals and competitions, the student might be ranked—"she has come in second place"—or graded on a scale—"the student has received a 91 out of 100." There are various methods for determining how students' assessments can be placed on a scale of measurement. However, the most common are criterion-referenced scores, in which there is a standard that students meet individually. Because of this standard, the scores are not compared to one another. All students can score high or low. Contrasted with this are norm-referenced scores, which are placed in reference to one another. "Grading on a curve" is an example of norm-referenced scoring. Currently, criterion-referenced scoring is more common grading in education. Table 6.1 lists examples of assessment, evaluation, and measurement.

> Assessment, evaluation, and measurement are different. *Assessment* uses data to form decisions on student learning quality; *evaluation* uses judgment to determine quality; and *measurement* uses preestablished criteria and to provide a grade or rating

While the road from assessment to evaluation to measurement becomes more specific, this does not mean that measurement is necessarily superior to evaluation, which is then superior to assessment. Instead, as assessment moves toward specificity, it becomes more inflexible and controversial. The measurement of a musical performance serves as an example. On many solo and ensemble grading sheets, the performance is broken down into criteria. The criteria might include, for example, accuracy of rhythm, pitch, and dynamics. This approach allows judges, teachers, and performers to agree upon what aspects of performance will be evaluated so that the students and teachers know how to prepare and there are established criteria for how the performers will be ranked. However, it creates at least two problems. First, if followed strictly, the process does not allow judges to pursue learning opportunities outside the confines of the judging criteria. If a student has stage fright, but such a category is not on the judging sheet, then the judge does not have the flexibility to address this issue with the student unless she bends the rules stated on the sheet. Second, a good performance is not

TABLE 6.1.

Examples of assessment, evaluation, and measurement

Assessment	Evaluation	Measurement
• Asking students questions and receiving answers. • Listening to a student perform. • Watching students move to music to gain their understanding of form. • Listening to a student's composition.	• Giving feedback on an essay. • Providing feedback on a performance on areas that need improvement. • Determining if students' movements demonstrate successful understanding of form. • Providing feedback on how a student can improve his or her composition.	• Grading an essay. • Using a rubric to score a performance. • Grading or ranking students' abilities to move as a demonstration of knowledge of form. • Giving a student first place or a perfect score in a composition competition.

necessarily reducible to these categories, so the categories may then become controversial. There are times when a performer can execute all the correct categories well—the pitches, rhythms, and dynamics are all accurate—but the performance feels lifeless and sterile. Conversely, there might be a performance that is "rough around the edges," but the performer is engaging and audiences still want to listen. Measurement, in attempting to categorize and rank performances, makes value judgments that some might not agree with about what constitutes a good performance (Hash, 2012). Some types of performers and performances will be advantaged and others disadvantaged. Measurement, compared to assessment and evaluation, is more controversial.

Assessment and evaluation are not bogged down by these problems—at least not to the same degree. General assessment and evaluation allow teachers greater flexibility to use their judgment as they listen to a performance. A teacher may be able to address the stage fright of a student when observing him, rather than being confined to the criteria on a grading sheet. Similarly, evaluation and assessment allow teachers to explore and debate with students what makes a good performance. The ambiguity of what constitutes a good performance and discussion about whether it can be broken down into discrete parts provide an educational moment for students. The problem, of course, is that without measurement criteria, a teacher might become unfocused and the criteria for judgment not well defined. A compromise, then, might be to form general criteria that teachers can comment on but also leave space for them to discuss other issues. This might suggest that general assessment, evaluation, and measurement each have their strengths and weaknesses, and teachers might employ them judiciously, using them at opportune times.

Application to teaching: Use general assessment, evaluation, and measurement at appropriate times. Knowing the differences among these forms of assessment can help music teachers build vocabulary, locate places where they assess, and communicate with evaluators. By expanding assessment to include areas beyond just measurement, music educators might realize that they assess more often than they thought. This enables music teachers to find the multiple areas where they already assess and then communicate to evaluators where and how they evaluate. In addition to helping music teachers advocate for their teaching and programs it provides them with more variety to best assess students. Music teachers need not always measure students' growth. Sometimes providing students' progress on a scale or in a ranking can be useful to help them develop and know where and how much they need to grow. However, music educators might acknowledge that measurement can create inflexibility. In addition to measurement, there are times when simply gathering information through general assessment is most appropriate. Similarly, gathering information through evaluation without measurement might provide flexibility in assessing where and how students need to grow and provide feedback tailored to their individual needs. By acknowledging and employing the differences among general assessment, evaluation, and measurement, music educators can develop the vocabulary to communicate with evaluators and strengthen their assessment strategies.

APPLYING TO PRACTICE 6.3

- In the work you do in your classroom, do you tend to favor assessment, evaluation, or measurement?
- What types of assessment have you used?
- What types of evaluation have you used?
- What types of measurement have you used?

TRIANGULATION OR VARYING ASSESSMENT

If assessment, evaluation, and measurement have strengths and weaknesses, then teachers might use them to assess student learning in different ways. This is a form of what is sometimes called *triangulation* (Reeves, 2009). In geography, the term denotes the practice of using three known coordinates to situate someone's location. For example, in global positioning systems (GPS), to find a location, the devices find information from three satellites to pinpoint the exact location of the device. In social sciences, triangulation means gathering information from different sources to make sure it accurately represents what one is looking for (Golafshani, 2003). For example, a historian might determine whether a reported historical event actually took place. The researcher might interview some people, look at newspapers from the time, and look at police reports or other government documents. The point of triangulation in both geography and social sciences is that one can be more certain about the accuracy of the evidence she is seeking if she gathers it from several sources.

Triangulation as a means to be sure of evidence is also applicable in educational assessment. To prove evidence of students' learning and abilities and to better gather data, the teacher might collect evidence from multiple sources. The differences among assessment, evaluation, and measurement are useful here. To return to assessing a musical performance as an example, a teacher might combine the different forms of assessment. There are times when the teacher might use a general form of assessment, others when she uses a general evaluative sheet for guidance, and others when a measurement instrument is helpful. Music teachers do this quite often. They use assessment in rehearsals, they form rubrics to give feedback to students, and they send their students to solo and ensemble festivals. As always, it is important that when music teachers do this they recognize these practices as forms of assessment, and that they can articulate and defend these processes to evaluators.

Application to teaching: Vary assessments. Triangulation might suggest that teachers provide students with multiple opportunities to demonstrate their knowledge, skill, or growth. Performing, composing, moving, writing, discussing, and creating multidisciplinary projects are some of the varied ways students might demonstrate their knowledge about the content of a course. This could include asking students to complete a written test, perform, present a project, or work in small groups or individually, all on the same content. For example, in elementary general music, where students often learn the basics of rhythm, there is a variety of ways they could demonstrate what they have learned. They might perform rhythms on Orff instruments, sing, create, and notate a composition, or make graphic representations of rhythms using Legos. Each one of these activities shows another facet of students' understanding and ability to use rhythms. While one student may struggle with performing rhythms, she might excel at composing or creating graphic representations. Triangulation provides a more robust way of assessing what students know and can do.

Consider a recent unit or piece of music taught. What are some ways you might triangulate your assessment to provide multiple opportunities for students to demonstrate their knowledge, ability, and growth?

FORMATIVE ASSESSMENTS, SUMMATIVE ASSESSMENTS, AND DATA

Some readers might be confused by the examples of demonstrating rhythms through performing on Orff instruments, composing, singing, or manipulating Legos. They might argue, "Those aren't assessments; they're activities." It is important that teachers do not conceive of instruction and assessment as separate acts.

> Assessment and instruction are *not* separate acts. Instruction allows teachers to constantly assess and provide evidence of student learning and knowledge.

Assessment is usually thought of as a test at the end of a unit or lesson plan that determines whether students learned the material and assigns the student a grade. Instead, educators might think of every moment in the classroom as an opportunity to assess student learning. Every question answered, every note played, and every assignment provides evidence of what students know and what they can do (Wesolowski, 2014).

The difference between assessment embedded throughout instruction and an assessment at the end of instruction is the difference between summative assessment and formative assessment (Wiggins, 1998). *Summative assessment* is what is commonly thought of as assessment: an test or evaluation at the end of a learning segment that gauges and evaluates what students have learned or can do. This is important and necessary, but just as important is to assess along the way during learning. This is *formative assessment*. All teachers formatively assess. Effective teachers do it purposefully and often.

Teacher evaluation is sometimes worded in ways that do not make apparent these different forms of assessment. For example, the Marzano system uses the word *data*. This term usually refers to teachers using the results of assessments to make judgments about future learning as well as helping students gather and interpret information about their learning. The use of the science-derived word *data* might lead some educators and evaluators to think it refers only to the outcomes of summative assessment and measurement. They might think that only numbers count as data. However, it is important to think of data more as "evidence." This evidence might come from the results of general assessment, evaluation, and measurement. For general assessment, this might include conversations with students. Evaluations might include rubrics or general written comments to students. Measurements might include formal tests that are graded. All of these provide data or evidence. Teachers often use these forms of assessment, and sometimes teachers need to acknowledge the varied ways they gather data.

Application to teaching: Assess continually and seamlessly with instruction. The distinctions between summative and formative assessments might suggest that music teachers can think of instruction and assessment as simultaneous, blended processes, rather than separate entities (Earl, 2013). Every moment in the classroom is an opportunity to assess students. Every moment students do anything observable—answer a question, play, sing, move, write, or even misbehave— is an opportunity for a music teacher to assess their abilities and understanding and the effectiveness of instruction. When assessment is always part of instruction, then observations by evaluators, whether announced or unannounced, will demonstrate a teacher's assessment practices.

It is also important for teachers to create many formative assessments as they instruct. Providing many opportunities for students to demonstrate their understanding is a strong assessment strategy. Teachers need not think of these assessment moments as stopping instruction to take a quiz to measure student growth, although that may be appropriate at times. Instead, music teachers might use rich activities and assignments that provide evidence or data. For example, in a music theory class, music teachers might provide many opportunities to learn triads. They might ask students to play different triads on a piano, notate them, and write a composition as a way to become familiar with and use these chords. Each of these activities, in addition to serving as an instructional strategy, has the potential to be a formal or informal assessment. In addition, if documented in ways that are required of teacher evaluation, these examples can also serve as evidence of student growth.

To find examples of assessment, music teachers might consult the Model Cornerstone Assessments (MCA), developed by NAfME, for more samples of integrating assessment seamlessly with instruction. The MCA "provide an instructional and assessment framework into which teachers integrate their curriculum to help measure student learning" and demonstrate student growth through both formative and summative assessments (NAfME, 2014). Using the *National Core Arts Standards* (NCCAS, 2014) as a basis, the MCA outline tasks students might do as they create, perform, respond, and make connections. As NAfME describes, these assessments are not meant to be used to evaluate the quality of teaching;

rather, they are tools to improve student learning, curriculum planning, and instruction in a process-oriented way.

We have argued that music educators should assess students regularly and often. Good teachers do this consciously, and they also vary, or triangulate, how they assess. Good teachers use assessment, evaluation, and measurement, including formative and summative assessments, and they vary the types of assessments that reveal students' different understandings of the content of what is being assessed. While these are good practices, they rely on another practice of good assessment: assessing the right things. Consider the following absurd scenario:

> A music theory class has been working diligently on the fundamentals of music all year. The students have studied for their final examination, and they arrive to class on the day of the test. The teacher hands out the exam, which contains the following prompt: Demonstrate your knowledge of the causes of World War I by writing either an essay, a script for a documentary on the topic, or the lyrics to a song.

Everyone would surely agree that this test is not appropriate because it does not assess whether the students understand and can use the content of the class. If a student does not do well on this test, it does not mean he or she has not learned the material of the course. Conversely, if a student does well on the test, it only shows that she knows about World War I, not music theory.

Whether an assessment accurately assesses what it is intended to is called "validity" (Reynolds et al., 2010). Making sure a test has validity is ensuring that it specifically assesses what it is intended to with the students who are taking it. More specifically, the absurd theory test on World War I lacks "content validity" because it does not accurately assess the content of the course.

While the example of taking a history exam at the end of a music theory course is an unrealistic exaggeration, there are more subtle ways that teachers make mistakes regarding validity. A common one is grading students on behavior rather than the content or objectives of the class (Dueck, 2014). In other words, teachers often use grades as a classroom management strategy, rather than evaluating students' learning and abilities (Kohn, 1999, 2011). While teachers might have reasons to do this, from an assessment perspective this threatens the validity of assessments. For example, in elementary band or orchestra, the goal of a unit is usually for each student to demonstrate that he or she learned his or her part in the ensemble and that he or she can play three major scales and a short solo. The grade is determined by two criteria: 50 percent attendance at rehearsals, sectionals, and concerts, and 50 percent practice log. While these are valuable criteria, from an assessment perspective neither might be considered valid categories for assessing the larger goals. While attendance and practice logs may be important components of the unit and the larger music course, music teachers should be careful to make sure the assessment tool matches what is being assessed. Neither a student's attendance nor the amount of time a student practiced guarantees or demonstrates with validity whether he or she successfully completed the unit goal. There could be a student who consistently attends rehearsals and practices a great deal but is not able to play his or her music. Conversely, a student might be inconsistent in attendance or practicing but plays all the assigned music perfectly.

Teachers have good reason to encourage punctuality and establish a consistent practice routine. These are important skills that students need to develop and teachers will want to encourage and support. However, tying them to assessment when they are not the goals of the course, unit, or lesson lacks validity, and this is problematic for several reasons. First, it assumes that grades motivate students (Kohn, 1999). While some students certainly are motivated to achieve a higher grade, many students—frankly, those who often need extra help in these areas—are often not motivated to improve their grades in the way these criteria intend. The result is that such a process is ineffective.

Second, and perhaps more damaging, these grading criteria might contain bias against certain groups of people, giving them an unfair disadvantage. For example, in middle school general music, clarity, punctuality, and neatness are categories that students with attention deficit hyperactivity disorder (ADHD) struggle with (Zentall, 2006). In an ensemble, students who come from families that struggle financially might have difficulty securing transportation to rehearsals and might not be able to practice at home because they live in an apartment and might disturb their neighbors. And while they might be able to practice at school after the instructional day is over, or the teacher might secure transportation, there is still a disadvantage. In both these cases, the teacher is grading the students on something they cannot control. This only reinforces the inequalities in society. While teachers might not be able to control the disadvantages in society, they can control whether they reinforce them in their assessment practices and grading.

Application to teaching: Create valid assessments that accurately and fairly assess students' abilities, knowledge, and growth. Teachers, then, within assessment aspects of teacher evaluation, can make sure that their assessments assess what they hope to understand about students' abilities and knowledge. They can create pointed assessments that have validity and attempt to remove any aspects of their assessment that would not give an accurate picture of what students know and are able to do in regard to the aims and objectives of the class. This requires that music teachers be clear to themselves and to their students what the criteria for assessment are and that the latter are tightly aligned with the course objectives and/or district, state, or national standards.

To check for validity, teachers could look for ways that the assessments might be disadvantaging certain students or setting them up to not be successful. Do procedures that are put in place disadvantage students with learning disabilities? Does assessments favor students who have access to more resources? Are students required to practice at home or consult or use resources like a computer, the library, or books that they might not have access to? Does the assessment favor certain cultural practices? It is often difficult to find these factors that threaten validity, but as teachers create and revise assessments, they might ask: Does this assessment potentially penalize students for processes they cannot control? If the answer is yes because of disability, socioeconomic status, cultural background, or any other factor that does not directly assess the objectives, then the validity of the assessment is in question, and the teacher should aim to make it more accommodating to students' abilities and backgrounds.

APPLYING TO PRACTICE 6.5

- Consult a rubric or other evaluation criteria you have used in the classroom. What are the categories? How many are content related? How many are related to other areas, such as participation, clarity of speaking, etc.?
- Consider making two changes to this criteria to be more "content valid." What other content-specific categories would you add?

LISTENING AS A FORM OF ASSESSMENT

Listening to students' performances and providing feedback is a cornerstone of assessment in music education. The ability to listen and immediately provide feedback to students is unique to music education and is a strength. By standing in front of an ensemble or group of students, a music teacher can listen and get a general sense of students' performing strengths and areas that need improvement. This way of assessing, it seems, is easier than, say, a math teacher having to look at each student's work individually. Reviewing student work individually is not as immediate and is more time-consuming than the relatively efficient process that music teachers use. Also, this process of listening to students in the act of making music is perhaps a more authentic assessment than a multiple choice test. In the vignette that began this chapter, Sarah was attempting to make this argument when she said, "the concert is my test."

While pure listening as a form of assessment is an asset for music teachers, it has some problems from an assessment perspective. First, it does not precisely capture individual growth of students. Students can easily hide when the teacher listens to the whole group. Second, even if a teacher listens to each student individually, listening does not result in documented evidence of student performance and teacher feedback. A performance is ephemeral; there is no evidence that remains after it takes place. All that remains is the teachers' informed, but still subjective, experience of the performance. This is different than the math example we used. A math teacher has a record of what the student produced. Third, as we have described, a performance is not always an accurate representation of what is learned. It might not have validity as an evaluative tool. If performance is used as an improper assessment, there is no guarantee that it demonstrates knowledge of the information. It provides evidence, but that evidence may not be the best indicator of what students know.

Application to teaching: Understand the strengths and weaknesses of listening as assessment in music education. Music educators must weigh these positives and negatives when devising assessment strategies and communicating with evaluators. This includes advocating for the strengths of assessment as it is commonly used in music education, through listening, especially with an evaluator without a music background. An evaluator might look to measure a student performance. However, this might not be appropriate for music education. Using the language of assessment, evaluation, measurement, validity, and data and other terms will give teachers the vocabulary to advocate for listening and other forms of assessment that are central to music education.

While music teachers may advocate for performance as a means of assessment, they may also acknowledge its limitations. When teachers use group performance as a form of assessment, students can hide, performance is not documentable, and it might not best demonstrate what student know. To address these limitations, music teachers might form assessments that capture individual student growth. This could include triangulating performances with other sources of evidence, including journal prompts, presentations, verbal descriptions, and so forth. In addition, music teachers might find ways to document students' products as well as teacher feedback. Recordings of rehearsals or students' individual performances and the verbal feedback teachers give might be a way to capture students' progression over time. Teachers might also create a system whereby they provide written feedback to students. This could include keeping a file for each student that collects rubrics or other forms of feedback. This could also be achieved electronically. A teacher might create a digital portfolio, including recordings of a student—both individually and in the ensemble—and written feedback to that student. Commercially available online portfolio systems like MusicFirst and SmartMusic can help teachers generate, keep track of, and grade student work.

STRATEGIES FOR INCORPORATING ASSESSMENT IN MUSIC

These terms—assessment, evaluation, measurement, validity, data, and formative and summative assessments—and listening as assessment are only the tip of the iceberg of the concepts of assessment. Such terminology can become overwhelming for teachers. This creates problems and frustration for music teachers, who often assess through more authentic means like performance and projects like compositions. How do music educators continue to assess in authentic ways but make that work in systems of teacher evaluation?

We now turn to two situations in which teachers might have some control over the evaluation system. First, we discuss strategies to fulfill the assessment requirements found in the observational component of many teacher evaluation systems. Second, we address ways educators might create or select assessments that assess the student growth component of teacher evaluation. This includes forming assessments alone and how to approach situations in which teachers have no input on the assessments used.

CREATING ASSESSMENTS FOR OBSERVATIONS

As mentioned previously in the chapter, observation components often include the evaluation of teachers' assessment practices. As music teachers prepare for this aspect, they might keep in mind some of the tenets, best practices, and limitations described in the preceding section: (1) assessing continually and seamlessly with instruction; triangulating and varying assessment data; (2) creating valid assessments that accurately and fairly assess students' abilities, knowledge, and growth; (3) understanding the strengths and weaknesses of listening as assessment in music education; and (4) communicating effectively about assessment to evaluators. Table 6.2 summarizes these guidelines for assessment practices for observations and provides examples and questions music teachers can ask themselves about their assessments to improve their practice.

TABLE 6.2.

Guidelines for assessment practices for observation, examples, and questions

Criteria for Creating Assessments for Observation	Questions to Improve Assessment Practices
Use general assessment, evaluation, and measurement at appropriate times.	• Does a lesson, unit, or course include all three forms of assessment? • Does the teacher's instruction rely too heavily on one assessment strategy? • Is the form of assessment used the most appropriate to gather information on students and provide them with feedback? • Does instruction include opportunities to generally assess students and times to use stricter criteria to evaluate and possibly measure their learning?
Vary assessments.	• Are students given opportunities to demonstrate their knowledge and abilities in at least three different ways?
Assess continually and seamlessly with instruction.	• Is the teacher continually assessing? • Looking at each activity as an opportunity to formatively assess, what information does the activity provide about students' knowledge or abilities? If a teacher cannot answer that question, then the activity needs to be modified so that students are doing more and providing more evidence, or it needs to be eliminated and replaced with a different activity.
Create valid assessments that accurately and fairly assess students' abilities, knowledge, and growth.	• Do all assessments accurately and fairly assess students' abilities, knowledge, and growth? • Looking through summative assessments, do they have any criteria like those previously mentioned—punctuality, neatness, etc.—that might penalize students even if they know the content? If so, how can the teacher change the assessment so that it focuses on the content? • Noncontest aspects such as punctuality and neatness are important, so how can educators teach these skills without enforcing them through grading? • Do the assessments put certain students at a disadvantage: students with differing cultural backgrounds, learning disabilities, ADHD, or other disabilities?

(continued)

TABLE 6.2.

Continued

Criteria for Creating Assessments for Observation	Questions to Improve Assessment Practices
Understand the strengths and weaknesses of listening as assessment in music education.	• Does the teacher rely too heavily on listening to students' performances to assess? • Does listening to students' performances completely represent their knowledge of the content of the course? Are there other ways students can demonstrate their knowledge of the content? • When the teacher listens and provides feedback, how does he or she document student progress and feedback? • How does a teacher ensure that he or she gathers evidence from all students and provides feedback to all students?

APPLYING TO PRACTICE 6.6

Using your curriculum, answer the questions in table 6.2. Evaluating the entire curriculum at first might be too difficult or overwhelming. Therefore, you might want to reflect on and revise one unit or even one lesson plan at a time.

CREATING AN ASSESSMENT FOR THE STUDENT GROWTH COMPONENT OF TEACHER EVALUATION

As we have mentioned, in addition to the observation component, sometimes teachers are required to create their own assessment systems. For example, in schools in R2T states, for academic subjects where there are no standardized tests, a district must create SLO assessments. An SLO is a strategy to gather and document student growth. The practices on this vary, but often the general requirements are to assess students at the beginning of a course, create and implement a pedagogical strategy to help students grow, and then at the end of the course again assess student learning to see the results of that strategy.

Figure 6.2 represents a process that music educators may take to create SLOs or other assessments that fulfill the assessment of student growth components of teacher evaluation system. We describe each of these steps in detail here.

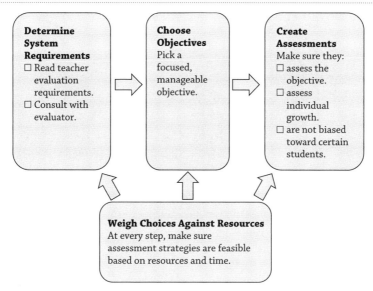

FIGURE 6.2. Process for creating and implementing an assessment for the student growth component of teacher evaluation

Determine system requirements. First, it is important for teachers to understand the language used in the requirements for these types of assessments. Do the requirements specify assessment, evaluation, or measurement? Often, teachers feel that an assessment must be a measurement. However, unless it is specifically stated that the SLO or other assessment must have a measurement component, then the teacher might have more flexibility than at first glance. Understanding the specific language can free music teachers to choose from a variety of assessment approaches. If measurement is not required, then teachers may not be required to provide a formalized pre- and post-test. Instead, they might be able to create a more flexible and authentic assessment system to gather information on students' abilities and knowledge at the beginning and end of the course. It is important to read the requirements carefully to come to an informed interpretation.

When making decisions about which assessment strategies to use, it is important that music educators communicate with their evaluators about the processes and reasons for selecting those strategies. It is essential to make sure that the evaluator is in agreement with the music teacher's interpretation. Sometimes this requires music teachers to communicate their perspectives. Often evaluators themselves are not fully aware of the differences among assessment, evaluation, and measurement. Their conception of assessment, particularly within teacher evaluation, might be to create a measurement. Being informed about the differences among these approaches, as well as having the ability to weigh the strengths and weaknesses of these differing ways to assess, will help music teachers advocate for themselves when speaking with evaluators. Afterward, if the music teacher disagrees with the evaluator's interpretation, he or she might come ready with specific language from the policy to support the interpretation and have a civil, constructive dialogue.

Choose objectives. After determining the parameters, music teachers might pick a focused, manageable objective to assess. Teachers hope to accomplish many objectives throughout a course. Some of these are better suited for evaluation systems than others. The objectives that are best to choose for the student growth component are easily assessed and do not take much time to administer. For that reason, the objective assessed should be as targeted as possible.

The objective of expressivity serves as an example. Expressivity is an important, common long-term objective of ensembles. However, this objective is not well suited to evaluation systems when measurement is required. Expression is too ambiguous a concept and is too difficult to measure. For that reason, it might be better to choose a more modest and less ambiguous objective like identifying dynamics. Performing and identifying dynamics is an essential part of playing expressively. Focusing on this aspect of expressivity for the student growth component is more developmentally feasible and easier to measure. In this way, a music teacher can address expressivity but focus on one aspect that is better suited to evaluation systems. A music teacher can conduct pre- and post-tests or other assessments in a way that conforms easily to the rules of SLOs while still working on larger goals.

This does not mean that expressive performances should not be a goal for young musicians or that expressivity is reduced to the correct performance of dynamics. Students are entirely capable of thinking and performing expressively in developmentally appropriate ways. A music education, even from the very beginning, would be incomplete if students were not required to engage with the concept of expressivity. What this does mean is that it might not be the best objective to choose to assess for an SLO or measurement of student growth. The logistics of capturing students' performances via recording or other means and rating those performances often do not elide well with SLOs and other assessments of student growth in teacher evaluation systems.

To be sure, this brings up a dilemma. If teacher evaluation systems' assessment and measurement of growth fail to capture an essential and perhaps the central goal of music education, expression, then why should music teachers continue to participate in such a system? This is indeed an important question. We advocate that music teachers be able to communicate these issues of validity to their evaluators, something we address in more detail in the next chapter. However, it is just as important to remember that teacher evaluation is a requirement that music teachers must fulfill, and they might not necessarily aim to have it completely capture and assess all aspects of their instruction. Instead, teachers might aim to assess objectives that are focused, manageable, and unambiguous, even if they do not completely capture the heart of music education.

Create assessments. After music teachers determine the objectives they think are appropriate to assess, they then might create valid assessments. These guidelines follow the same advice given throughout this chapter on strong assessment strategies. First, music teachers should take care to ensure that their assessments evaluate what they aim to assess and not something else. This means that the objective lines up with the assessment. Also, if music teachers have the flexibility within the requirements, they might choose not to measure and instead choose an evaluation strategy to best assess the objective. They might also make sure not to assess aspects like punctuality and neatness if those are not the lesson objectives. Second, music teachers might ensure that the assessment captures individual components. Each student must be directly assessed and there must be evidence of the student's performance. Finally, music teachers might also ensure that assessments are not biased toward or against certain students. They may consider students' socioeconomic, racial, and gender identities, as well as in what ways the assessment may disadvantage students with learning and physical disabilities.

Weigh choices against resources. At every step of this process, it is important that music teachers check for any other hindrances that might affect the administering of the assessment. For example, the teaching schedule might determine what sort of objectives to assess and how to assess them. For classes that meet only once a week or for part of the year, the teacher might choose manageable objectives and assessments that are quick to administer. Similarly, there might not be sufficient resources, like materials or instruments, to effectively administer the assessment. If there are any limitations, the music teacher can take these into consideration when selecting the best objectives and assessment strategies to employ. For example, a teacher might have the flexibility to capture student growth through an online portfolio and feels that it authentically demonstrates students' learning throughout the year. However, because the class meets only once a week, there are performances to prepare for, and the school computers and software are difficult to secure, the teacher might ultimately choose a more modest pre- and post-test.

Weighing resources and time is particularly important if teachers are required to create assessments in committees that include multiple teachers and serve different schools. Once again, teachers might pay particular attention to the validity of assessments in terms of whether a proposed assessment might favor certain teachers or settings over others. In this process, it is important to understand the differences between teachers' resources and contexts. Do some teachers' classes meet for less instructional time than others'? Is there less access to resources? For example, if within a district one teacher's middle school ensemble meets ninety minutes every other day, while another teachers' group meets after school every other week, then educators might form assessments that account for that inequality in time. Similarly, if students are required to take the same assessment across different subareas of music education, teachers might pay attention to any biases that could arise. A proposed assessment, for example, might favor orchestra students over general music students. Music teachers might aim to devise an assessment that fairly assesses the students (and teacher) regardless of the course in which the students are enrolled.

ADDRESSING ASSESSMENTS MANDATED BY THE DISTRICT OR STATE

There are times when teachers do not have control of how student growth is assessed. Teachers might be required to administer a standardized test determined by administration, policy, or even law. Unfortunately, there are times when students' growth is measured by factors that have little or nothing to do with their music education. Sometimes growth is determined by standardized test scores in other subjects. A teacher might be evaluated on, say, how students perform on a standardized English test. Sometimes the student growth component of a teacher's evaluation might be determined by school-wide factors, including students' attendance or the performance and climate of a school. These seem like lamentable and inappropriate measures; they have little validity because they do not measure student growth in music and are beyond the control of music teachers.

In these situations, the teacher might specifically focus on the criteria and targets of the measures of student growth. Teachers can do this by focusing on the aspects that they can control: the observation component and improving instruction to make changes in student growth. For example, if teachers are required to use a standardized test that measures student growth in music, then it is important to understand what the test evaluates. Understanding specifically what the test aims to measure and how it does so can help teachers create curricula that best prepare students for that test. Similarly, if growth is measured in areas besides music, then the teacher might find out specifically what is measured. For example, if student attendance is a component in the measure, music teachers might make efforts to help students attend school. Talking with students during class about the importance of attendance, including any barriers they might encounter that inhibit them from attending, can be useful in targeting the attendance component. If school climate is a measure, then a teacher might work on improving the climate in the classroom along the measures that are articulated. Finally, if the measures are in standardized tests in other subjects, teachers might work to incorporate parts of those subjects into their class. If English scores are a measure, then teachers might incorporate issues of literacy as reading and writing; see chapter 5 on literacy for more information.

While these approaches are not perfect, and some music teachers might feel it is unfair to contribute their instructional time to nonmusical objectives, others might ultimately want or need to choose such strategies. Some music teachers might like the certainty of having a clear objective to focus their curriculum and instruction. For others, tailoring instruction to meet the needs of these assessments might be unappealing. They might conclude that agreeing to participate in what they see as an unfair system "feeds the beast," legitimizing unfair measurements and normalizing these means of evaluating teachers. In that situation, teachers might opt to advocate for themselves and their programs. In the final chapter we address how teachers might go about advocating within teacher evaluation.

SUMMARY

Assessment is a critical component of teacher evaluation. Often teachers must demonstrate practices of assessment in their teaching through observation by an evaluator, and students' "growth" must be evaluated. The assessment of student growth is often controversial because it is difficult to assess growth in valid ways. In preparation for assessment in teacher evaluation, music teachers might create a variety of assessment strategies. These strategies (1) use general assessment, evaluation, and measurement at appropriate times; (2) are valid by assessing content and not penalizing things students cannot control, like disabilities or cultural backgrounds; and (3) use both formal and summative assessments that blend assessment and instruction. By using these principles in instruction; creating assessments of student growth; and communicating with evaluators, administrators, and other colleagues, music educators can succeed in teacher evaluation systems. By using these strategies from the beginning, Sarah the chorus teacher, who in the vignette was unable to successfully complete the assessment component of teacher evaluation, can take a more proactive and ultimately successful approach.

Sarah the chorus director meets with her principal to discuss teacher evaluation for the year. As they discuss her goals together, Sarah listens to her principal's advice and makes changes to her plans. Eventually they come to a place of disagreement. The principal voices concerns about Sarah's assessment strategies. "Your plans for the year do not include any evidence of your assessing students," he says. "That's interesting," replies Sarah, "because I have been purposeful in my preparation for assessment for the coming year. I value and appreciate your perspective. So can you tell me more, so I can understand? What evidence do I lack?" "Where's the paperwork from your students?" he replies. "When I taught math, the final exam provided documented proof of how each student did in the course. I don't see any of that. I suggest you give more multiple choice tests and regularly give students the scores of their tests so they know their progress." "OK," replies Sarah. "As you know, music and math are different in many ways. Assessment tends to be a little different in music, particularly in chorus. We often do not have tangible proof like a paper-and-pen test. This is a blessing and a curse; it tends to be a more authentic form of assessment, but you're right, the results aren't as document-able. Because of that, I want the concert to serve as a good, authentic indicator of whole group progress. But, I realize that this doesn't always capture individual growth the whole year. So after the concert I will have them fill out a reflection sheet that discusses how they think they individually performed on the concert. Also, throughout the year I have had the students keep a portfolio of their playing. They have articulated their goals for the year and regularly recorded themselves to document progress. I periodically check their portfolios and give them written feed-back. The first performance serves as a way to gather their initial level and the last recording to gauge their results at the end." "OK, fine," the principal responds. "But that's not a pre-test and post-test model. You haven't measured student progress." "True," replies Sarah, "I haven't measured; you're correct. But as I understand it, the evaluation doesn't require measurement. It asks for assessment of students at the beginning, to devise a learning plan based on that assessment, and then to do another assessment to assess whether the objectives of the learning plan were met. I think this more open assessment is more appropriate because it is more re-sponsive to the needs of the students and captures the ambiguity of music making, in which there is often interpretation and subjectivity in whether a performance is good." "Hmm, I have to think about this," the principal says. "It seems like you might have some reservations," Sarah responds, sensing that he needs more con-vincing. "What if we continue to dialogue about this throughout the year? I can show you the goals I have devised for the students based on the first recordings after I've collected them, in two weeks. Then we can continue to discuss ways that we both think they'll satisfy the teacher evaluation requirements for student growth." "All right" says the principal. "This is different, but you've always been open to my suggestions, so I'm willing to see how this goes."

ADDITIONAL RESOURCES ON ASSESSMENT

Assessment is a large area of study. We have only covered some basic areas and how they apply to teachers' use of assessment within teacher evaluation systems. Readers interested in additional explanations of the terms used or more information on how practicing music teachers might create more valid assessments and detect bias might consult the following resources on assessment in music education and education in general.

Brophy, T. (2010). *The practice of assessment in music education: Frameworks, models, and designs*. Chicago, IL: GIA Publications.

Barbot, B., & Lubart, T. (2012). Creative thinking in music: Its nature and assessment through musical exploratory behaviors. *Psychology of Aesthetics, Creativity, and the Arts*, 6, 231–242. doi:10.1037/a0027307

Brophy, T. S. (2000). *Assessing the developing child musician: A guide for general music teachers*. Rochester, NY: Boydell & Brewer Ltd.

Denis, J. M. (2017, November 7). Assessment in music: A practitioner introduction to assessing students. *Update: Applications of Research in Music Education*. doi:10.1177/8755123317741489

Dueck, M. (2014). *Grading smarter, not harder: Assessment strategies that motivate kids and help them learn*. Alexandria, VA: ASCD.

Fautley, M. (2010). *Assessment in music education*. New York, NY: Oxford University Press.

Fautley, M., & Savage, J. (2008). *Assessment for learning and teaching in secondary schools*. Thousand Oaks, CA: Sage.

Giudici, C., Rinaldi, C., & Krechevsky, M. (2001). *Making learning visible: Children as individual and group learners*. Cambridge, MA: Project Zero, Harvard Graduate School of Education.

Hughes, D., & Keith, S. (2015). Linking assessment practices, unit-level outcomes and discipline-specific capabilities in contemporary music studies. In D. Lebler, G. Carey, & S. Harrison (Eds.), *Assessment in music education: From policy to practice* (pp. 171–193). New York: Springer. doi:10.1007/978-3-319-10274-0_12

Wesolowski, B. (2014). Documenting student learning in music performance: A framework. *Music Educators Journal*, 101(1), 77–85. doi:10.1177/0027432114540475

PLANS FOR TRACKING STUDENT GROWTH

The following are plans that track student growth in ways similar to SLOs and other assessments. These plans demonstrate scenarios in which the teacher initially assesses students, reviews the evidence or data, creates a teaching plan to address areas of misunderstanding, and finally reassesses to determine if the strategy was effective and students have improved. The first plan includes a scenario in which a beginning instrumental teacher must measure using a paper-and-pen test. In the second, an elementary general music teacher must create and use a district-wide assessment, but can use students' musical performance as data for the assessment. The third plan involves a high school choral teacher who has great flexibility and applies innovative student-led forms of documenting and assessing student growth.

ELEMENTARY BAND OR ORCHESTRA

One of Jacob's yearly goals is to have his beginning orchestra students play with expression. His teacher evaluation system, however, does not allow the flexibility to record students' abilities through performance tests that might capture students' nuanced knowledge of expression in music or their ability to perform with expression. Instead, the requirements for assessment of student growth are quite restrictive, in which student growth must be measured and assessment be administered through a written test. In order to meet these criteria and to keep his assessment of student growth measurable, Jacob focuses on an essential component of playing expressively: dynamics. He decides that his assessment of students' growth will measure their knowledge of the traditional terms of dynamics and how to produce them on the instruments. The following plan does not assess all of his goals for the first year, nor does it display or assess a complete picture of their abilities to play expressively. However, it does meet the criteria for the student growth requirement of teacher evaluation and is a manageable, targeted assessment that allows him to focus on an aspect of one of his goals for the first year. It also provides him with some data to help plan his instruction.

Plan

1. **Administer pre-test on expression.** Students are given a written pre-test of dynamics. Jacob ensures the test is valid by making sure it is worded appropriately for fifth-grade students' reading abilities. This test consists of multiple choice questions like the following:

    An *f* written in music means the player (performer/musician) should:
    a. Play loud
    b. Play soft
    c. Play medium loud
    d. Play medium soft

2. **Analyze the results to create and teach lesson plans.** Jacob scores the pre-test. He notices that some students have some knowledge of these terms while others do not. Based on this knowledge, he creates lesson plans that are adequately differentiated to help students learn these terms. He is also careful to sequence the lessons so that he starts simple, slowly adding complexity. For example, he develops flash cards with dynamic markings on one side and definitions on the other. He helps students apply the new knowledge of dynamics to interpret music, to be able to perform the dynamics on their instruments, and ultimately to play with expression appropriate for the abilities of beginning instrumentalists. Jacob starts the class by playing for

students, asking them what dynamic he was performing. A group of students is selected in each class to perform a scale for the class, deciding how they will alter dynamics in their performance. Students in the class need to identify the dynamic changes. Jacob does this to assess the students in two ways: in both their performance (the group playing the scale) and their description/response to the performance (the rest of the class).

3. **Administer a post-test on expression.** At the end of the semester, Jacob administers a post-test similar to the pre-test. While the questions are not identical, he asks similar multiple choice questions about dynamics. After scoring the tests, he creates a chart of students' individual growth, marking each student's score on the pre- and post-tests. While not every student improved significantly, the majority of the class showed significant growth, demonstrating Jacob's ability to pre-assess, devise a teaching plan, and assess the effectiveness of the plan.

ELEMENTARY GENERAL MUSIC

One of the goals of Maria's district's curriculum is for kindergarteners to sing in tune by the end of the year. Her teacher evaluation system allows some flexibility in how data or evidence is recorded and how teachers can use their professional judgment in interpreting this evidence, but all music teachers must evaluate in the same way. The committee decides that all teachers will evaluate kindergartners' ability to sing in tune through singing games.

Plan

1. **Pre-assess students' singing ability.** On the first day of class, the teachers teach a song that prompts the students to individually echo the teacher. This song could be a hello song or the "Who Has the Penny?" singing game. This activity enables the teachers to assess the students' individual singing abilities. Within the first month of classes, Maria videorecords the students singing the song. After class, she watches the video and grades the students using a rubric that she and the other teachers have crafted.

2. **Analyze the evidence to create and teach lesson plans.** Based on the rubric, Maria creates lesson plans that will help students develop their singing voices. These plans include activities she knows are effective every year, like siren exercises and her favorite songs in a variety of styles. She also continues to address other aspects of her curriculum, including listening, keeping a beat, and experimenting with different sounds through simple composition exercises. Another teacher also decides to periodically sing the original singing game she used to assess the students. She does this informally, without the rubric, but listens through the lens of the rubric, keeping track of where the students are showing signs of improvement and what else might

be worked on. Instead of assigning a score, she writes short evaluative notes about her students to document areas of progress and areas of her planning she might modify to further help students. Meanwhile the other teachers also use the songs and activities they have found effective. Throughout the year they share these ideas and borrow from one another, but each teacher has his or her unique way to improve students' singing abilities.

3. **Post-assess students' singing ability.** Toward the end of the school year Maria repeats the process she used at the beginning of the year. She has students sing the song, videorecords it, and then scores the students' performances using the rubric. Through this process, she has documented student growth.

HIGH SCHOOL CHORUS

Sarah is given great flexibility in her teacher evaluation system. Through ongoing dialogue, in which she points to specific language in the teacher evaluation policy, she is able to convince her evaluator that assessment need not be measurement. They agree that she is required to pre-assess, create a plan, and re-assess. As part of the Danielson (2013) framework, she is also encouraged to help students to contribute input and drive the direction of instruction, including devising assessment criteria and tracking their own progress. She wants to highlight this aspect, because including student input is also a principle she values as an educator. Sarah decides to devise the assessment and plan with the students that captures these student-centered components.

Plan
1. **Articulate parameters to the students.** In the first week of class Sarah explains that the students are required to put on a performance at the end of the year. She lets them pick the repertoire they want to play, with her guidance. Sarah wants to take care to coach her students about repertoire selection. She encourages them to think about music they are passionate about, what they like to listen to, and the types of music they enjoy performing. She warns them that selecting only music they like may limit their broadening of interests and asks them to think about diverse selections of style and time period. Sarah also asks that they consider their audience, the strengths and weaknesses of their ensemble, and how much time they realistically have to prepare all of the music.

2. **Determine goals with students.** The students decide that they want to sing some popular songs, both as a group and as solos. In addition, with a little bit of nudging by Sarah they also decide to sing a motet by Palestrina. Based on the music they choose, she has a discussion with them about what will be the challenges of performing these compositions. Through discussion facilitated by Sarah, the students realize that for the pop songs they need to arrange

the music, because an arrangement suitable for their voice parts is not available, or arrangements are too difficult to read. For the Palestrina motet, they need to select an edition. They also realize that they need to be able to switch between these styles, and that the intonation on all the pieces will be particularly tricky. Based on these observation, they make a list of goals for the year.

3. **Devise instruction with students to achieve goals.** Throughout the year, Sarah and the students devise ways to address their goals through rehearsals and classroom activities. They document this process in a portfolio, which includes recordings of rehearsals and students' solos, write-ups of rehearsals and goals, and students' arrangements. The portfolio also includes student self-assessments of their goals. The students are asked to write reflections on their own individual performances and also on the group as a whole. Sarah also contributes to the class and student portfolio and asks that students respond to her critiques verbally or in writing to demonstrate knowledge of what she is asking them to improve.

4. **Evaluate with students to what degree the students achieved the goals.** At the end of the year, after the performance, the class reviews their goals to evaluate the degree to which they have achieved them for the year. Each student writes up a one-page summary detailing his or her views on his or her individual progress as well as the progress of the entire class. Sarah submits all of these materials as documentation of her assessment of student growth.

7

TALKING TO EVALUATORS

THROUGHOUT THIS BOOK we have stressed the need to understand the history, uses, and language of teacher evaluation in order to successfully maneuver through the process, improve practice, and grow professionally. As we described in chapter 1, teachers may encounter different uses of teacher evaluation. Sometimes the evaluation process may be a support and develop model (Gabriel & Woulfin, 2017), in which the teacher is viewed as a professional learner and observations are used to collect data on what and how to support teachers. At other times the evaluation may be a measure and sort model, in which the teacher is seen more as an employee and observations are used to assess the quality of teaching and provide a rating.

Looking at both the support and develop and measure and sort approaches, in chapters 1 and 2 we provided an overview of education policy and teacher evaluation. We stressed the importance of music teachers understanding policies in order to navigate them in their practice. We framed teacher evaluation through three types of knowledge: content knowledge, pedagogical knowledge, and pedagogical content knowledge (Shulman, 1987). Content knowledge is the teacher's knowledge of the subject material. In music, this includes the ability to play an instrument, correct errors, or recall historical information about a composer or text, among other knowledge of music. Pedagogical knowledge is knowledge of how to teach. It can be an understanding of learning theories, creating and implementing lesson plans, or changing classroom management techniques based on students. Pedagogical content knowledge combines content and pedagogical knowledge, with careful attention to the ways in which content informs how students learn. In music, this includes ways to introduce fast and slow, create an ostinato, or help students interpret the text painting of a piece, as well as other pedagogical techniques and strategies unique to music education.

As we described in chapter 2, knowing the differences between general pedagogical knowledge and pedagogical content knowledge provides a way to balance advocacy and openness. This allows music teachers to be open to what an evaluator says while also advocating for their pedagogical choices and identifying strengths and weaknesses. We then extended general pedagogical knowledge and pedagogical content knowledge to practice. In chapters 3 through 6 we explored large ideas related to teacher evaluation that often puzzle music teachers—including questioning, differentiation, literacy, and assessment—and offered strategies to implement them in music classrooms. As a whole, in the previous chapters we have introduced a framework for how to engage with teacher evaluation and then looked at how music teachers might navigate these systems in areas that are particularly difficult.

In this final chapter we synthesize these themes to delve deeper into music teachers' discussions with evaluators. First, we describe the key components of teacher evaluation discussions: the rules and procedures required of teacher evaluation systems, the evaluator, and the music teacher. Second, we provide advice for preparing for meetings. Next, we provide a framework for listening to and responding to feedback during meetings. Finally, we describe steps music teachers can take after meetings to spark growth and maintain communication with evaluators.

KNOWING THE KEY COMPONENTS OF TEACHER EVALUATION DISCUSSIONS

Every interaction within teacher evaluation, including meetings and observations, includes three key components: (1) the rules and procedures of the evaluation system, (2) the evaluator, and (3) the teacher. First among these is the evaluation system itself, including the rules, procedures, and context that are part of that evaluation system. In addition to the teacher evaluation system are both the evaluator and the teacher, who interpret the rules and procedures. Both the evaluator's and the

> Navigating teacher evaluation requires a balance of knowing the rules and procedures of the evaluation system; knowing the evaluator's background, biases, and pressures; and knowing your own biases and pressures.

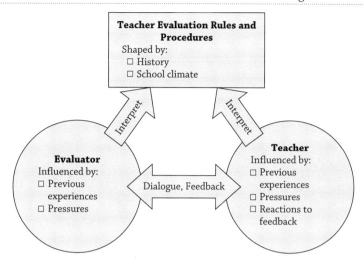

FIGURE 7.1. The components of teacher evaluation interactions

teacher's interpretations of those rules and procedures are influenced by pre-vious experiences, biases, and personal traits. Finally, the evaluator and teacher share—or sometimes fail to share—their interpretations with each other through dialogue and feedback. Figure 7.1 represents these three components and their influence. By knowing these three main components, music teachers can begin to engage in the final component—dialogue and feedback, described in detail later in this chapter.

KNOW THE TEACHER EVALUATION SYSTEM

As a starting place, music teachers may benefit from knowing the official policies about what is required of them and how they are assessed in teacher evalua-tion. As we discussed in chapter 1, knowing the structure of school or district evaluation policies and systems can help music teachers navigate the evaluation process. Music teachers need to know the components of the system, such as how many times they are required to be observed and how many observations are announced or unannounced. It is also useful to know the requirements for writing and demonstrating yearly goals and how they play a part in the evalu-ation rating. Sometimes a percentage of a teacher's overall evaluation score is based on outcomes, or students' test scores. Music teachers also need to know what comprises the evaluation system, including what components of teaching and professional practice are being evaluated and how the rubrics are structured. Some frameworks scale their rubrics from "ineffective" to "highly effective" or on a numerical basis. Some provide teaching examples to demonstrate and explain what counts as adequate demonstration for these criteria. Finally, music teachers may know the history and competing uses of these systems by policymakers, administrators, teachers, and others. By reviewing chapter 1, music teachers can begin to gather a deep knowledge of the official rules of the system as well as the unwritten procedures that surround teacher evaluation in their schools.

APPLYING TO PRACTICE 7.1

- If you have been through the evaluation process before, recall a situation in which you had a conversation with your evaluator about a teaching tool or technique not written in the evaluation rubric (the "unwritten procedures" such as assessment, differentiation, and literacy). What did your evaluator tell you about this? How did you respond? Where would your knowledge of the rubric and teaching tool help you to speak with your evaluator about implementing the technique?
- Take your evaluation system and look for places where certain teaching aspects (questioning, differentiation, literacy, assessment) might be implied or applied. How might you use your pedagogical content knowledge to help your evaluator know *what* to observe in terms of musical content?

KNOW THE EVALUATOR

While knowing the requirements of the evaluation system is an important first step toward actively participating in the evaluation process, it is also important to realize that the evaluator is responsible for interpreting the protocols and procedures. As we also noted in chapter 1, these interpretations are often influenced by evaluators' pressures and biases. An evaluator might be dealing with the pressures of raising standardized test scores, keeping graduation rates high, maintaining a safe learning environment, or creating school-wide goals and improvement plans. Evaluators, like teachers, also have many responsibilities and may not have sufficient time to implement teacher evaluation effectively. As we noted in the vignette at the beginning of the introduction, this lack of time sometimes leads to "doorknob" observations, in which the evaluator spends little time in the classroom.

Evaluators also have previous experiences as teachers. As we noted in chapter 2, sometimes evaluators have previous experience as, say, English teachers or math teachers, and no experience teaching music. This may provide them with general pedagogical knowledge but not pedagogical content knowledge in music. These experiences may lead evaluators to have biases and expectations about what counts as good teaching.

Pressures, experiences, and biases influence how an evaluator interprets the procedures, rules, and assessment criteria of teacher evaluation systems. Teacher evaluation is aimed at assessing and helping each teacher individually. However, evaluators often use teacher evaluation as a means to accomplish school-wide goals rather than to develop individual teachers. Evaluators often hope that connecting teacher evaluation to school-wide goals can potentially encourage teachers to "understand their work within the larger contexts of which it is a part . . . and support a school culture of continuous organizational learning" (Holland, 2005, p. 73). For example, if a school is labeled as a school in need of improvement by the state for having low test scores, the principal may be concerned with "norming" instruction. "Norming" is a tactic whereby teachers are required to use similar, consistent instructional techniques, such as incorporating "turn and talks" into their daily instruction or administering an exit slip at the end of each class as a quick assessment. So, in an observation an evaluator may be looking for "norming" traits that will contribute to large-scale improvement. In this way, even though teacher evaluation is supposed to be aimed at the improvement of an individual teacher's growth, the evaluator is using teacher evaluation as a way to accomplish larger organizational goals.

It is important for music educators to know, as much as possible, these pressures, biases, and experiences that influence evaluators. Sometimes this is easy to accomplish because the evaluator is self-aware and a clear communicator. However, often evaluators are not aware of how their biases and pressures influence their interpretations, or they are not effective at communicating. We discuss in detail later in the chapter how educators can discover and successfully deal with the biases of evaluators who do not communicate well.

APPLYING TO PRACTICE 7.2

Take a moment to create a comprehensive picture of your evaluator. What pressures does he or she have in his or her roles and responsibilities? What biases do you feel he or she carries? Does he or she tend to favor or look for particular pedagogical practices?

KNOW "YOURSELF"

Just as evaluators have pressures, experiences, and biases that influence how they interpret evaluation system requirements, so do music educators. Music teachers have expectations for and from the community, including concerts and competitions. These expectations may influence what a music teacher prioritizes in teacher evaluation, and this may differ significantly from the evaluator's expectations. Music teachers also have biases and preferred methods or philosophies of music education. While teachers might have these pressures, it is often difficult to be self-aware and pinpoint them. It is important for music teachers to discover and acknowledge their pressures and expectations so that they can clearly articulate them to evaluators.

In addition to having these pressures and biases, music teachers, like everyone else, respond to feedback in varying ways. Without being aware, people often play subconscious psychological tricks on themselves to avoid criticism. Sometimes, because of this, music teachers can misinterpret feedback or blow comments out of proportion. Feedback specialists Stone and Heen (2015) refer to the factors that cause these types of reactions as "triggers." They have identified three triggers that inhibit people from accurately hearing and implementing feedback: truth triggers, relationship triggers, and identity triggers.

Truth triggers are comments that cause someone to become defensive about the content of feedback. Upon hearing feedback about incorporating more choice in his classroom, a teacher might have a knee-jerk reaction and say, "That's not going to work. My students are too disrespectful to be given freedom. What's wrong with that evaluator?!" *Relationship triggers* are interactions that cause reactions based on the relationship with the person who gives the feedback. A teacher might say, "Sure, he wants me to incorporate more choice, but what does he know, he's never taught music. Also, he doesn't seem to follow his own advice when he runs faculty meetings!" Finally, *identity triggers* are factors that cause someone to attach criticism to his or her self-worth, rather than seeing the feedback as a comment on one aspect of his or her performance. A teacher might say, "Oh no, he wants me to incorporate student choice. I can't do anything right; I'm just bad at teaching. I should just give up!"

These triggers add a psychological dimension to the bridging of general pedagogical knowledge and pedagogical content knowledge that we have advocated throughout this book. Truth and relationship triggers can inhibit bridging the gap as well as explain why people use it as an excuse to not receive feedback. A response like, "I'm not listening to him, he's never taught music" is a result of a relationship trigger, while saying, "What he says won't work in music" results from a truth trigger. In order to bridge the gap between general pedagogical knowledge and pedagogical content knowledge, music teachers must acknowledge these triggers. However, this works the other way as well. Music teachers can use the differences between general pedagogical knowledge and pedagogical content knowledge as a way to justify their triggers and not receive feedback. For music educators to bridge this gap, they need to know themselves by understanding when they might face these triggers in feedback.

APPLYING TO PRACTICE 7.3

Think about some feedback you have received from an evaluator. How have you responded? Did the feedback trigger particular responses for you? Was it more reactive, such as a truth trigger; a relationship trigger, in which you positioned your evaluator in an opposing light; or an identity trigger, turning more inward and questioning your teaching value?

PUTTING IT TOGETHER: KNOWING THE COMPONENTS OF DISCUSSIONS

By knowing the requirements of teacher evaluation as well as an evaluator's pressures, expectations, and biases, music teachers can anticipate the types of questions that an evaluator might ask. Primary to this is understanding the requirements on paper. However, it is important to understand that the evaluator might focus on specific areas of those requirements. Table 7.1 lists some questions a music teacher might want to seek answers to before speaking with an evaluator, as well as the sources that may provide some answers.

PREPARING: ANTICIPATING QUESTIONS

In addition to understanding the components of teacher evaluation, music teachers may also try to anticipate specific questions evaluators could ask. In both formal and informal conversations with teachers, we have found that evaluators often ask four common questions to begin dialogue in a pre-observation:

- What do you hope to accomplish?
- How do you know whether students have accomplished that goal?
- How will you let students know their progress toward achieving those goals?
- What information should I know about the students in this class?

TABLE 7.1.

Questions to consider and sources to consult regarding an evaluator's background and pressures

- **Components:** What are the actual requirements of the teacher evaluation?
  - *Sources to consult*: teacher evaluation system, state laws, policies
- **Evaluator's Background:** What is the evaluator's background? Find out the following:
  - What academic subject he or she taught.
  - Where he or she taught (suburban, urban, rural, or other characteristics of the community).
  - What age level(s) he or she taught.
  - What evaluation approach he or she favors–measure and sort vs. support and develop model—and what type of communicator he or she is.
  - *Sources to consult*: ask the evaluator; discuss with colleagues
- **Evaluator's Pressures:**
  - Are there any initiatives that are required of the evaluator? These may include norming instruction, raising test scores, or targeting learning goals for specific student demographics.
  - Is the evaluator required to do an abundance of teacher observations?
  - *Sources to consult*: newsletters from the principal and superintendent, memos to faculty, the topics of required professional development sessions, state policies and laws

It makes sense for an evaluator to ask these questions. The first—"What do you hope to accomplish?"—is asking the teacher to state the objectives of the class. The second—"How do you know whether students have accomplished that goal?"—is a matter of assessment. The evaluator wants to determine if the music teacher has considered how to assess the objectives, how to accurately determine if a student has accomplished a goal, and other qualities of strong assessment practices that we discussed in chapter 6. The third question—"How will you let students know their progress toward achieving those goals?"—is a matter of feedback. An evaluator asks this question to know if the music teacher is using information from the assessments to help students improve and achieve the objectives. Finally, the fourth question—"What information should I know about the students in this class?"—helps the evaluator gather any specific information on students and the class. This includes whether any students have individual education plans (IEPs) or other special education modifications, classroom management issues, issues that arise because of scheduling, or other factors that evaluators might not know about, but that might help them provide feedback to the teacher.

In post-observation meetings, we have seen evaluators ask three overarching questions:

- What was your goal?
- What do you think went well?
- What would you change if you had the opportunity?

These questions help the teacher demonstrate the ability to reflect on and improve his or her teaching. Asking the last question—"What would you change if you had the opportunity?"—gives the evaluator an idea of what the teacher thinks happened in the class and, just as important, what comes next (Cote & Bernard, 2017). This question also provides the opportunity for both evaluator and teacher to plan for the future and implement the feedback.

Music teachers may want to come prepared to answer these questions in a conversation with evaluators. At first thought, a music teacher might focus on the aspects that are common to music education; in other words, concerns of pedagogical content knowledge. However, music educators may answer such questions differently depending on the evaluator. It is important to shape the answers in ways that (1) demonstrate general pedagogical knowledge and (2) take into account the background and pressures of the evaluator. Table 7.2 provides a way to organize how music educators can create effective answers tailored to different types of evaluators.

While this table might help music teachers focus and tailor their responses, it is important to mention some notes of caution. First, this table (and particularly the last column) is not a device for music educators simply to figure out what the evaluator wants to hear. As we discussed in chapter 3 on using questions with students, if answers are focused toward figuring out the answer that the questioner has in mind, the exercise does not become a learning experience. Instead, this is a device for music educators to translate their sincere concerns

> When music teachers anticipate the questions that might be asked in a meeting, they can better prepare and exhibit their pedagogical content knowledge in their responses to an evaluator's feedback.

and thoughts into language that evaluators will understand. Second, music teachers should not think that evaluators will automatically ask these questions. The chart

TABLE 7.2.

Ways music teachers and evaluators might respond to overarching reflection questions

	How a music teacher or evaluator with a music background might answer (PCK, CK)	How an evaluator whose background is not in music might answer (PK)	Other answers to nuance these answers based on an evaluators' pressures and background
What do you hope to accomplish?			
How do you know whether students have accomplished that goal?			
How will you let students know their progress toward achieving those goals?			
What information should I know about the students in this class?			
What do you think went well?			
What would you change if you had the opportunity?			

merely provides a way to think through possible questions an evaluator *might* ask. For music teachers who would like to better anticipate questions, it might be beneficial to consult with colleagues who have worked with a particular evaluator to better understand that person's perspectives and areas that he or she has focused on in the past.

APPLYING TO PRACTICE 7.4

- Using table 7.2, think about how you might respond to the questions. Recall the "third turn" of questioning from chapter 3. How might your evaluator respond to your answers? How would you then respond to the evaluator's responses?

DURING THE MEETING: MAKING THE MOST OF FEEDBACK

Throughout this book we have emphasized the balance of advocacy and openness, in which music teachers demonstrate the ability to show that their decisions in the classroom are informed and that they are open to improving their practice. Nowhere is this as crucial—and as difficult—as in meetings with evaluators. While ultimately what teachers do in the classroom is the most important work with which they engage, a teacher's ability to respond to evaluators' feedback in constructive ways is paramount. In this way, all the ideas and advice in this book lead up to this significant moment.

While receiving and responding to feedback is an important moment in teacher evaluation, it is deceptively difficult to do. It is hard for teachers to receive criticism of their instruction, because they are passionate about their work and care for their students and therefore want to do a good job. In addition, because the stakes are high in teacher evaluation and teachers can lose their jobs or face other punitive measures based on the evaluators' judgments, listening to the evaluator's feedback becomes even more difficult. Finally, as we discussed earlier, triggers might inhibit teachers from truly hearing and acting upon feedback. It is much more reassuring to hear a generic "good job" from an evaluator. However, this does not lead to professional growth, as targeted, friendly, critical comments aimed at improving practice do.

In addition to the inherent difficulty of hearing feedback, unfortunately, sometimes evaluators are not good at providing feedback. Sometimes evaluators are not strong communicators (Bernard, 2015; Darling-Hammond, 2013; Gabriel & Woulfin, 2017; Katz-Cote, 2016). They might have valuable feedback but do not

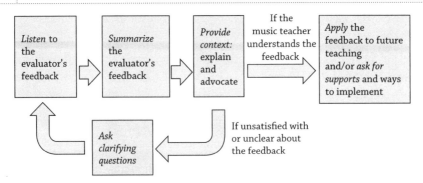

FIGURE 7.2. Process for listening to and responding to feedback

know how to convey it clearly or constructively. Sometimes evaluators provide generic, "copycat" feedback. Because they do not know what to say or because they do not have sufficient time, evaluators might give the same feedback to all teachers regardless of subject. In addition to poor communication skills and copycat feedback, sometimes the content of evaluators' feedback is simply not good. To put it plainly, there are some evaluators who are not strong educators; they lack content knowledge, general pedagogical knowledge, or pedagogical content knowledge. As a result, their feedback might focus on areas that are not important or might make identified problems in the classroom worse.

> Listening and responding to an evaluator is key to digesting and implementing feedback.

Regardless of the quality of an evaluator's comments, for teachers to thrive in teacher evaluation, it is their responsibility to build upon all feedback in constructive ways. How do music teachers complete this crucial but difficult task of teacher evaluation? Here we present and explain a process for listening to and responding to feedback. In this process the music teacher listens carefully, summarizes the evaluator's feedback, justifies his or her choices, asks clarifying questions and for elaboration if needed, and finally demonstrates how he or she will implement the feedback and/or asks for support. Figure 7.2 represents this process.

LISTEN

Obviously, the first step in receiving feedback is to listen carefully to what the evaluator says. While listening is crucial, it is deceptively difficult. As we have noted, because of the high stakes of teacher evaluation, it is easy to mishear information or selectively hear unintentionally. Take, for example, the following comment from an evaluator:

Great job today. I thought your project serving as a summative assessment was quite strong. However, I think you need to find more opportunities to incorporate formative assessments leading up to that summative assessment.

Instead of hearing both the positive and constructively critical comments in this feedback, some teachers might focus on one or the other. Some teachers might only hear the first part and think that their assessment strategy is adequate and there is nothing to fix. Conversely, other teachers might focus on the second part and think that there was nothing positive about their teaching. Instead, it is important to hear both the positive and the negative within this feedback.

Key to hearing this feedback in its entirety is "knowing yourself." The truth, relationship, and identity triggers might impede music teachers from hearing certain feedback. A truth trigger might compel teachers to disregard the assessment comment as "that's not how we do it in music." A response to a relationship trigger might be to criticize how the evaluator demonstrated an assessment critique in a recent meeting and therefore dismiss everything the evaluator says. A teacher might have a great deal of pride and identify as a strong teacher, but an identity trigger might cause him or her to perceive as a threat any criticism of practice; the teacher might either disregard criticism or take it as a comment on his or her worth. Because of this, it is important to know how these triggers affect the process of listening.

SUMMARIZE

After music teachers have listened to all the information in feedback, it is important that they outwardly demonstrate that they have heard what the evaluator said. Evaluators are like everyone else; they want to be heard and validated and to be helpful. By summarizing what the evaluator has said, music teachers demonstrate an ability to listen to feedback.

What should be part of this summary? It is important for teachers to describe, as accurately as possible, what the evaluator said, and not to editorialize. By listening carefully, "knowing oneself," and identifying possible triggers, music teachers can differentiate among what happened, what was really said, and what they're telling themselves happened and was said. This is what Stone and Heen (2015) call "separating the strands" of the feedback. By separating out impressions created by triggers from what happened and what the evaluator said, music teachers can give a more "even-keeled" summary. Providing a summary that separates out what was said from what one *thought* was said allows teachers to see an evaluator's perspective and provides a starting point for discussion.

While it is important to try to separate what was said from what was heard, it is not possible to give a completely accurate account; perception always colors how information is received. That is why it is important that the music teacher acknowledge he or she might be mishearing the information. While it is a cliché, starting with "what I think I hear you saying is . . ." is a useful way to begin the summary. It signals to the evaluator an attempt to give a balanced summary, while also signaling that the interpretation might be different than the intent.

PROVIDE CONTEXT AND ADVOCATE

After summarizing the evaluator's feedback, music teachers might then be in a position to provide context for the choices they made and to advocate for themselves. In this aspect of responding to feedback, it is important to have much knowledge of the key components of teacher evaluation dialogues. First, it is important for teachers to "know themselves" and to make sure that advocacy is not driven by triggers and insecurities, but by the desire to engage in professional development. Second, it is important for teachers to know the actual requirements. When advocating for themselves, music teachers will strengthen their arguments when they point to specific requirements. Finally, knowing the evaluator's pressures, perspectives, and biases will help how a music teacher advocates. Starting a justification by acknowledging the concerns of the evaluator is helpful. For example, a music teacher might say in response to feedback to incorporate more reading to prepare for standardized tests:

> I know the district administration is focused on raising standardized test scores in literacy. This is obviously important. However, I haven't focused on reading texts because I am interested in developing "music literacy," which to me is the ability for students to participate in music making including performance, composing, and listening.

Such a justification acknowledges the evaluator's pressures but provides a rationale for disagreeing.

In addition to knowledge of these key components of teacher evaluation discussions, the music teacher should have command of general pedagogical knowledge and pedagogical content knowledge. Music teachers may have many justifications for their choices that are driven by pedagogical content knowledge. However, in order to communicate to the evaluator and to make the link to the teacher evaluation requirements, the music teacher may need to translate that pedagogical content knowledge into general pedagogical knowledge.

Finally, when advocating, using positive language is central. Language can have hidden negative connotations, even when the speaker is not completely aware of the words' negativity and their effect on others. When discussing students' attributes and backgrounds, music teachers may want to avoid phrases like "slow learners" or referring to a student as a "problem." Music teachers can positively discuss students who are not at target level, how students support one another, and what models they have in place for supporting students who struggle. Again, this can provide music teachers with a chance to discuss differentiation strategies, as referenced throughout chapter 4, giving the evaluator context for their teaching. Positive language conveys to the evaluator the ways in which students are supported to thrive and to engage actively in musical endeavors.

Of course, if a music teacher sees value in the evaluator's feedback, then he or she may ultimately choose to skip this step. However, even when a music teacher finds the feedback adequate, explaining context and advocating provides an opportunity to educate the evaluator about issues, concerns, and other aspects that are unique to the music teacher's classroom. For evaluators without a music background, this step provides an opportunity for the music teacher to educate them about unique aspects of music education and pedagogical content knowledge in music education.

ASK CLARIFYING QUESTIONS

After listening to feedback, summarizing, and then advocating, music teachers may choose to question and perhaps challenge the feedback. As we have noted, there are times when evaluators are not effective communicators. They might not provide sound feedback because of lack of pedagogical content knowledge or even general pedagogical knowledge. In those cases, a music teacher might elect to gather more information by asking clarifying questions.

As in the previous areas, knowledge of the components, the evaluator, and oneself will help guide these questions. It is important for the teacher to point to the components to ground these questions. It is also important to word questions in ways that communicate directly to evaluators in language they will understand. Finally, and most importantly, questions should be used to gather more information, not to make veiled comments. Questions should not be used as a compensation tools for triggers. If questions are used as defenses rather than to gather more information, an evaluator might become defensive; as a result, the conversation can become unproductive and harmful to professional growth.

Similar to what we mentioned in the previous section about providing context, when asking questions, using positive language is key. For that reason, discussions with an evaluator should focus on strengths. For example, if an evaluator asks, "What are you bad at?," it may be helpful for the teacher to rephrase the question in his or her mind as, "What are my goals and what do I hope to improve upon?" If the evaluator tends to word questions negatively, the music teacher might even ask this question and answer it aloud to reframe the conversation in more positive language. In addition to reframing the question in a positive way, this wording provides a concrete talking point that can be steeped in observable data, instead of talking about interpretive (such as "good" or "bad") feedback. Also, focusing on improving, rather than dwelling on negatives in the past, keeps the conversation positive. Music teachers might ask their evaluator, "What do you think is a good next step to improve?" This positive language allows the teacher to move the conversation forward by thinking about applying the feedback to future action.

Finally, just as asking questions is a sound pedagogical approach, asking questions of evaluators is useful in continuing and sustaining dialogue. Asking open, guided, and closed questions might help music teachers generate different types of questions, depending on the types of information or the responses that are needed. The advice in chapter 3 on questioning can provide further strategies for forming and wording questions. Table 7.3 provides some examples of questions music teachers might ask in various scenarios.

> Structuring questions to evaluators as open, guided, and closed can give clarity to feedback.

After asking these questions, it is important for the teacher to repeat the previous steps of listening, summarizing, and advocating. Truly listening to the responses shows the evaluator that the music teacher is interested in sustaining dialogue in order to grow professionally, rather than using questions to be defensive and launch passive-aggressive criticisms of the evaluator.

APPLYING TO PRACTICE 7.5

- Recall a recent post-observation. What feedback did your evaluator give you? What made sense, and what didn't? Did you agree or disagree with any of the feedback, and why? How did you respond to your evaluator?
- Now, consider how listening, summarizing, providing content, and asking questions could have aided you in the post-observation conversation. How might this have changed the conversation or the ways in which you responded to or interpreted the feedback? Consider how you might have responded to the unwarranted feedback you received. What questions could you have asked your evaluator to clarify the feedback?

TABLE 7.3.

Various forms of clarifying questions

When feedback is unclear:
"You said that you want me to assess more. Can you explain more what you mean by that? Are you looking for formal assessments? Do you think these assessments should be on paper, or do you think other forms are acceptable?"

When feedback does not align with requirements:
"I noticed you're asking me to present more concerts throughout the year. What aspects of the teacher evaluation requirements does doing this fulfill?"

When suggested strategies appear to be unsound:
"You're suggesting that I ask fewer questions and that I 'drill and kill' more. This does not seem to line up with all of the things I've learned about student-centered teaching and engaging students. Am I missing something? Why do you think this will help students learn the music better?"

When students give nonverbal answers to questions:
"You mentioned that you saw a lot of conducting and playing and not a lot of talking, so you didn't know if students were 'getting it.' The students were responding to my conducting and changing their sound; it seemed to me that each time, they improved. Do you want me to ask students specific questions about how the sound changed?"

DEMONSTRATE HOW TO APPLY THE FEEDBACK AND/OR ASK FOR SUPPORT

After music teachers have listened, summarized, advocated, and (if necessary) asked clarifying questions, they may demonstrate to evaluators that they are open to professional growth by applying the feedback to their teaching. Optimally, a music teacher should be able to show the ability to synthesize all of the information and how to proceed. For example, an evaluator might advise the teacher to incorporate more differentiation strategies in order to fulfill the requirements of "demonstrating knowledge of students" and "reaching students with special needs." Music teachers might identify some strategies they will implement based on this feedback. Remembering the different types of differentiation described in chapter 4, the teacher might respond:

I think differentiating instruction to make composing more accessible to students is important. For me, it is important to keep the process of composing using notation because I think that is an important literacy for students to develop. So I think that I'm going to keep that a requirement for all students and differentiate other aspects. I think one parameter I can differentiate is student interest. I'll give them greater choice in what they write about, what instruments they choose, and if they want to write it out or use notation software. I'm going to look at my instruction and assignments and see if I can modify them along these lines.

This sort of response shows the evaluator that the teacher has listened and is willing to improve practice based on feedback.

Key to moving forward is bridging general pedagogical knowledge and pedagogical content knowledge. In the example above, the response requires the music teacher to engage in general pedagogical knowledge language about differentiation, but then translates that into specific strategies within music, using pedagogical content knowledge. In this way, the music teacher is able to inhabit the worlds of general education and music education and meld the two through reflection and action in order to improve practice. Teachers might not be able to provide this information in the actual meeting. Sometimes responding, "I will have to think about your feedback" might be appropriate. This will give the music teacher time to think of ways to implement the evaluator's ideas. If this happens, it is important for the teacher to follow up with the evaluator and demonstrate some ways he or she has thought about implementing the feedback.

> A process for receiving feedback should include listening, summarizing, providing context, asking questions, and demonstrating how to apply feedback

Demonstrating a way to move forward might be ideal, but we recognize that this is not always possible. Sometimes evaluators might ask the teacher to take on a practice that seems too overwhelming or foreign, or that does not seem to be effective. For example, sometimes the strategies are too vague. An evaluator might ask a teacher to assess in a new way, revamp questioning techniques, or try new differentiation strategies, but not provide enough specifics. As we described in chapter 3 on questioning, Jacob the orchestra teacher was asked to incorporate more questioning into his high school orchestra, but there was no discussion about what this meant or what it could look like. When a situation like this happens and feedback cannot be implemented, it is important that music teachers ask for support. It is most useful to ask the evaluator to demonstrate in more detail what he or she is looking for. This is not a weakness on the teacher's part; rather, it is responding to the evaluator's comments and openly demonstrating how to make changes. Additionally, this gives the evaluator an opportunity to clarify and set concrete expectations with the teacher.

There may be times that an evaluator asks for a change in practice that does not feel comfortable to the music teacher's teaching style or beliefs. If an evaluator asks to apply feedback outside of the teacher's comfort zone, it is appropriate and necessary for the teacher to ask for support in implementing the strategy. Asking for support to implement strategies will look different depending on the evaluator's feedback. For example, it might be helpful to ask for release time to go observe and talk to teachers, either in the school or in other schools that exemplify the practices suggested by the evaluator. Other times, it might be helpful to ask to have an instructional leader come in and meet, plan, and observe to help implement the strategies that the evaluator is suggesting. This might be the evaluator or someone with music-specific content knowledge.

Music teachers might also ask for support in forming professional learning communities in which they can plan and work with one another. These professional learning communities (PLCs) can be music or arts based, or perhaps even grade-based. For example, if an elementary music teacher has classroom management issues with a third-grade class, he or she might benefit from participating in a third-grade PLCs to see how other teachers are dealing with the class's behavioral issues. The teacher may also ask for resources—books, websites, curricula, or videos—that can aid in shifting practice.

Finally, demonstrating the ability to implement the feedback and asking for support are not mutually exclusive; there may be times when music teachers do both. It is possible to demonstrate some ways to implement the feedback but also ask for additional support to aid in that implementation.

APPLYING TO PRACTICE 7.6

Recall a post-observation in which you were not sure what the evaluator wanted you to do with his or her feedback. How would you ask for help with this particular evaluator? Keep in mind the person's communication skills, pressures, and background. Is there a resource to ask for, or is there a teacher in the building to assist you?

This process of listening to and responding to feedback is a strategy to use meetings with evaluators as an opportunity to facilitate professional growth. By listening, summarizing, providing advocacy and justification, asking clarifying questions, and then applying the feedback and/or asking for support, music teachers can achieve the balance of advocacy and openness we have encouraged throughout this book. This process uses teacher evaluation not as a tool to measure and sort, but as a way to support and develop teachers. Finally, it connects the general pedagogical knowledge language of teacher evaluation systems and non-music evaluators with the pedagogical content knowledge of music teachers.

For this feedback to work and accomplish these goals, however, it is important that the process end in the final step of applying and/or asking for support. If the process ends with advocacy alone, then the music teacher might give the impression that he or she is defensive and not open to growing professionally. Only by signaling a desire to move forward by completing the final step can music teachers balance advocacy and openness. Table 7.4 provides an example of how dialogue between the music teacher and the evaluator might unfold. It is annotated to show which parts of the process the music teacher's response fulfills.

As readers might notice in the table, this process is not always as linear as we have described. The music teacher in this example asked clarifying questions before providing context. Sometimes it is important to modify this process. It is important to realize that evaluators are human; they are not going to respond in ways that will fit neatly into a music teacher's process. They, too, might ask clarifying questions, or offer their own ideas for implementation or support. In fact, some music teachers might be lucky and get an evaluator who naturally guides the discussion in this direction with little effort from the teacher. However, the framework provides some general ways of guiding conversations toward professional growth. The important aspect is to respond to conversation in a natural way while keeping in mind a general agenda of improving practice by listening, reflecting, and generating solutions.

AFTER THE MEETING: APPLYING FEEDBACK

The most important part of receiving feedback is using the information to improve future practice. Feedback is not useful if a person does not use it to improve future actions. After the meeting, it might be helpful for the teacher to show the

TABLE 7.4.

Example of dialogue with an evaluator

Evaluator: *(L)* I want to talk to you about students taking more of a role in the direction of the class during band rehearsal. You asked a lot of yes/no questions. You also didn't have students give input into the class. You set the agenda, you gave the feedback, and students weren't asked to be evaluative about their own playing and the playing of peers. I think you need to incorporate those ideas more.

Teacher: *(S)* Okay, I'm hearing a few things and want to make sure that I address them all. You want students to be more involved in the class activities; there should be different types of questions for students to give input and evaluate themselves and each other. *(Q)* Is that correct?

Evaluator: Yes, that's basically it. What I'm saying is that I want to see more student engagement.

Teacher: *(P)* Thanks for clarifying. Today we spent a lot of time on score navigation and locating where people play at certain times in the piece. So a lot of the questions I asked pertained more to finding the answers in the score, rather than interpreting; for example, "If we play the crescendo at measure 63, what dynamic level do we need to start from?" drew students' attention to the crescendo. *(A)* But I think I could take this a step further and ask them perhaps why the crescendo is there so they can look at their part and see the notes going up in pitch, which signifies getting louder. And then I could ask them to evaluate their crescendo and watch me for different types of crescendos. I'm wondering if you have any teachers in mind that do this well. Perhaps I could get some release time to observe them.

Key (Note that the letter precedes the sentence(s) it refers to.)
(L) = *Listen* carefully, looking to separate the strands, distinguishing between what is really said and the triggers that might cause the teacher to selectively hear or mishear.
(S) = *Summarize* what the evaluator says
(P) = *Provide* context
(Q) = Ask clarifying *Questions*
(A) = *Apply* and ask for supports

evaluator that he or she is intent on improving by immediately applying the feedback, informing the evaluator of the results, and inviting him or her to participate in future dialogue and observation. This process might help music teachers both when they are receiving sound feedback and when they do not agree with the advice.

IMPLEMENTING FEEDBACK TO IMPROVE PRACTICE

It is important to implement feedback as soon as possible. Evaluators are expected to conduct post-observation meetings as soon as possible after an observation. They are trained to be "prompt, timely, and thorough" (Goodwin & Miller, 2012) in their feedback because it is courteous, and because the closer to an event a person hears feedback, the more likely it is that the feedback will be helpful. While many evaluators are not consistent in this practice because of time constraints, prompt-ness is a good practice for teachers to follow as well when applying feedback. Music teachers might consider implementing any type of feedback—whether they agree or disagree with it—the next day. After implementing this feedback, it is also a good idea for teachers to let their evaluators know that they have done so, what happened, and how students responded. Sending an email or dropping by the evaluator's office or classroom to inform him or her of the results shows that the teacher is interested in using teacher evaluation as a tool of professional development.

Equally important when informing the evaluator of the results is for music teachers to use their pedagogical content knowledge to use feedback to move forward. Take the following example. After an observation of a choral rehearsal, Sarah's evaluator suggested that she differentiate instruction by asking students to work in groups to figure out their vocal lines. Sarah did not think students were ready to immediately work individually with little teacher guidance. She knew that students would be unable to learn their parts in small groups because they would have issues navigating the score and their own vocal lines. Because she had these concerns, but also wanted to implement more differentiation, Sarah mod-ified the feedback so that it was developmentally appropriate for young singers. She had students work together to follow their vocal lines while they listened to a recording, noting any repeat signs or other road maps in the piece. After that, she put students in parts, implementing the principal's feedback. Sarah then wrote to her principal:

> I think the students need to grasp the idea of following a piece of music from beginning to end—score navigation—and locating the proper measure numbers a little more before they figure out their own voice parts. They need to see where repeats are, if their part breaks into small vocal parts, where they sing or don't sing, and so on. If they can follow a vocal line—their own line—throughout the score noting these issues, they can begin figuring out their parts. If you have time, I'd love to have you observe me teach using this process.

Here, Sarah demonstrated to her evaluator that she had listened to and applied the feedback, but also inserted her pedagogical content knowledge to give context about how the feedback could be modified.

Finally, as Sarah demonstrated in her email, music teachers can show that they are focused on professional growth and continued dialogue by inviting evaluators to visit their classrooms again. Asking evaluators to see how a music teacher is implementing the feedback shows the continued desire to improve. Because evaluators are often busy, they may not elect to visit again. However, by voluntarily inviting evaluators into their classrooms again, music teachers show they are listening to feedback, are applying it to their teaching practice, and are not afraid to receive continued guidance.

STRATEGIES WHEN THE TEACHER DISAGREES WITH THE FEEDBACK

There might be times when music teachers fundamentally disagree with the feedback, and no modifications will make the advice workable. In this difficult situation, it is most important for the teacher to balance the advocacy and openness that we have encouraged throughout this book. Music teachers can aim to demonstrate the willingness to improve practice but also advocate for what they think is sound music pedagogy.

General music teacher Maria had to carefully maneuver this balance when she received feedback that she did not agree with. Maria's principal has been receiving pressure from upper administration to increase students' academic vocabulary to prepare for tests. Because of these pressures, in a meeting after an observation of a first-grade general music class in which students sang and played circle games, the principal suggested that they stop "playing games" and instead read out of the textbook more.

Maria had concerns about this advice and tried to communicate them to her evaluator. She knew from experience as well as her foundations in music methods that when she incorporated musical play into her teaching, students were more engaged and learned the content better. The students were doing much more than playing; they were listening, singing, moving, and responding to the music and lyrics. The games served as a basis for students to use musical material from the song, such as figuring out a rhythm or melody from the song by ear or using manipulatives or notation, learning new vocabulary, composing, arranging, and playing accompaniments to the song.

Despite Maria's reservations, the principal was adamant about these changes, and Maria implemented this feedback to show she was interested in trying new strategies and improving practice. She eliminated some games and had students read from the textbook. As she had anticipated, the students were not as engaged. She sent an email to the principal, recounting as accurately as possible what happened:

> I thought about your advice, and I omitted two games during the lesson. The students were very chatty and moving around a lot. Many of them asked if they could play a game, but I responded, "not today." About four students asked to go to the bathroom during the class—students who usually never ask. I was wondering if you had any ideas for moving forward. Maybe I didn't implement the way you had envisioned. Perhaps you could observe me teaching this lesson to help me implement the feedback the way you envision it.

Maria's first reaction was to respond, "The idea didn't work at all" or "This tanked." Instead, she used positive language, writing, "I was wondering if you had any ideas for moving forward. Maybe I didn't implement the way you had envisioned." She also invited the principal to observe and provide more feedback. In response, Maria's principal rethought her advice. She thought about Maria's justifications as well as the results and realized play could incorporate vocabulary and other school-wide aims that she wanted the teachers to accomplish.

The result—the evaluator re-examining her position—was an ideal conclusion. However, this sort of result does not happen often. Evaluators may continue to provide feedback and provide additional resources. Because evaluators are busy, they might not have the time to accept the offer to observe again or might not even respond. In a worst-case scenario, an evaluator might continue down a path of measure and sort by continuing to conduct drop-in observations to see if the teacher is making the changes the evaluator expects.

In these most difficult situations, teachers may need to seek ways to resolve disputes outside of discussions with the evaluator. If necessary, they should know the specific details of the appeals processes and other ways disputes are resolved in schools. Seeking out the help of a teachers' union if there is one may be necessary. These are, of course, last options, and probably should be avoided. However, even in this process, it is necessary for the music teacher to show the evaluator and others that he or she is open to continued professional growth and improved practice. By finding the right balance of advocacy and openness to growth, music teachers can minimize the likelihood of these negative interactions with evaluators.

Regardless of the situation, it is important to continue to use the advice we have given throughout this chapter. Know the components of teacher evaluation, seek to understand the pressures and expectations of the evaluator, and know "yourself" and triggers that might inhibit a teacher accepting feedback. In dialogue with the evaluator, continue to listen carefully, summarize, ask for clarification, provide context, and continue to implement ideas employing pedagogical knowledge, while using positive language throughout. These processes may help teachers through difficult situations. Going through these processes continually leads teacher evaluation from measure and sort to support and develop and keeps the process focused on professional development.

APPLYING TO PRACTICE 7.7

- How much time typically passes between your observations? Is the feedback given still relevant by the next observation? How can you make your response to feedback timely and relevant?
- What steps have you taken to apply your evaluator's feedback? Has your evaluator followed up on the feedback? Have you followed up on your implementation of feedback in your communication with the evaluator?

SUMMARY

Speaking with evaluators is a crucial yet delicate balance of openly listening to feedback while advocating for one's current teaching practices. In order to speak with evaluators in a productive manner, music teachers should be aware of the key components of teacher evaluation discussions: (1) the evaluation system's makeup and requirements; (2) the evaluator's background, pressures, and biases; and (2) identifying any triggers that might prevent music teachers from hearing feedback in an open way.

When preparing for a meeting with an evaluator, music teachers can anticipate the questions that might be asked and how both they and the evaluator might answer them. Being able to anticipate what an evaluator will ask can help music teachers better prepare for meetings. During meetings, it is important to build on the evaluator's feedback. This includes listening carefully to what the evaluator has to say, even if the feedback is unwarranted or unsought. We have suggested a process to follow to speak with the evaluator to improve communication, which entails (1) summarizing what the evaluator said, (2) providing context to advocate for the teaching decisions made, (3) asking clarifying questions if unsure of or in disagreement with the feedback, and (4) asking for support to take steps toward applying feedback in practice. This process for communication allows music teachers to advocate for themselves and also to openly receive feedback. Throughout these conversations, music teachers should focus on using positive language to fuel the conversation during the post-observation meeting.

Finally, applying feedback is the culmination of preparing for and participating in meetings with evaluators. Applying feedback demonstrates that the music teacher was actively listening in the meeting. Implementing feedback in a timely manner after it is given can also be used to improve practice. When feedback is lacking, music teachers may modify its application in the classroom by using their pedagogical content knowledge and should report back to evaluators on how the application went. Reporting back to the evaluator on the implementation experience might show him or her that the teacher has mindfully taken the ideas into consideration and might encourage the evaluator to provide additional support. These actions point toward overall, long-term professional development and growth, rather than taking a measure and sort approach to evaluation.

Postlude

The world of high-stakes evaluation is not disappearing from the climate of education anytime soon. Policymakers will continue to watch over the schools with a careful eye to ensure "productivity" and "growth." This points to the need for music teachers to realistically and thoughtfully examine their teaching, not for the sake of survival or for a high evaluation rating, but to address the complex issues associated with music teaching practice in order to better navigate evaluation systems.

Throughout this book we have explored ways that music teachers might navigate teacher evaluation, its parts, and processes in this climate. We have discussed the pedagogical and political implications of teacher evaluation and sorted through the parts of evaluation that music teachers can control: both pedagogical and reflective practice. The chapters have looked at policies and at pedagogical techniques in questioning, differentiation, literacy, and assessment, and have provided a framework for speaking with evaluators about practice. We have stressed the importance of being open to receiving feedback and improving professional practice while also advocating for teaching practices. The book has explored the tension of pedagogical content knowledge in music with general pedagogical knowledge and how music teachers may advocate for the uniqueness of music teaching. This pedagogical content knowledge can help music teachers remain open to the suggestions of others to improve the execution of their general pedagogical knowledge. Music teachers can invite evaluators into their world to begin a productive dialogue and to thrive in teacher evaluation systems. Properly balancing these tensions increases the likelihood that the teacher evaluation process—despite all its negatives—may yield a constructive rather than a destructive experience.

Such an approach might help music teachers become full members of their professional communities. Music teaching is not completely removed from other forms of teaching. While there are some aspects that make it a form of teaching unlike others, there are practices and strategies that are effective regardless of the content, age of students, or setting. Rather than siloing themselves off from educators in other disciplines and evaluators without music backgrounds, music teachers might begin to dialogue with them to improve teaching. In this interchange between music teachers and educators of other disciplines, music educators might envision new music pedagogies. In addition, by sharing their general pedagogical knowledge and pedagogical content knowledge, music teachers might contribute to the professional knowledge and improvement of other educators and help them better understand the values, pressures, and joys of music education.

In this spirit of dialogue and improvement, in closing we want to reorient readers toward the broader goal that the advice in this book aims to support. For us, "thriving" in a teacher evaluation is not achieving high scores or the admiration of evaluators, or obtaining pay raises, but rather a more noble and substantial aim: teacher growth and to reflect on teaching to improve students' education. The famous education philosopher John Dewey (1933) considered the act of reflection to be an important, if not the most important, capacity humans have: "Reflection emancipates us from merely impulsive and merely routine activity, it enables us to direct our activities with foresight and to plan according to ends-in-view or purposes of which we are aware, to act in deliberate and intentional fashion, to know what we are about when we act" (p. 17). For Dewey, reflection meant to break out of routines, to act deliberately and intentionally, and to better know who we are. Dewey also believed that this reflection could only be done with others. Through careful deliberation with others, we can become better versions of ourselves. For us, participation in teacher evaluation should be aimed squarely at this work of reflection with other professionals in the service of students. This is the true mark of a superior educator, a mark more accurate and rewarding than any "highly effective" rating.

References

Affholder, L. P. (2003). *Differentiated instruction in inclusive elementary classrooms* (Unpublished EdD thesis). University of Kansas, Lawrence, KS.

Amrein-Beardsley, A. (2014). *Rethinking value-added models in education: Critical perspectives on tests and assessment-based accountability*. New York, NY: Routledge.

Aronson, B., & Laughter, J. (2016). The theory and practice of culturally relevant education: A synthesis of research across content areas. *Review of Educational Research, 86*(1), 163–206. doi.org/10.3102/0034654315582066

Baum, S. M., Cooper, C. R., & Neu, T. W. (2001). Dual differentiation: An approach for meeting the curricular needs of gifted students with learning disabilities. *Psychology in the Schools, 38*, 477–490. doi:10.1002/pits.1036

Baxter, M., & Allsup, R. E. (2004). Talking about questions: Better questions? Better discussions! *Music Educators Journal, 91*(2), 29–33. doi:10.2307/3400046

Bernard, C. F. (2015). Ensemble educators, administrators, and evaluation: support, survival, and navigating change in a high-stakes environment (Doctoral dissertation). Teachers College, Columbia University, New York, NY.

Brandt, C., Mathers, C., Oliva, M., Brown-Sims, M., & Hess, J. (2007). *Examining District Guidance to Schools on Teacher Evaluation Policies in the Midwest Region. Issues & Answers.* REL 2007-No. 030. Regional Educational Laboratory Midwest.

Brophy, J. E. (1979). Teacher behavior and its effects. *Journal of Educational Psychology, 71*(6), 733.

Civic Impulse. (2017). H.R. 1532 (112th [Congress]): Race to the top act of 2011. Retrieved from https://www.govtrack.us/congress/bills/112/hr1532

Coggshall, J. G., Ott, A., & Lasagna, M. (2010). *Convergence and contradictions in teachers' perceptions of policy reform ideas* (Retaining Teacher Talent, Report No. 3). Naperville,

IL: Learning Point Associates and New York: Public Agenda. Retrieved from http://www. learningpt.org/expertise/educatorquality/genY/ CommunicatingReform/index.php

Coiro, J., Knobel, M., Lankshear, C., & Leu, D. (2008). *Handbook of research on new literacies.* Mahwah, NJ: Erlbaum.

Coleman, D. (2011). *Guiding principles for the arts, grades K–12.* New York: New York State Education Department. Retrieved from http://si2012leadertools.ncdpi.wikispaces.net/ file/view/Arts+Guiding+Principles.pdf/338363332/Arts%20Guiding%20Principles.pdf

Cote, H., & Bernard, C. (2017). Standard II, Teaching all students: Authentic questioning techniques in the ensemble rehearsal through the lens of teacher evaluation. *Massachusetts Music Educators Journal*, 65(3), 46–47.

Cubberley, E. P. (1915). *The superintendent of schools. The Elementary School Journal, 16*(3), 147–154.

Danielson, C. (2007). *Enhancing professional practice: A framework for teaching.* Alexandria, VA: Association for Supervision and Curriculum Development (ASCD).

Danielson, C. (2013). *The framework for teaching evaluation instrument, 2013 edition: The newest rubric enhancing the links to the Common Core State Standards, with clarity of language for ease of use and scoring.* Princeton, NJ: The Danielson Group.

Danielson Group, The. (n.d). *General questions about the framework.* Retrieved from https:// danielsongroup.org/questions-about-the-framework-for-teaching/

Darling-Hammond, L. (2013). *Getting teacher evaluation right: What really matters for effectiveness and improvement.* New York, NY: Teachers College Press.

David, J. L. (2010). What research says about using value-added measures for evaluate teachers. *Educational Leadership, 67*(8), 81–82.

Dewey, J. (1933). *How we think: A restatement of the relation of reflective thinking to the educative process* (2nd ed.). Boston, MA: Houghton-Mifflin.

Donaldson, M. L. (2009). So long, Lake Wobegon? Using teacher evaluation to raise teacher quality. *Center for American Progress*, 1–32.

Dueck, M. (2014). *Grading smarter, not harder: Assessment strategies that motivate kids and help them learn.* Alexandria, VA: Association for Supervision and Curriculum Development (ASCD).

Duke, R. A., Prickett, C. A., & Jellison, J. A. (1998). Empirical description of the pace of music instruction. *Journal of Research in Music Education, 46*(2), 265–280. doi:10.2307/3345628

Earl, L. M. (2013). *Assessment as learning: Using classroom assessment to maximize student learning.* Thousand Oaks, CA: Corwin Press.

Engelmann, S., & Bruner, E. C. (1969). *DISTAR reading I: Teacher's guide.* Chicago, IL: Science Research Associates.

Engelmann, S., & Carnine, D. (1969). *DISTAR arithmetic I* (Teacher's presentation book, student material, and teacher's guide). Chicago, IL: Science Research Associates.

Engelmann, S., & Osborn, J. (1977). *DISTAR language II: An instructional system.* Chicago, IL: Science Research Associates.

Finley, S. (2011). Critical arts-based inquiry: The pedagogy and performance of a radical ethical aesthetic. In N. Denzin & Y. Lincoln (Eds.), *The Sage handbook of qualitative research* (pp. 435–450). Thousand Oaks, CA: Sage.

Fisher, D., & Frey, N. (2014). *Better learning through structured teaching: A framework for the gradual release of responsibility* (2nd ed.). Alexandria, VA: Association for Supervision and Curriculum Development (ASCD).

Gabriel, R., & Woulfin, S. (2017). *Making teacher evaluation work: A guide for literacy teachers and leaders*. Portsmouth, NH: Heinemann.

Gardner, H. (2006). *Multiple intelligences: New horizons*. New York, NY: Basic Books.

Gay, G. (2002). Preparing for culturally responsive teaching. *Journal of Teacher Education, 53*(2), 106–116. doi:10.1177/0022487102053002003

Gay, G. (2010). *Culturally responsive teaching: Theory, research, and practice*. New York, NY: Teachers College Press.

Geake, J. (2008). Neuromythologies in education. *Educational Research, 50*(2), 123–133. doi:10.1080/00131880802082518

Gershwin, G., & Heyward, D., Heyward, D., & Gershwin, I., (2002). *Summertime*. New York, NY: Aladdin.

George, P. S. (2005). A rationale for differentiating instruction in the regular classroom. *Theory into Practice, 44*(3), 185–193. doi:10.1207/s15430421tip4403_2

Ginsberg, M. B. (2005). Cultural diversity, motivation, and differentiation. *Theory into Practice, 44*(3), 218–225. doi:10.1207/s15430421tip4403_6

Golafshani, N. (2003). Understanding reliability and validity in qualitative research. *Qualitative Report, 8*(4), 597–607. Retrieved from http://nsuworks.nova.edu/tqr/vol8/iss4/6

Goldstein, L. S. (2008). Kindergarten teachers making "street-level" education policy in the wake of No Child Left Behind. *Early Education & Development, 19*(3), 448–478. doi: 10.1080/10409280802065387

Good, T. L., & Grouws, D. A. (1979). The Missouri Mathematics Effectiveness Project: An experimental study in fourth grade classrooms. *Journal of Educational Psychology, 71*(3), 335–362.

Goodwin, B., & Miller, K. (2012). Good feedback is targeted, specific, timely. *Educational Leadership, 70*(1), 82–83. Retrieved from http://www.ascd.org/publications/educational-leadership/sept12/vol70/num01/Good-Feedback-Is-Targeted,-Specific,-Timely.aspx

Goolsby, T. W. (1996). Time use in instrumental rehearsals: A comparison of experienced, novice, and student teachers. *Journal of Research in Music Education, 44*, 286–303. doi:10.2307/3345442

Goolsby, T. W. (1997). Verbal instruction in instrumental rehearsals: A comparison of three career levels and preservice teachers. *Journal of Research in Music Education, 45*, 21–40. doi:10.2307/3345463

Hall, G. E., Dirksen, D. J., & George, A. A. (2008). *Measuring implementation in schools: Levels of use*. Austin, TX: Southwest Educational Development Laboratory.

Hash, P. M. (2012). An analysis of the ratings and interrater reliability of high school band contests. *Journal of Research in Music Education, 60*, 81–100. doi:10.1177/0022429411434932

Heacox, D. (2012). *Differentiating instruction in the regular classroom: How to reach and teach all learners* (Updated anniversary ed.). Minneapolis, MN: Free Spirit Publishing.

Hertberg-Davis, H. (2009). Myth 7: Differentiation in the regular classroom is equivalent to gifted programs and is sufficient; Classroom teachers have the time, the skill, and the will to differentiate adequately. *Gifted Child Quarterly, 53*, 251–253. doi:10.1177/0016986209346927

Hodge, P. H. (1997). *An analysis of the impact of a prescribed staff development program in differentiated instruction on student achievement and the attitudes of teachers and parents toward that instruction* (Unpublished doctoral dissertation). University of Alabama, Tuscaloosa, AL.

Holland, P. (2005). The case for expanding standards for teacher evaluation to include an instructional supervision perspective. *Journal of Personnel Evaluation in Education, 18*(1), 67–77. doi:10.1007/s11092-006-9009-0

Hunter, M. C. (1982). *Mastery teaching*. Thousand Oaks, CA: Corwin Press.

Johnsen, S. (2003). Adapting instruction with heterogeneous groups. *Gifted Child Today*, 26(3), 5–6. doi:10.1177/107621750302600302

Kanevsky, L. (2011). Deferential differentiation: What types of differentiation do students want? *Gifted Child Quarterly*, 55(4), 279–299. doi:10.1177/0016986211422098

Katz-Cote, H. M. (2016). *A matrix of music supervisors' stories in the midst of school reform* (Doctoral dissertation). Boston University, Boston, MA. Retrieved from https://hdl.handle.net/2144/16848

Kohn, A. (1999). *Punished by rewards: The trouble with gold stars, incentive plans, A's, praise, and other bribes*. Boston: Houghton-Mifflin.

Kohn, A. (2011). *Feel-bad education and other contrarian essays on children and schooling*. Boston, MA: Beacon Press.

Konstantopoulos, S. (2014). Teacher effects, value-added models, and accountability. *Teachers College Record*, 116(1), n1.

Ladson-Billings, G. (2009). *The dreamkeepers: Successful teachers of African American children*. San Francisco, CA: John Wiley & Sons.

Landrum, T. J., & McDuffie, K. A. (2010). Learning styles in the age of differentiated instruction. *Exceptionality*, 18(1), 6–17. doi:10.1080/09362830903462441

Lapp, D., Moss, B., Johnson, K., & Grant, M. (2012). *Teaching students to closely read texts: How and when?* (IRA E-ssentials). Newark, DE: International Reading Association.

Learning Sciences International. (2017). *Marzano focused teacher evaluation model*. Retrieved from https://www.learningsciences.com/wp/wp-content/uploads/2017/06/Focus-Eval-Model-Overview-2017.pdf

Lee, Y. A. (2007). Third turn position in teacher talk: Contingency and the work of teaching. *Journal of Pragmatics*, 39(6), 1204–1230.

Library of Congress. (n.d.). *About Shenandoah*. Song of America Project. Retrieved from https://www.loc.gov/creativity/hampson/about_shenandoah.html

Lind, V. R., & McKoy, C. (2016). *Culturally responsive teaching in music education: From understanding to application*. New York, NY: Routledge.

MacLeod, R. B., & Nápoles, J. (2015). The influences of teacher delivery and student progress on experienced teachers' perceptions of teaching effectiveness. *Journal of Music Teacher Education*, 24(3), 24–36.

Martin, L. D. (2014). *An exploratory study of music teacher evaluation practices in multiple states with Race to the Top funding: K–12 music educators' experiences, perspectives, and recommendations* (Unpublished doctoral dissertation). University of Colorado, Boulder.

Marzano, R. (2011). *Art and science of teaching: Teacher evaluation model, Domain 3, Reflecting on teaching*. Learning Sciences International. Retrieved from http://www.marzanoevaluation.com/files/domain-docs/Marzano_AST_Domain3_ShortForm_102711.pdf

Marzano, R. (2013). *Developing a passion for professional teaching: The Marzano teacher evaluation model*. Learning Sciences Marzano Center. Retrieved from https://www.learningsciences.com/wp/wp-content/uploads/2017/06/Marzano-Teacher-Evaluation-Model-2013.pdf

Marzano, R., & Toth, M. D. (2013). *Teacher evaluation that makes a difference: A new model for teacher growth and student achievement*. Alexandria, VA: Association for Supervision and Curriculum Development (ASCD).

McAdamis, S. (2001). Teachers tailor their instruction to meet a variety of student needs. *Journal of Staff Development*, 22(2), 1–5.

McREL International. (2017). *Personnel evaluation*. Retrieved from https://www.mcrel.org/personnel-evaluation/

Moje, E. B. (2008). Foregrounding the disciplines in secondary literacy teaching and learning: A call for change. *Journal of Adolescent & Adult Literacy, 52*(2), 96–107. doi:10.1598/JAAL.52.2.1

Morrison, K. A., Robbins, H. H., & Rose, D. G. (2008). Operationalizing culturally relevant pedagogy: A synthesis of classroom-based research. *Equity & Excellence in Education, 41*, 433–452. doi:10.1080/10665680802400006

Nassaji, H., & Wells, G. (2000). What's the use of "triadic dialogue"?: An investigation of teacher-student interaction. *Applied Linguistics, 21*, 376–406. doi:10.1093/applin/21.3.376

National Association for Music Education(NAfME). (2014). *Student assessment using Model Cornerstone Assessments*. Retrieved from https://nafme.org/my-classroom/standards/mcas/

National Association for Music Education (NAfME). (2016a). *Workbook for building and evaluating effective music education in ensembles*. Reston, VA: National Association for Music Education.

National Association for Music Education (NAfME). (2016b). *Workbook for building and evaluating effective music education in general music*. Reston, VA: National Association for Music Education.

National Coalition for Core Arts Standards (NCCAS). (2014). *National core arts standards*. Dover, DE: State Education Agency Directors of Arts Education. Retrieved from http://www.nationalartsstandards.org/sites/default/files/NCCAS%20%20Conceptual%20Framework_4.pdf

National Governors Association Center for Best Practices & Council of Chief State School Officers. (2010). *Common Core State Standards for English language arts and literacy in history/social studies, science, and technical subjects*. Washington, DC: Authors

Oakes, J., & Lipton, M. (2003). *Teaching to change the world* (2nd ed.). Boston, MA: McGraw-Hill.

Otterman, S. (2011, May 23). Test for pupils, but the grades go to teachers. *New York Times*. Retrieved from http://www.nytimes.com/2011/05/24/education/24tests.html?pagewanted=all&_r=0

Pashler, H., McDaniel, M., Rohrer, D., & Bjork, R. (2008). Learning styles concepts and evidence. *Psychological Science in the Public Interest, 9*(3), 105–119. doi:10.1111/j.1539-6053.2009.01038.x

Polikoff, M. S., & Porter, A. C. (2014). Instructional alignment as a measure of teaching quality. *Education Evaluation and Policy Analysis, 36*(4), 399–406. Retrieved from http://epa.sagepub.com/content/early/2014/04/11/0162373714531851.full.pdf+html?ijkey=Uwvo4Eg6.hQHI&keytype=ref&siteid=spepa

Prince, C. D., Schuermann, P. J., Guthrie, J. W., Witham, P. J., Milanowski, A. T., & Thorn, C. A. (2009). *The other 69 percent: Fairly rewarding the performance of teachers of nontested subjects and grades*. Washington, DC: Center for Educator Compensation Reform. Retrieved from http://www.cecr.ed.gov/guides/ other69Percent.pdf

Ravitch, D. (2013). *Reign of error: The hoax of the privatization movement and the danger to America's public schools*. New York, NY: Vintage.

Reeves, D. B. (Ed.). (2009). *Ahead of the curve: The power of assessment to transform teaching and learning*. Bloomington, IN: Solution Tree Press.

Reinhorn, S. K., Johnson, S. M., & Simon, N. S. (2017). Investing in development: Six high-performing, high-poverty schools implement the Massachusetts teacher evaluation policy. *Educational Evaluation and Policy Analysis, 39*(3), 383–406.

Reis, S. M., Burns, D. E., & Renzulli, J. S. (1993). *Curriculum compacting: The complete guide to modifying the regular curriculum for high ability students.* Mansfield Center, CT: Hawker Brownlow Education, Creative Learning Press.

Reynolds, C. R., Livingston, R. B., Willson, V. L., & Willson, V. (2010). *Measurement and assessment in education.* Upper Saddle River, NJ: Pearson Education International.

Robinson, M. (2015). The inchworm and the nightingale: On the (mis)use of data in music teacher evaluation. *Arts Education Policy Review, 116*(1), 9–21. doi:10.1080/10632913.2014.944966

Rosenshine, B. (1987). Explicit teaching and teacher training. *Journal of Teacher Education, 38*(3), 34–36.

Santamaria, L. J. (2009). Culturally responsive differentiated instruction: Narrowing gaps between best pedagogical practices benefiting all learners. *Teachers College Record, 111*(1), 214–247.

Shanahan, T., & Shanahan, C. (2008). Teaching disciplinary literacy to adolescents: Rethinking content-area literacy. *Harvard Educational Review, 78*(1), 40–59. doi:10.17763/haer.78.1.v62444321p602101

Shaw, R. D. (2016). Music teacher stress in the age of accountability. *Arts Education Policy Review, 117*(2), 104–116. doi:10.1080/10632913.2015.1005325

Shuler, S. C. (2012). Music assessment, part 2: Instructional improvement and teacher evaluation. *Music Educators Journal, 98*(7), 7–10. doi:10.1177/0027432112439000

Shulman, L. S. (1986). Those who understand: Knowledge growth in teaching. *Educational Researcher, 15*(2), 4–14. doi:10.3102/0013189X015002004

Shulman, L. (1987). Knowledge and teaching: Foundations of the new reform. *Harvard Educational Review, 57*(1), 1–23. doi:10.17763/haer.57.1.j463w79r56455411

Sizer, T. R. (1997). *Horace's hope: What works for the American high school.* New York, NY: Houghton Mifflin Harcourt.

Spillane, J. P. (2006). *Standards deviation: How local schools misunderstand policy.* Cambridge, MA: Harvard University Press.

Steinberg, M. P., & Donaldson, M. L. (2016). The new educational accountability: Understanding the landscape of teacher evaluation in the post-NCLB era. *Education Finance and Policy, 11*, 340–359. doi:10.1162/EDFP_a_00186

Stone, D., & Heen, S. (2015). *Thanks for the feedback: The science and art of receiving feedback well (even when it is off base, unfair, poorly delivered, and frankly, you're not in the mood).* New York, NY: Penguin.

Strickland, C. A. (2007). *Tools for high quality differentiated instruction: An ASCD action tool.* Alexandria, VA: Association for Supervision and Curriculum Development (ASCD).

Stronge & Associates. (2016). *Stronge teacher effectiveness performance evaluation system performance standards.* Retrieved from https://www.strongeandassociates.com/files/components/Stronge+TEPES%20standards-for%20review.pdf

Taebel, D. K. (1990a). Is evaluation fair to music educators? *Music Educators Journal, 76*(6), 50–54.

Taebel, D. K. (1990b). An assessment of the classroom performance of music teachers. *Journal of Research in Music Education, 38*, 5–23. doi:10.2307/3344826

Tomlinson, C. A. (1995). Deciding to differentiate instruction in the middle school: One school's journey. *Gifted Child Quarterly, 39*(2), 77–87. doi:10.1177/001698629503900204

Tomlinson, C. A. (2001). *How to differentiate instruction in mixed-ability classrooms.* Alexandria, VA: Association for Supervision and Curriculum Development (ASCD).

Tomlinson, C. A. (2003). *Fulfilling the promise of the differentiated classroom.* Alexandria, VA: Association for Supervision and Curriculum Development (ASCD).

Tomlinson, C. A., Brighton, C., Hertberg, H., Callahan, C. M., Moon, T. R., Brimijoin, K., . . . Reynolds, T. (2003). Differentiating instruction in response to student readiness, interest, and learning profile in academically diverse classrooms: A review of literature. *Journal for the Education of the Gifted, 27*(2/3), 119–145. doi:10.1177/016235320302700203

Tomlinson, C. A., Moon, T. R., & Callahan, C. M. (1998). How well are we addressing academic diversity in the middle school? *Middle School Journal, 29*(3), 3–11.

Tuma, A. P., Hamilton, L. S., & Tsai, T. (2018). *A nationwide look at teacher perceptions of feedback and evaluation systems.* Santa Monica, CA: RAND Corporation. Retrieved from https://www.rand.org/pubs/research_reports/RR2558.html.

US Congress. (2001). *No child left behind act of 2001.* Washington, DC: Author.

US Congress. (2016). *Every student succeeds act.* Washington, DC: Author. Retrieved from https://www.congress.gov/bill/114th-congress/senate-bill/1177/text.

US Department of Education (USDOE). (1995). *Goals 2000: Educate America act* (Contract No. RR93002002). Washington, DC: US Government Printing Office.

US Department of Education (USDOE). (2001). *No child left behind act of 2001.* Retrieved from http://www.ed.gov/policy/elsec/leg/esea02/index.html.

US Department of Education (USDOE), Institute of Education Sciences, National Center for Education Statistics. (2015). *National assessment of educational progress* (NAEP). Retrieved from https://www.nationsreportcard.gov/reading_math_2015/#?grade=4

US National Commission on Excellence in Education. (1983). *A nation at risk: The imperative for educational reform; A report to the nation and the Secretary of Education, United States Department of Education.* Washington, DC: The Commission on Excellence in Education.

University of Washington Center for Educational Leadership. (2017). *5 dimensions of teaching and learning: Instructional framework 4.0.* Retrieved from http://info.k-12leadership.org/hs-fs/hub/381270/file-797242241-pdf/documents/5d_framework_v4.0.pdf?hsCtaTracking=47f9f379-b6f7-4147-9d65-342ddd015205%7Cob34b59d-44d0-47bb-8a81-f746ae468998

Vygotsky, L. S. (1978). *Mind in society: The development of higher psychological processes.* Cambridge, MA: Harvard University Press.

Weisberg, D., Sexton, S., Mulhern, J., Keeling, D., Schunk, J., Palcisco, A., & Morgan, K. (2009). *The widget effect: Our national failure to acknowledge and act on differences in teacher effectiveness* (2nd ed.). Brooklyn, NY: The New Teacher Project. Retrieved from http://tntp.org/assets/documents/TheWidgetEffect_2nd_ed.pdf

Wendell, H. (2007). The new Bloom's Taxonomy: Implications for music education. *Arts Education Policy Review, 108*(4), 7–16. doi:10.3200/AEPR.108.4.7-16

Wesolowski, B. (2014). Documenting student learning in music performance: A framework. *Music Educators Journal, 101*(1), 77–85. doi:10.1177/0027432114540475

Wiggins, G. (1998). *Educative assessment: Designing assessments to inform and improve student performance.* San Francisco, CA: Jossey-Bass.

Wiggins, G. P., & McTighe, J. (2005). *Understanding by design.* Alexandria, VA: Association for Supervision and Curriculum Development (ASCD).

Wormeli, R. (2006). *Fair isn't always equal: Assessing and grading in the differentiated classroom.* Portland, ME: Stenhouse Publishers.

Yarbrough, C., & Price, H. E. (1989). Sequential patterns of instruction in music. *Journal of Research in Music Education, 37*, 179–187.

Zentall, S. S. (2006). *ADHD and education: Foundations, characteristics, methods, and collaboration.* Upper Saddle River, NJ: Prentice Hall.

Index